STALIN
Man of Contradiction

To the memory of Ralph Hyndman, steelworker,
Gary, Indiana.

When he died
the New York Times obituary (very full coverage)
neglected to record the death,
for Ralph was not much for clipping coupons.
He was not that kind of steel man,
never forged a cartel
nor a war.

a gray man
gray as the steel he made,
with a great gray head, and eyes
blue as a blow-torch.
There was a well of kindness
in this man
his steelfellows felt it
and followed him
followed his silence and slow speech.

For Ralph was a listener,
when you talked you could see him
feed your talk into the gears of experience
to see if it fitted;
when he got something, it
stuck to him and became part of him
and he gave it to others
as he gave himself.

as steel is made
so was this man made;
as steel spreads to girders,
the spirit of this man
molds and holds.

(K.N.C.)

STALIN
Man of Contradiction

KENNETH NEILL CAMERON

NC Press Limited
Toronto, 1987

Cover illustration: Laura Benne
Author's photo: Howell Studios, Martha's Vineyard.

Permission to quote from Joseph E. Davies,
Mission to Moscow, Simon and Schuster, New York, 1941
has been granted by the Publishers

Canadian Cataloguing in Publication Data

Cameron, Kenneth Neill.
  Stalin, man of contradiction

Bibliography: p.
Includes index.
ISBN 0-920053-97-1 (bound). - ISBN 0-920053-95-5 (pbk.)

1. Stalin, Joseph, 1879–1953.   2. Heads of state—
Soviet Union—Biography.   I. Title.

DK268.S8C36   1986   947.084'2'0924   C86-094338-0

New Canada Publications, a division of NC Press Limited,
Box 4010, Station A, Toronto, Ontario, Canada, M5W 1H8

Printed and bound in Canada

Distributed in the United States of America by
Independent Publishers Group, One Pleasant Avenue,
Port Washington, New York, 11050

CONTENTS

About the Author

Kenneth Neill Cameron was born in England but early moved to Canada. He attended Maisonneuve School, Lower Canada College and McGill University in Montreal. In 1931 he went to Oxford as a Rhodes Scholar. In the summer of 1934 he made a tourist trip to the U.S.S.R. From 1934–35 he was Executive Secretary of the Canadian League Against War and Fascism in Toronto and edited its national magazine, *Action*. In 1939 he received his Ph.D. from the University of Wisconsin. From 1939 to 1952 he taught English at Indiana University. His first book, *The Young Shelley: Genesis of a Radical* (New York, 1950, London, 1951) was awarded the Macmillan-Modern Language Association of America Prize for the best work of scholarship in 1950. In 1952 he came to New York to work at the Carl H. Pforzheimer Library and published four volumes of the library's Shelley collection manuscripts—*Shelley and his Circle* (Harvard University Press, Oxford University Press, 1961 and 1970). In 1961 he made a second trip to the U.S.S.R., this time with his wife and daughter, and met with Soviet scholars in his field. In 1973—paperback, 1977—he published a Marxist history of the world—*Humanity and Society: A World History* (Indiana University Press, Monthly Review Press); and in 1974, *Shelley: The Golden Years* (Harvard), a study of Shelley's later works in prose and poetry. In 1976 he published *Marx and Engels Today: A Modern Dialogue on Philosophy and History*. In 1977 he brought out a volume of poetry, *Poems for Lovers and Rebels* (privately printed). In 1964 he became Professor of English at New York University and is now Professor Emeritus. In 1967 he was awarded a Guggenheim Fellowship. In 1971 he received an honorary D.Litt. from McGill University. In 1978 a "festschrift" volume of essays honoring his work— *The Evidence of the Imagination: Studies of Interactions Between Life and Art in English Romantic Literature*—was published by his fellow scholars and former students (New York University Press). In 1982 he was presented the Distinguished Scholar Award of the Keats-Shelley Association of America at the convention of the Modern Language Association of America. In 1985 he published *Marxism, The Science of Society: An Introduction* (Bergin and Garvey). He has recently completed a book on dialectical materialism and modern science. He lives in New York with his wife, Mary Owen Cameron, a sociologist and author of *The Booster and the Snitch: Department Store Shoplifting*. They have a summer house at Gay Head, Marthas Vineyard.

Preface

A few months ago I had lunch with a leading academic Marxist and faculty colleague. When I told him I had just finished a book on Stalin, he said, "Stalin! My God, every time I talk about socialism, some student brings up Stalin—and then, what can one say?" One can say quite a lot. One can say, for instance, that Stalin, more than any other single individual, built the first socialist society and built it on the wreck left by imperialist intervention and civil war. One can also say that Stalin, more than any other single individual, was responsible for ending Nazi imperialism; in doing so, he not only preserved socialism but helped to extend its foundations in Eastern Europe. These are immense accomplishments, accomplishments that place Stalin among the foremost historical figures of our century. They are, moreover, accomplishments in the interests of humanity as a whole and run counter to the plans of world reaction.

That a man of these accomplishments—no matter what else he did— would be subject to a concerted campaign of vilification could have been safely predicted. We could hardly, however, have predicted its scope. Its immediate purpose is to arbitrarily establish an image so monstrous as to make balanced evaluation suspect. Sometimes it employs simple fantasy, constructing for mass consumption the vision of a power-mad dictator wantonly slaughtering "millions" (from 4 to 60, depending on the estimator). Sometimes we get the more sophisticated picture of a cunning intriguer pushing aside the true, "democratic" socialists and installing a regime of grey regimentation.

What truth or fragments of truth there are in these often blending pictures, we shall try to see as we go along. What we must see at the outset is the deeper purpose of the campaign. The purpose is already apparent in my friend's comment: the vilification of Stalin serves to attack the Soviet Union and socialism, for clearly such a monster could only function in a nation

7

of moronic robots. As such, it becomes part of the current anti-Soviet campaign designed to sabotage disarmament and justify nuclear holocaust. The time has obviously come to do a little balancing-up, to try to make a serious analysis of Stalin, not only as a historical figure but as a Marxist. Stalin's theoretical views, not only influenced millions during his lifetime but are still influential, even though often unacknowledged as his. My intention in this book is to begin that balancing-up, in regard to both Stalin the historical figure and Stalin the Marxist theorist.

Chapter I
Prelude to Revolution

"The Russians," Frederick Engels wrote in 1885 to the Russian revolutionary, Vera Zazulich, "are approaching their 1789." Engels was not thinking of a socialist but of a bourgeois revolution, a revolution like the French Revolution led by the bourgeoisie (the capitalists and the professionals associated with them) against a feudal state, accompanied by peasant revolts in the countryside. Feudal tyranny had stifled Russian capitalist enterprise, as it had stifled the French economy a century before. In 1880 Russia produced but three million tons of coal, compared to 72 million in the United States; in 1885 it had but 16,000 miles of railroads, compared to the United States' 160,000. Furthermore, the railways were owned not independently but by the state, that is to say, by the feudal aristocracy and the tsar; most of the coal industry was leased out to French entrepreneurs. There were at mid-century 40 million serfs, 20 million of them on the royal estates. In the wealthier provinces there was one doctor for each 35,000 inhabitants and in the poorer, one for each 83,000. Only 30 percent of the population was literate.[1]

In spite of all feudal efforts to the contrary, however, capitalism had begun to develop. By 1913 Russia was producing 40 million tons of coal and 10 million tons of oil. In these conditions, a modern proletariat emerged with startling speed and thus the situation as seen by Engels changed rapidly. The possibility arose of not only a bourgeois revolution but a proletarian (primarily industrial working-class) revolution.

Stalin was born Joseph Vissarionovich Djugashvili in 1879, not in Russia proper but in the Russian colony of Georgia, a nation bordering the Black Sea and extending into the Caucasus. A small nation between large ones, it had been harassed for centuries by more powerful neighbors, especially Turkey, Persia, and Russia. Invaded over the centuries by the armies of Alexander the Great, Ghengis Khan, and Tamerlane, it became a Russian possession under Peter the Great. In the 19th century, with the coming of the railways and a discovery of oil, it developed several industrial centers, most notably Baku, the world's leading oil center, with a population of 250,000 and Tiflis (Tbilisi), an administrative and railway center of 150,000. When Marxist and other radical groups began to arise in the 1890s, they were subjected to a mixture of working-class and bourgeois nationalist influences, the latter aiming at an independent Georgian state to be ruled by native capitalists.

Stalin's parents came from poor peasant families and were born into serfdom. As a young man his father went to Tiflis and became a worker in a shoe factory, and then moved to the village of Gori, 45 miles away, to work as an assistant in a shoemaker's shop. As a boy Stalin was a brilliant student and, at his mother's urging, applied for and won a scholarship to the Tiflis theological seminary to train for the priesthood in the Russian Orthodox Catholic Church. The seminary, a large three-story institution with 600 students, was split between a reactionary administration and a rebellious student body, their rebellion rooted primarily in Georgian nationalism. The language of instruction was Russian. A rector who referred to Georgian as "a language for dogs" was murdered by a student. In 1893, just before Stalin entered, a student protest strike—among the demands was the establishment of a department of Georgian language—had resulted in the explusion of 87 students and the closure of the seminary for a time by the police.[2]

In his student years Stalin achieved some local fame as a poet (a poem of his was republished for years in an anthology of Georgian poetry). One of his best poems, "To the Moon," took the Promethean rebel as its theme. (Prometheus was chained to Mount Mkhinvari in the Caucasus, a mountain made "holy" by his suffering.) As in Aeschylus, Shelley and Byron, Stalin's Prometheus is viewed as the symbol of human rebellion:

> *Move on, O tireless one—*
> *Never bowing your head,*
> *Disperse the misty clouds,*
> *Great is the providence of the Almighty.*
> > *Smile tenderly upon the world*
> > *Which lies outspread beneath you,*
> > *Sing a lullaby to Mkhinvari,*
> > *Which hangs from the sky.*
> *Know well that those who once*
> *Fell to the oppressors*
> *Shall rise again and soar,*
> *Winged with hope, above the holy mountain.*

When we recall the poems of the young Marx and those of Mao-Tse-tung, it does not seem so strange that Stalin began his intellectual life as a poet. Like the young Shelley or Byron (or Pushkin), he was then an idealistic, humanitarian rebel. Soon a militant anti-clericalism superseded his religious views, making the parallel to Shelley and Byron still closer. A reading of Darwin's *Descent of Man* and Feuerbach's *Essence of Christianity* (which had strongly influenced the young Marx) soon had him preaching atheism to his fellow theological students.[3]

In 1931, the German author Emil Ludwig asked Stalin the usual question posed to radicals: whether he was driven to radicalism by his parents' ill-treatment. Stalin replied:

No. My parents were uneducated, but they did not treat me badly by any means. But it was a different matter at the Orthodox theological seminary which I was then attending. In protest against the outrageous regime and the Jesuitical methods prevalent at the seminary, I was ready to become, and actually did become, a revolutionary, a believer in Marxism as a really revolutionary teaching.

While he was still a student, then, the center of the young Stalin's radicalism shifted from Georgian nationalism to economic oppression, from a perspective of national freedom from tsarist rule—without basic social change—to one of social revolution. It was a change similar to that which occurred in Mao Tse-tung, Sean O'Casey, and other radical intellectuals brought up in oppressed nations. One of his fellow students at the seminary remembered that Stalin joined a rebel faction at the school that was studying Marxism and other radical works:

Of the books read by Stalin and his comrades in those years, I recall: *The Communist Manifesto*; Engels's *Condition of the Working Class in England*; Lenin's *What the "Friends of the People" Are and How They Fight the Social-Democrats*; Beltov's (Plekhanov's) *Development of the Monistic View of History*; Adam Smith's and David Ricardo's books on political economy; [M.I.] *Tugan-Baranovsky*; Spinoza's *Ethics*; Buckle's *History of Civilization in England*; Letourneau's *Evolution of Property*; [N.Y.] Zieber's *Social and Economic Researches of David Ricardo and Karl Marx*, and books on philosophy.

Stalin also, the same contemporary tells us, read widely in literature and was once reprimanded for reading Victor Hugo. This interest in literature persisted throughout his life. He was well-read in Georgian and Russian literature, admiring Tolstoy in particular, and also read such European writers as Goethe and Ibsen.[4]

Of the works listed as read by Stalin at the seminary, four place particular emphasis on the working class: those by Marx, Engels, Lenin, and Tugan-Baranovsky. These indicate the direction that his thinking was taking. *The Communist Manifesto* (1848) examines the social character of the working class and projects its historical direction. Engels's *Condition of the Working Class in England* (1845) not only gives a detailed account of the early British proletariat but stresses its power and potential (as demonstrated at the time under Chartist leadership). Tugan-Baranovsky's *The Russian Factory, Past and Present* (1898) performs a similar service for the Russian working class. Lenin's pamphlet (1894) attacked reformists and liberals who "want to make shift with darning and patching the system" and argued that the working class must struggle against both feudalism ("the remnants of medieval, semi-serf institutions") and capitalism. According to Lenin, the proletariat would organize itself, in the struggle, into a unified and cohesive social and intellectual force:

> The political activities of Social Democrats consist of assisting the development and organisation of the labour movement in Russia, of transforming it from the present state of sporadic attempts at protesting, "riots" and strikes lacking a leading idea, into an organised struggle of the whole of the Russian working class directed against the bourgeois regime and striving towards the expropriation of the expropriators and the abolition of the social system based on the oppression of the toilers. At the basis of these activities lies the general conviction among Marxists that the Russian worker is the sole and natural representative of the whole of the toiling and exploited population of Russia.

Although Lenin speaks here of "Social Democrats," there was at the time no social democratic or Marxist party but only scattered groups, one of which Lenin had himself organized in St. Petersburg. Lenin was at the time, we might note, virtually unknown, and it seems surprising to find his work being read in Georgia.[5]

The influence on Stalin of such works, particularly Lenin's, soon became evident. He set up Marxist study groups, not only for the seminary students but also for the railway workers in Tiflis. Not surprisingly, he was expelled from the seminary for his political activities, one year before he would have been eligible for university training.

After his expulsion, the young Stalin gave up all thoughts of a career in the Church. He took up the hard demanding life of a professional revolutionary, first among the railway workers:

> I recall the year 1898, when I was first put in charge of a study circle of workers from the railway workshops. That was some twenty-eight years ago. I recall the days when in the home of Comrade Sturua and in the presence of Djibladze (he was also one of my teachers at that time), Chodrishvili, Chkheidze, Cochorishvili, Ninua and other advanced workers of Tiflis, I received my first lessons in practical work. Compared with these comrades, I was then quite a young man. I may have been a little better-read than many of them were, but as a practical worker I was unquestionably a novice in those days. It was here, among these comrades, that I received my first baptism in the revolutionary struggle.

The year 1898 was, we might note, the year of the founding of the Russian Social-Democratic Party. Only nine delegates attended the founding convention, however, and soon thereafter virtually all the Party leaders were arrested by the tsarist police. Lenin was already in exile in Siberia. The struggle in which Stalin participated was then primarily a product of the particular situation in Georgia, with its already powerful movement of railway and oil workers and its seething anti-Russian nationalism. As we read the names of workers Stalin listed—all of them now unknown—we begin to get a sense of the extent and cohesion of this movement and, indeed of the immensity of the coming, total Russian revolution and the numbers of those who struggled in it at various stages of its unfolding.

We can also catch the flavor—and the fervor—of Stalin as a young revolutionary in his articles printed at the time, articles which show deep feeling not only for the workers but for the peasants and oppressed minorities:

> The working class is not the only class that is groaning under the yoke of the tsarist regime. The heavy fist of the autocracy is also crushing other social classes. Groaning under the yoke are the Russian peasants, wasted from constant starvation, impoverished by the unbearable burden of taxation and thrown to the mercy of the grasping bourgeois traders and the "noble" landlords. ... Groaning under the yoke are the eternally persecuted and humiliated Jews who lack even the miserably few rights enjoyed by other Russian subjects—the right to be employed in government service, and so forth. Groaning are the Georgians, Armenians, and other nations who are deprived of the right to have their own schools and be employed in the government offices, and are

compelled to submit to the shameful and oppressive policy of *Russification* so zealously pursued by the autocracy.[6]

Having begun with study groups among the railway workers, the young Stalin turned to leaflet writing and union organizing, and, as a result he was featured in a tsarist police report:

> In autumn 1901 the Tiflis Committee of the R.S.D.L.P. [Russian Social-Democratic Labor Party] sent one of its members, Joseph Vissarionovich Jugashvili (sic), formerly a pupil in the sixth form of the Tiflis Seminary, to Batum [an oil center] for the purpose of carrying on propaganda among the factory workers. As a result of Jugashvili's activities ... Social-Democratic organizations, headed in the beginning by the Tiflis Committee, began to spring up in all the factories of Batum. The results of the Social-Democratic propaganda could already be seen in 1902 in the prolonged strike in the Rothschild factory at Batum and in street disturbances.

In these years Stalin was sometimes known as Koba, a name he took from a character in a romantic Georgian nationalist novel, *The Patricide*, by Alexander Kazbegi. Later, about 1910, he added a last name "Stalin" (the Russian word for steel), apparently in imitation of "Lenin," and he began signing articles "K. Stalin." "J. Stalin" appeared only after the revolution.[7]

Georgia was not only oppressed as a colony of Russia, but its people also suffered, as did all the Russians, from the general feudal (tsarist) tyranny. Lenin had argued that all workers should therefore concern themselves not just with their economic struggles, but also with leading the fight against the tyranny, for only they—and not the bourgeoisie—could lead this struggle to a mass democratic solution, one beyond mere "constitutional" reforms. This applied equally to the Georgian workers. "The working class alone," Stalin wrote, "is a reliable bulwark of genuine democracy. It alone finds it impossible to compromise with the autocracy for the sake of a concession, and it will not allow itself to be lulled by sweet songs sung to the accompaniment of the constitutional lute."

In 1903 the second congress of the Russian Social-Democratic Party took place, in London. This time 43 delegates were present, representing 26 organizations. Lenin emerged as the leader of the Bolshevik (majority) faction, which advocated a disciplined, revolutionary party, in opposition to the Menshevik (minority) faction. The congress took the form that it did partly because the growing Russian working class had embarked on a massive strike movement. In 1903 more than 250,000 workers were on strike, including the oil and railway workers of Baku and Tiflis, many of the strikes being political in nature and run by the Party.

In 1904 Russia declared war on Japan. A humiliating defeat precipitated a revolution the following year against the tsarist regime. Soon 400,000 workers were on strike, peasant revolts broke out, and revolutionary councils ("soviets" in Russian) of workers arose in Moscow, St. Petersburg (later named Petrograd, still later Leningrad), and other cities. In Georgia the workers seized control of Tiflis and other cities and took over part of the railway system. By 1906 the number of strikers had gone up to a million, the greatest strike movement in European labor history up to that time. But the Czarist regime weathered the storm through a combination of terrorism and concessions, including the granting of a parliament possessed of limited powers (the Duma).

For Stalin, the defeat contained a bitter lesson:

Who does not recall the seething, insurgent populace of Tiflis, the West Caucasus, South Russia, Siberia, Moscow, St. Petersburg and Baku? How is it that the lackeys of the tsar could scatter this infuriated populace like a flock of sheep?... Our comrades were routed because the December insurrection was isolated and unorganized. While Moscow was fighting on the barricades, St. Petersburg was silent; Tiflis and Kutais were getting ready for the attack when Moscow had already been "subdued"; Siberia took to arms when the South and the Letts had been "vanquished." This means that the fighting proletariat was split into groups when it met the revolution, as a result of which the government was able to "vanquish" it with comparative ease.[8]

In spite of this defeat, the oil and marine workers in Baku, some 50,000 strong, declared a general strike—at a time when the rest of the Russian proletariat was in retreat. Stalin was one of the leaders:

I recall, further, the years 1907-09, when, by the will of the Party, I was transferred to work in Baku. Three years of revolutionary activity among the workers in the oil industry steeled me as a practical fighter and as one of the local practical leaders. Association with such advanced workers in Baku as Vatsek, Saratovets, Fioletov, and others, on the one hand, and the storm of acute conflicts between the workers and the oil owners, on the other, first taught me what it means to lead large masses of workers. It was there, in Baku, that I thus received my second baptism in the revolutionary struggle.

The "practical" workers were the Party organizers inside Russia. Leon Trotsky, then the leader of a splinter group between the Bolsheviks and Mensheviks, writes scornfully in his *History of the Russian Revolution* of such workers and of Stalin in particular:

> Whereas Kamenev as a publicist stayed for many years abroad with Lenin, where stood the theoretical forge of the party, Stalin as a so-called "practical," without theoretical viewpoint, without broad political interests, and without a knowledge of foreign languages, was inseparable from the Russian soil. Such party workers appeared abroad only on short visits to receive instructions, discuss their further problems, and return again to Russia.

In spite of Trotsky's disdain for the "practicals," they constituted the backbone of the Party. Without them Lenin and the other leaders abroad would have been talking to the air. Lenin recognized their paramount importance and, as Stalin noted, kept up a continuous correspondence with them until he was acquainted with the details of local work everywhere. Nor were the practicals, as Trotsky implies, automatons who were summoned abroad periodically to receive instructions. To judge by Stalin, Sverdlov, Molotov, Kaganovich, Voroshilov, Ordzhonikidze, and others, they were well-read in the Marxist classics and quite capable of working out tactical problems for themselves. Their understanding of events—as revealed, for instance, in the first analysis, by Molotov and others, of the March 1917 revolution—was probably more solid than that of most of those gathered around the Geneva intellectual "forge." True, they did not have the theoretical grasp of Lenin, but no one else did either.

Stalin first met Lenin in 1905 at a Party conference in Finland:

> It is accepted as the usual thing for a "great man" to come late to meetings so that the assembly may await his appearance with bated breath; and then, just before the "great man" enters, the warning whisper goes up: "Hush!...Silence!...He's coming." This ritual did not seem to me superfluous, because it creates an impression, inspires respect. What, then, was my disappointment to learn that Lenin had arrived at the conference before the delegates, had settled himself somewhere in a corner, and was unassumingly carrying on a conversation, a most ordinary conversation with the most ordinary delegates at the conference. I will not conceal from you that at that time this seemed to me to be something of a violation of certain essential rules.
>
> Only later did I realise that this simplicity and modesty, this striving

to remain unobserved, or, at least, not to make himself conspicuous and not to emphasize his high position, this feature was one of Lenin's strongest points as the new leader of the new masses, of the simple and ordinary masses of the "rank and file" of humanity.[9]

The continuation of the working-class struggle in Georgia, after the revolution had been hurled back in the rest of Russia, brought Stalin recognition by the Party center. As G.K. Ordzhonikidze, later a Bolshevik leader, wrote in remembering these events: "While all over Russia black reaction was reigning, a genuine workers' parliament was in session at Baku." Stalin was selected as a delegate to two national congresses of the Party, one in Stockholm in 1906 and one in London in 1907, at both of which he supported the Bolsheviks' position against the Mensheviks in the bitter inner Party struggles of the time. With the defeat of the revolution, some Party leaders and others advocated liquidating the Party, a position that both Stalin and Lenin vigorously attacked. Others turned toward philosophical idealism, a move countered by Lenin in *Materialism and Empirio-criticism*. Stalin, back in Georgia, took a similar position to Lenin's in this dispute also: "So-called 'god-building' as a literary trend and, in general, the introduction of religious elements into socialism is the result of an interpretation of the principles of Marxism that is unscientific and therefore harmful for the proletariat."

Nevertheless, Stalin was aware of the desperate situation faced by the Party at the time, and he discussed it in the style of blunt realism that was to become his hallmark:

It is sufficient to point to St. Petersburg, where in 1907 we had about 8,000 members and where we can now scarcely muster 300 to 400, to appreciate at once the full gravity of the crisis. We shall not speak of Moscow, the Urals, Poland, the Donets Basin, etc., which are in a similar state.

But that is not all. The Party is suffering not only from isolation from the masses, but also from the fact that its organizations are not linked up with one another, are not living the same Party life, are divorced from one another. St. Petersburg does not know what is going on in the Caucasus, the Caucasus does not know what is going on in the Urals, etc.; each little corner lives its own separate life. Strictly speaking, we no longer have a single Party living the same common life that we all spoke of with such pride in the period from 1905 to 1907. We are working according to the most scandalously amateurish methods. The organs now published abroad—*Proletary* and *Golos* on the one hand, and *Sotsial-Demokrat* on the other—do not and cannot link up the organizations scattered over Russia, and cannot endow them with a single Party life. Indeed, it would be strange to think that organs published abroad, far removed from Russia reality, can co-ordinate the work of the Party, which has long passed the study-circle stage.

Stalin proposed a solution:

It will be possible to unite the organizations scattered over Russia only on the basis of common Party activity. But common Party activity will be impossible unless the experience of the local organizations is col-lected at a common centre from which the generalized Party experience can later be distributed to all the local organizations. An all-Russian newspaper could serve as this centre, a centre that would guide, co-ordinate and direct Party activity. But in order that it might really guide the Party's activity it must receive from the localities a constant stream of inquiries, statements, letters, information, complaints, protests, plans of work, questions which excite the masses, etc.; the closest and most durable ties must link the newspaper with the localities; acquiring in this way adequate material, the newspaper must note in time, comment on and elucidate the necessary questions, distil from this material the necessary directions and slogans and bring them to the knowledge of the entire Party, of all its organizations.... [10]

In these comments the unique strengths of Stalin begin to emerge. Just returned at the time from exile in Siberia and still hounded by the tsarist police, he confronted the situation realistically and looked for practical solutions. Nor was he just following the lead of Lenin. On the contrary, he was partly taking issue with Lenin, who was the editor of *Proletary*. Without disagreeing with its general line, Stalin challenged the adequacy of a press published abroad. Only by establishing a press within Russia and, even more important, a strong Russian political center could the Party be built and the workers rallied. This, he implies, could be carried on even in conditions of tsarist terror, if proper methods were used and determination and courage were high.

In 1910 Stalin began to see the beginning of a revival: "The state of depression and torpor into which the driving forces of the Russian revolution had fallen at one time is beginning to pass off." He again pushed for a native press, this time to include papers in all the main areas: "The Urals, Donets Basin, St. Petersburg, Moscow, Baku." And he now openly advo-cated "the transference of the [leading] practical centre to Russia." Lenin evidently agreed with Stalin and may have been thinking along similar lines himself, for in 1912 he co-opted Stalin to the Central Committee of the Party, set up a Russian bureau of four with Stalin in charge, and supported the idea of a Russian newspaper. Stalin recorded its founding:

> It was in the middle of April 1912, one evening at Comrade Poletayev's house, where two members of the Duma (Bokrovsky and Poletayev), two writers (Olminsky and Baturin) and I, a member of the Central Committee (I, being in hiding, had found "Sanctuary" in the house of Poletayev, who enjoyed "parliamentary immunity") reached agreement concerning *Pravda's* platform and compiled the first issue of the newspaper.[11]

When Stalin began to emerge in the early 1920s as Lenin's successor, observers in the outside world were astonished at the sudden rise of the "unknown." But, although Stalin had not been in the national or international limelight, he had long been known within the Party as one of its leaders, especially by the Party members in Russia. What came as a surprise to the outside world came as no surprise to the Party—and the Party was the center of power. Nor was this rise to power of people unknown to the international socialist movement and others limited to Stalin. Within a few years, in fact, the basic Party leadership was in the hands of the old "practicals," the Party organizers who had operated within Russia under conditions of tsarist terror.

The picture that emerges of Stalin during these years is that of a growing Party leader devoted to the working class, a determined and courageous revolutionary, and a staunch supporter of Lenin. First arrested by the tsarist police in 1902, he was sentenced to exile in Siberia. Escaping and returning to Georgia, he succeeded in evading the police for four years. There followed once again prison, exile, and escape, and then still again; altogether he was arrested six times and exiled six times. From the final exile, beyond the Arctic Circle, he was released by the March revolution in 1917, and immediately returned to Petrograd. It was a hard and bitter life, the dreariness of Siberian exile graphically revealed in a passage in a letter from Stalin to Olga Alliluyeva, the mother of the woman he was later to marry:

> I received the parcel. Thank you. I ask only one thing: do not spend money on me: you need money yourselves. I should be happy if you would send me, from time to time, postcards with views of nature and so forth. In this forsaken spot nature is reduced to stark ugliness—in summer, the river, and in winter, the snow, and that is all there is of

nature here—and I am driven by a stupid longing for the sight of some landscape even if it is only on paper.

There is heroism and dedication in this record of Stalin's, a dedication to the working class which is, essentially, a dedication to humanity. If others also showed heroism and dedication, their strengths do not detract from Stalin's. The Bolsheviks were magnificent people.[12]

In 1850, after the defeat of the 1848 revolutions, Marx discussed the problem of the relationship of the working class to the bourgeois, anti-feudal revolution. The workers, he argued, must not allow themselves "to form the chorus of bourgeois democracy"; but should continue their own anti-bourgeois struggles: "From the first moment of victory we must no longer direct our distrust against the beaten reactionary [feudal] enemy, but against our former allies."

> While the democratic petty bourgeoisie would like to bring the revolution to a close as soon as their demands are more or less complied with, it is our interest and our task to make the revolution permanent, to keep it going until all the ruling and possessing classes are deprived of power, the governmental machinery occupied by the proletariat, and the organisation of the working classes of all lands is so far advanced that all rivalry and competition among themselves has ceased; until the more important forces of production are concentrated in the hands of the proletarians.[13]

Lenin and other Bolshevik leaders were aware of the general parallel between their own situation in 1905-07 and that examined by Marx. But there were also, as Lenin noted, specific differences:

> At the same time the Russian revolution was also a proletarian revolution, not only in the sense that the proletariat was the leading force, the vanguard of the movement, but also in the sense that the specifically proletarian means of struggle—namely, the strike—was the principal instrument employed for rousing the masses and the most characteristic phenomenon in the wave-like rise of decisive events.[14]

The main ally of the proletariat was no longer the bourgeoisie or petty bourgeoisie, but the peasantry. Both propositions—proletarian dominance and the role of the peasantry as main ally—were disputed by the reformist wing of the Party, which thought of the bourgeoisie as the leader in what they considered essentially a bourgeois revolution. Stalin sided with Lenin:

The only leader of our revolution, interested in and capable of leading the revolutionary forces in Russia in the assault upon the tsarist autocracy, is the proletariat. The proletariat alone will rally around itself the revolutionary elements of the country, it alone will carry through our revolution to the end. The task of Social-Democracy is to do everything possible to prepare the proletariat for the role of leader of the revolution.

This is the pivot of the Bolshevik point of view.

To the question: who, then, can be the reliable ally of the proletariat in the task of carrying through our revolution to the end, the Bolsheviks answer—the only ally of the proletariat, to any extent reliable and powerful, is the revolutionary peasantry. Not the treacherous liberal bourgeoisie, but the revolutionary peasantry will fight side by side with the proletariat against all the props of the feudal system.

By the proletariat carrying the revolution through "to the end," Stalin did not mean the socialist but the bourgeois-democratic revolution, as he made clear in reporting on the London congress: "That our revolution is a bourgeois revolution, that it must end in the rout of the feudal and not of the capitalist system, and that it can culminate only in a democratic republic—on this, everybody seems to be agreed in our Party."

In this struggle Stalin supported the direct seizure of the land by the peasants; but this policy was not intended to be permanent:

True, after capitalism has sufficiently established itself in the rural districts, division of the land will become a reactionary measure, for it will then be directed against the development of capitalism. Then Social-Democracy will not support it. At the present time Social-Democracy strongly champions the demand for a democratic republic as a revolutionary measure, but later on, when the dictatorship of the proletariat becomes a practical question, the democratic republic will already be reactionary, and Social-Democracy will strive to destroy it.

"Later on," but how much later? Clearly Stalin was envisaging a long period during which capitalism would become "sufficiently established." And he implies a rather rigid division between a "democratic republic" and "the dictatorship of the proletariat."

In later rejecting some of these views, Stalin commented that they were based on:

... the premise that was accepted among Russian Marxists, including
the Bolsheviks, that after the victory of the bourgeois-democratic revolution there would be a more or less long interruption in the revolution,
that between the victorious bourgeois revolution and the future socialist
revolution there would be an interval, during which capitalism would
have the opportunity to develop more freely and powerfully and em-
brace agriculture too; that the class struggle would become more intense
and more widespread, the proletarian class would grow in numbers,
the proletariat's class consciousness and organization would rise to the
proper level, and that only after all this could the period of the socialist
revolution set in.[15]

That Stalin was correct in his contention that a long-lapse theory was
current among the Bolsheviks is clear from Lenin's *Two Tactics of Social
Democracy*, written in the summer of 1905:

A decisive victory of the revolution over tsarism is the revolutionary-
democratic dictatorship of the proletarist and peasantry.... But of course
it will be a democratic, not a socialist dictatorship. It will not be able
(without a series of intermediary stages of revolutionary development)
to affect the foundations of capitalism.

As the struggle mounted, however, Lenin began to see that the two stages
of the revolution, anti-feudal and socialist would blend more closely than
had been thought: "From the democratic revolution we shall at once, according to the degree of our strength, the strength of the class conscious
and organised proletariat, begin to pass over to the socialist revolution. We
stand for continuous revolution. We shall not stop half way."[16]

The difference in views on this issue between Lenin and Stalin reveals a
difference in degree of what we might call Marxist imagination. Stalin was
almost entirely absorbed by the immediate struggle and was not realistically
projecting a transition to a socialist revolution. Lenin, on the other hand,
possessed a continual sense of historical perspective. The socialist revolution
was real to him. To Stalin it was remote and theoretical, even though
inevitable and desirable. No doubt the more Lenin thought about it, the
more a situation of workers and peasants calmly building capitalism after
having gone through a massive anti-feudal revolution began to seem unreal.
Such a situation would, in fact, have eroded revolutionary gains and induced
social stagnation instead of further strivings toward socialism. Stalin had
clearly not thought the problem through. But the contradiction must go
deeper than this. It must indicate some general theoretical Marxist deficiency

in Stalin in these years, despite his organizational and tactical skills. And this, indeed, is what an examination of his works at the time reveals.

In the course of intense bourgeois nationalistic rebellion in Georgia, a number of intellectuals turned to anarchism. Stalin answered the anarchist arguments in a series of articles written in 1906-1907, which were later reprinted as a separate work, *Anarchism or Socialism*. In it he discussed dialectical and historical materialism, both of which had come under anarchist attack. Although Stalin skillfully demolishes the anarchists' misconceptions, he introduces some of his own:

> That in life which is born and grows day after day is invincible, its progress cannot be checked. That is to say, if, for example, the proletariat as a class is born and grows day after day, no matter how weak and small in numbers it may be today, in the long run, it must triumph.

Stalin's view leaves out what Lenin (and Marx) considered the essence of dialectics, namely "the 'struggle' of opposites." Applied to nature, Stalin's view omits or plays down the basic clash of negative and positive processes, in matter, living matter, and life forms. Applied to society it mutes the class struggle. Stalin, in fact, comes close to saying that all a class needs to do in order to "triumph" is to grow. He did not, of course, really believe this, as his organizing of the oil and railway workers showed, but he was unable to adequately project his daily "practical" work into general theory. This dichotomy continued in his later life.[17]

We also find in this early article the germ of his future (1950) concept of "the superstructure":

> And as, in Marx's opinion, economic development is the "material foundation" of social life, its content, while legal-political and religious-philosophical development is the "ideological form" of this content, its "superstructure," Marx draws the conclusion that: "With the change of the economic foundation the entire immense superstructure is more or less rapidly transformed."

Stalin, then, at this time considered "superstructure" as "ideological." He makes a metaphysical (abstractionist) distinction between the economic foundation as "content" and superstructure as "form," a concept for which there is no basis in Marx, Engels, or Lenin.[18]

The best known of Stalin's theoretical works in this period is *Marxism and the National Question*, written during a brief stay in Vienna in 1913. The Russian empire contained many nations, including Stalin's native Georgia, and their role in the revolutionary movement needed to be examined. In attempting this task—sponsored by Lenin—Stalin ventured again into general theory: "A nation is a historically evolved, stable community of language, territory, economic life, and psychological make-up manifested in a community of culture." As Stalin believed that nations were first formed by capitalism—"The process of elimination of feudalism and development of capitalism was at the same time a process of amalgamation of people into nations"—he is here referring to modern capitalist states. But a Marxist cannot, even in a brief definition, leave out the class division of such nations or the economic foundation for this division.

True, there exist certain common psychological and other national characteristics, but Marx clearly regarded them as of secondary historical significance and the divisions as fundamental. It is primarily the divisions that determine both the nature of life within a nation and its historical direction. Capitalist nations, far from being economically "stable," are, as Marx and Engels pointed out, "anarchic" in production and racked by periodic crises. Far from having a stable "psychological make-up," which Stalin equates with "national character," they are torn apart by class in these respects as in every other; what is called "national character" is, as the *Communist Manifesto* indicates, essentially the "character" of the ruling class. And so, too, with language and culture. It is true, for instance, that English is the language of Britain but working-class English is very different from upper-class English.[19]

Stalin, in other parts of his essay, recognized the danger of "lying propaganda regarding 'harmony of interests'" and notes other class struggle factors but he omits such matters from his general theory and general definition. His emphasis is on "the nation" as a kind of monolithic unity; and something of this outlook has lingered on in some Marxist circles today. We should note also that it is not true, as Stalin contends, that nations were first formed by modern capitalism; Roman Italy was a nation and the city-states of ancient Greece or medieval Italy were small nations. The commercial-feudal England of Chaucer was a nation. So was the kingdom of Lady Murasaki. Stalin, although a dedicated working-class revolutionary, seems sometimes in these years of anti-tsarist battle to imply some admiration for capitalism, something which we do not find in Lenin, who had a fierce, unrelenting hatred of all ruling classes and an unremitting sense of class struggle. Stalin's writings in these years, although usually oriented toward the working class and often impassioned, sometimes exhibit bourgeois attitudes—the result, no doubt, of the all-pervasive, bourgeois nationalism of Georgia and the compelling fact of the anti-tsarist struggle. However, before we emphasize Stalin's theoretical weaknesses too strongly, we should note that his general level of Marxist understanding was as high as that of any Party member at the time with the exception of Lenin. Only Lenin seems to have achieved a truly deep and creative grasp of Marxism and dialectical materialism.

Chapter II
Revolution and Civil War

The revolution began suddenly and spontaneously. March 8, 1917 was International Women's Day, a holiday observed by the parties of the Second International. On that day the women textile workers of Petrograd (now Leningrad) defied the ban on strikes and left their factories, calling on men workers to join them and marching to the municipal council to demand bread. By the next day one third of the workers in the city had joined the strike. On March 10 the city was in the grip of a general strike. The strikers raided the police stations in the working-class districts and disarmed the police. On March 11 the police and soldiers opened fire; 150 workers were shot. But even this armed assault failed to break the strike. On the contrary it led to a most significant development: several regiments joined the strikers.

A great role is played by women workers in the relation between workers and soldiers. They go up to the cordons more boldly than men, take hold of the rifles, beseech, almost command: "Put down your bayonets—join us." The soldiers are excited, ashamed, exchange glances, waver; someone makes up his mind first, and the bayonets rise guiltily above the shoulders of the advancing crowd.

When the strike movement broke out, the parliament was in session; on March 12 it was prorogued, but before dispersing, its members elected a provisional executive committee, "to restore order and to deal with institutions and individuals." On March 15 the tsar abdicated and this committee announced the formation of a Provisional Government. The head of this government was Prince G. E. Lvov, a "wealthy landowner" from "an ancient aristocratic family." Among its leading members were P. N. Miliukov, leader of the Constitutional Democratic Party, the party of the Russian businessmen, and "chairman of the central war industries committee"; A. I. Guchkov, who came from a "family of wealthy Moscow merchants" and was "prominent in business as well as in municipal and national affairs"; M. T. Tereschenko, a wealthy capitalist and estate owner, "chairman of the Kiev war industries committee"; and Alexander Kerensky, a lawyer.

The ancient pattern was apparently being repeated: the masses make the revolution and a new ruling class of exploiters takes over. This time, however, the pattern was truncated. On March 12, the day on which parliament was prorogued, the revolt spread to Moscow. In Petrograd a meeting was held by the members of the strike committee, which was in charge of the general strike in the city, along with workers from the Workers Group of the War Industries Committee (recently released from prison), Social Democratic members of parliament and others—a total of 250—and set themselves up as the Provisional Executive Committee of the Soviet of Workers' Deputies. This provisional committee called for the election of a Petrograd Soviet (Council) of Workers' Deputies, which was to elect a permanent Executive Committee. These deputies were to be elected by workers and also by soldiers:

> All those troops that have joined the side of the people should immediately elect their representatives, one for each company. Factory workers should elect one deputy for each one thousand. Factories with less than one thousand workers should elect one deputy each.

Thus the working class of Petrograd, recalling 1905, established a committee or council to represent its interests, a council which was the top of a pyramid whose essential base was in the factories.[1]

When the revolution broke out, Lenin was abroad and Stalin in exile. Stalin, returning to Petrograd a month before Lenin, took over leadership of the Party from V. M. Molotov, until then the acting head of its Russian Bureau, and confronted a complex situation of dual power in which the Provisional Government faced a Soviet of Workers', Soldiers', and Peasants' Deputies dominated by Menshevik and other non-Bolshevik forces. This Soviet not only represented a network of local soviets (elected committees) in factories, farms, districts, and regiments but also represented the Russian people in general. Even while viewing these events from abroad, Lenin had argued that the network of soviets represented the potential state form for the dictatorship of the proletariat predicted by Marx and Engels. When he arrived in Petrograd in April, he urged that the Party, even though it did not have a majority in the Petrograd Soviet, advocate the transfer of governmental power to it, under the slogan "All Power to the Soviets." True, such a government would not immediately be a socialist one, but it would necessarily become so as it faced the problems of economic dislocation, peasant revolt, and the continuation of a war marked by accumulating military disasters. Lenin put forward his ideas clearly and forcefully:

> As long as we are in the minority we carry on the work of criticising and exposing errors and at the same time advocate the necessity of transferring the entire power of state to the Soviets of Workers' Deputies, so that the masses may by experience overcome their mistakes.
> Not a parliamentary republic—to return to a parliamentary republic from the Soviets of Workers' Deputies would be a retrograde step— but a republic of Soviets of Workers', Agricultural Labourers' and Peasants' Deputies throughout the country, from top to bottom.

The army must be turned into a people's army, all police forces must be disbanded, and "all landed estates" must be confiscated by the soviets: "Nationalisation of *all* lands in the country, the disposal of such lands to be in the charge of the local Soviets of Agricultural Labourers' and Peasants' Deputies."[2]

Before Lenin returned, there was considerable confusion in the ranks of the Party, in which Stalin, as he later frankly admitted, shared (as his old view of long-gap transition from the bourgeois-democratic to the socialist revolution rose again to the surface):

> In the conditions of struggle a new orientation of the Party became necessary. The Party (its majority) gropingly proceeded to this new orientation. It adopted the policy of having the soviets exercise pressure on the Provisional Government in the question of peace, and did not venture all at once to take any step beyond the old slogan of the dictatorship of the proletariat and the peasantry to the new slogan of the rule of the soviets. This half-way policy was intended to enable the soviets to perceive the truly imperialist nature of the Provisional Government from the concrete questions of peace and thereby rip the soviets loose from the Provisional Government. However, this position was utterly erroneous, for it begot pacifist illusions, poured water on the mill of defencism and hampered the revolutionary education of the masses. In those days I shared this erroneous position with other Party comrades, and completely renounced it only in the middle of April, when I endorsed Lenin's theses.

That the Party was indeed "groping" toward Lenin's position is clear from Stalin's first *Pravda* article after his arrival in Petrograd: "The revolutionary

Social-Democrats must work to consolidate these Soviets, form them every-where, and link them together under a Central Soviet of Workers' and Soldiers' Deputies as the organ of revolutionary power of the people." By "revolutionary power of the people," however, Stalin did not mean actual, ruling political power but, for the time being, the power of pressure upon the Provisional Government: "The solution is to bring pressure on the Provisional Government to make it declare its consent to start peace negotiations immediately." And he concluded his article with a call for "a democratic republic." By April 25, however, after Lenin's return, he was writing:

> Who shall we regard as our government: the Soviet of Workers' and Soldiers' Deputies or the Provisional Government?
> Clearly, the workers and soldiers can support only the Soviet of Workers' and Soldiers' Deputies which they themselves elected.

Stalin's growing importance in the Party was shown when at its April Conference he was elected to the Central Committee by the highest number of votes after Lenin and Gregori Zinoviev.[3]

By July the situation had become extremely dangerous. The reformist parties in control of the Petrograd Soviet collaborated with the Provisional Government to launch an armed attack on the Bolsheviks. Lenin, on Party orders, went into hiding. Of the militarists who had taken over he wrote: "These butchers are the real power." The slogan "All Power to the Soviets," he argued, must now be discarded because the peaceful transition to pro-letarian rule which it implied had become impossible. A new revolutionary movement, aimed at gaining power by force, must be developed. No support should be given to the existing soviets: "Soviets may, indeed are bound to, appear in this new revolution, but *not* the present Soviets, not organs of compromise with the bourgeoisie, but organs of a revolutionary struggle against the bourgeoisie."[4]

It was in this situation that Stalin was asked by the Central Committee to make the main political report to the Sixth Congress in Lenin's absence. His report was clear and incisive, in general following positions earlier agreed upon in consultation with Lenin: "The peaceful period of the revolution has ended. A period of clashes and explosions has begun." But on one point he differed somewhat from Lenin:

> The fact that we are proposing to withdraw the slogan "All power to the Soviets!" does not, however, mean "Down with the Soviets!" And although we are withdrawing the slogan, we are not even resigning

from the Central Executive Committee of the Soviets in spite of the wretched role it has lately been playing.

As Stalin wrote later: "The Central Committee and the Sixth Congress adopted a more cautious line [than Lenin], holding that there was no reason for believing a revival of the soviets impossible." And he added: "Subsequently Lenin acknowledged that the line taken by the Sixth Congress was correct."[5]

During the debate on Stalin's speech, a delegate took issue with the line of a forceful proletarian revolutionary advance and proposed an amendment: "To direct it [the state power] towards peace and, in the event of a proletarian revolution in the west, towards socialism." Stalin replied:

I am against such an amendment. The possibility is not excluded that Russia will be the country that will lay the road to socialism. No country hitherto has enjoyed such freedom in time of war as Russia does, or has attempted to introduce workers' control of production. Moreover, the base of our revolution is broader than in Western Europe, where the proletariat stands utterly alone face to face with the bourgeoisie. In our country the workers are supported by the poorer strata of the peasantry. Lastly, in Germany the state apparatus is incomparably more efficient than the imperfect apparatus of our bourgeoisie, which is itself a tributary to European capital. We must discard the antiquated idea that only Europe can show us the way. There is dogmatic Marxism and creative Marxism. I stand by the latter.

"Uneven economic and political development," Lenin had written in 1915, "is an absolute law of capitalism. Hence, the victory of socialism is possible, first, in a few or even in one single capitalist country." Whether Stalin knew of this comment in 1917—he noted it in 1924—is not clear, but even if he did, he was certainly thinking "creatively" and, indeed, boldly in a difficult and complex situation.

Stalin's report gives credence to his statement that it was in 1917, following his experiences in Tiflis, Baku, and Petrograd, "in the society of the Russian workers, and in direct contact with Comrade Lenin," that he "first learned what it means to be one of the leaders" of the Party. And it is clear that his leadership was recognized in the Party.[6]

One gets the impression from some accounts that the Russian revolution was run by a small group of conspirators led by Lenin, with Stalin as a subservient but ambitious tool, Lenin periodically issuing diktats and directing matters with a political cunning that resulted in the overthrow of the government. The implication seems to be that if that government, led by Alexander Kerensky, had only been a bit smarter things might have gone the other way. In fact, of course, the revolution was a mass movement responding to exploitation and tyranny. After its initial surge in March 1917—as a "bourgeois-democratic" revolution—it came more and more under the dominance of the working class. In March and April, more than 2,000 trade unions were established. In July, an All-Russian Conference of Trade Unions registered 1,475,000 workers in 976 unions. The metal workers in Petrograd had 16,000 members in March, 70,000 in June, 138,000 in August.

The Bolsheviks party—later the Communist Party—which from its beginnings had been predominantly working-class oriented, became the party to which this mass of workers, new and old, turned; and the Party led them toward the seizure of the means of production and socialism. In spite of depictions to the contrary, the Bolshevik Party was a democratically run, working-class party that little by little became a dominant political force. Its power was based on nothing but the trust of the masses, a trust won by months of struggle in the soviets, factories, unions, and streets. When the March revolution broke out, the Party had 24,000 members; in October, 400,000. In elections in November it received nine million votes. Before the July attack on the Bolsheviks, *Pravda* had a circulation in Petrograd of 100,000; in addition the Party had 41 other publications.[7]

Lenin was away—on orders of the Central Committee—from July to October. In the meantime, the Party was run by the Central Committee and other top committees, whose minutes show that Stalin was one of the five or six top leaders. Lenin was, of course, in touch by mail with the committee. But the minutes also show that he was not regarded as a "boss" or an oracle but as "Comrade Lenin" (or "Il'ich"), the most respected member of a collective whose affairs were conducted democratically, usually with considerable debate. In these debates Stalin again seems to have been generally on Lenin's side. For instance, when Lenin in September and October was urging the necessity of insurrection and some members, notably Zinoviev and Kamenev, disagreed, Stalin moved that Lenin's letters be distributed to the leading Party organizations. And when Lenin returned, Stalin supported his position.[8]

Stalin, however, like Sverdlov and other leaders, was by now perfectly able to analyze events for himself, and his writings in the period of Lenin's absence contain a number of interesting points either not emphasized or viewed somewhat differently by Lenin. In August, the government was planning a new assault, conspiring with General L. G. Kornilov to invade

Petrograd and crush the workers' movement. Stalin perceived the danger and issued a call for action:

> Today when the country is stifling in the clutches of economic disruption and war, and the vultures of counterrevolution are plotting its doom, the revolution must find the strength and the means to save it from crumbling and disintegrating.

The "means" were indeed found, and the workers and the soviets rallied to defeat Kornilov's battalions.

In the struggle it became apparent to the people that the government, which pretended neutrality, was supporting Kornilov—a perception that seriously undermined the government. Stalin, in considering these events, made a wry observation:

> Marx attributed the weakness of the 1848 revolution in Germany among other things to the fact that there was no strong counterrevolution to spur on the revolution and to steel it in the fire of struggle.
>
> We, Russians, have no reason to complain in this respect, for we have a counterrevolution, and quite a substantial one. And the latest actions of the counterrevolutionary bourgeois and generals, and the answering tide of the revolutionary movement demonstrated very graphically that the revolution is growing and gaining strength precisely in battles with counterrevolution.

In later writings, looking back on the course of the revolution, Stalin made an interesting analysis with possible implications for other revolutions:

> One unique feature of the tactics of the revolution during this period deserves to be noted. This feature consists in this: that the revolution tries to make every, or almost every, step of its offensive look like a defensive measure. The refusal to evacuate the army was undoubtedly a serious offensive step of the revolution, yet this offensive was effected under the slogan of the defence of Leningrad against a possible attack by the foreign enemy. Undoubtedly the formation of the Military-Revolutionary Committee was an even more grave offensive step, directed against the Provisional Government, yet it was carried out under the slogan of organizing Soviet control over the activities of the district military headquarters. Undoubtedly the open passing over of the garrison to the side of the Military-Revolutionary Committee and the organization of a network of Soviet commissars betokened the

beginning of an uprising, yet these steps were carried out by the revolution under the slogan of the defence of the Leningrad Soviet against any possible action by the counter-revolution. The revolution seemed to camouflage its offensive steps with a smoke-screen of defence, in order to draw the hesitant, vacillating elements the more easily within its orbit.

In these months Stalin began to call for the reintroduction of the slogan "All Power to the Soviets," arguing that it had acquired a new significance:

> Thus, "Soviet power," proclaimed in April by a "small group" of Bolsheviks in Petrograd, at the end of August obtained the almost universal recognition of the revolutionary classes of Russia.
> It is now clear to all that "Soviet power" is not only a popular slogan, but the only sure weapon in the struggle for the victory of the revolution, the only way out from the present situation. . . .
> Power to the Soviets means the dictatorship of the proletariat and revolutionary peasantry . . . a dictatorship which does not coerce the masses, a dictatorship by the will of the masses, a dictatorship for the purpose of curbing the will of the enemies of the masses.[9]

When Lenin returned to Petrograd in October, he complained—according to the Central Committee minutes—that "since the beginning of September a certain indifference to the question of insurrection has been noticeable." He urged the establishment of a special committee to direct the insurrection. The committee then set up "a Military Revolutionary Center consisting of the following: Sverdlov, Stalin, Bubnov, Uritsky, and Dzerzhinsky," a Party committee to work in conjunction with the Revolutionary Committee of the Petrograd Soviet, of which Leon Trotsky was president. On November 7, "Red Guards and revolutionary troops occupied the railway stations, post office, telegraph office, the Ministries and the State Bank." The power of state, then in the hands of the Petrograd Soviet, was handed over to the All-National Congress of Soviets in which the Bolsheviks had a majority of delegates. The Congress elected a Council of People's Commissars, all of them Bolsheviks.

The actions of the Congress were vividly recorded by John Reed in *Ten Days That Shook the World:*

> Other speakers followed, apparently without any order. A delegate of the coal-miners of the Don Basin called upon the Congress to take measures against Kaledin, who might cut off coal and food from the

capital. Several soldiers just arrived from the Front brought the enthusiastic greetings of their regiments.... Now Lenin, gripping the
edge of the reading stand, letting his little winking eyes travel over
the crowd as he stood there waiting, apparently oblivious to the long-
rolling ovation, which lasted several minutes. When it finished, he
said simply, "We shall now proceed to construct the Socialist order!"
Again that overwhelming human roar.[10]

Reed brings us back to the human reality of the revolution, that human
magnificence which had impressed Krupskaya, Lenin's wife, on her first
glimpse of Petrograd as she arrived with Lenin after years of exile, and to
a sense of mass-democratic power. It was to this that Lenin and Stalin and
the rest had dedicated their lives. This was the result of their Marxist insight
and tactical planning. This was what the meetings of the Central Committee
were all about. Reed helps to show us how petty and how wrong is the
scurrilous gossip-column approach to history, which depicts these leaders
as self-serving conspirators mad for power for power's sake and each driven
by personal ambition. Not, of course, that personal ambitions were absent,
but they were minuscule parts of an overwhelming collective dedication to
the revolution. And the spirit in which these men met, as even the scanty
minutes reveal, was essentially one of good comradeship, in spite of some
differences between them.[11]

Scarcely was the 1917 revolution concluded than civil war and armed
intervention began. British, French, and American troops invaded northern
Russia through Murmansk, and the port of Archangel was captured. British,
Japanese, and American troops occupied Vladivostok. British armed forces
seized the Georgian oil centers of Baku and Batum, where the young Stalin
had led the oil workers' struggles. The French army occupied Odessa. Polish
forces invaded and occupied the Ukraine. In the meantime, reconstituted
tsarist armies, supported by the imperialist governments, had begun a full-
scale civil war. An army of 150,000 led by General Anton Denikin advanced
into south Russia, seizing Kiev and Kharkov. General Yudenich menaced
Petrograd. In Siberia, Admiral Alexander Kolchak, with an army of 125,000,
seized Perm and other towns, proclaimed himself Supreme Ruler of Russia,
and threatened to advance upon Moscow.

On the assumption of power by the Bolshevik government, Stalin, as a
Georgian and the author of *Marxism and the National Question*, had been
appointed Commissar of Nationalities. His main task, however, as with
other Bolshevik leaders, soon became that of organizing and leading the
Soviet forces against the interventionist and tsarist armies. In December
1918, Stalin and another leading Bolshevik, Felix Dzerzhinsky, were sent

by the Central Committee of the Party—on Lenin's motion—to investigate the situation on the Siberian front, where the capture of Perm by Kolchak's forces had particularly alarmed the Bolsheviks. The flavor of the situation and of Stalin's work in the civil war period may be gathered from a letter which he and Dzerzhinsky sent to Lenin from the front shortly after their arrival:

To Comrade Lenin,
Chairman of the Council of Defence.

The investigation has begun. We shall keep you regularly informed of its progress. Meanwhile we consider it necessary to bring one urgent need of the Third Army to your attention. The fact is that of the Third Army (more than 30,000 men), there remain only about 11,000 weary and battered soldiers who can scarcely contain the enemy's onslaught. The units sent by the Commander-in-Chief are unreliable, in part even hostile, and require thorough sifting. To save the remnants of the Third Army and to prevent a swift enemy advance on Vyatka (according to all reports from the command of the front and the Third Army, this is a very real danger) it is absolutely essential urgently to transfer at least three thoroughly reliable regiments from Russia and place them at the disposal of the army commander. We urgently request you to exert pressure on the appropriate military authorities to this end. We repeat, unless this is done Vyatka runs the risk of suffering the same fate as Perm. Such is the general opinion of the comrades concerned, and all the facts at our disposal lead us to endorse it.

It is apparent from the documents published in Volume IV of Stalin's Works that he played a most important role in the civil war. He made numerous visits to all the fronts at the request of the Central Committee, and his reports back to them and to Lenin and others show that the same organizational talents demonstrated in the pre-revolutionary period and in the revolution were applied to the war situation. Everywhere he showed his characteristic common-sense realism, unerringly pointing to key weaknesses and proposing practical solutions. He shuttled between the eastern front, against Kolchak, the southern front, against Denikin, and the Petrograd front, against Yudenich. Nor was his role confined to that of organizational specialist. It was his plan for the attack on Denikin—approved by the Central Committee—that resulted in the final defeat of his armies and the freeing of Kiev and Kharkov. Even when the forces of reaction might have seemed overwhelming to an outsider, he kept a clear basic political perspective:

The Denikin-Kolchak rear is falling to pieces, and is sapping the foundations of the front, because the Denikin-Kolchak government is a government which spells bondage for the Russian people, a government which arouses the maximum distrust among the broad strata of the population.[12]

After three years of determined, courageous struggle by the Bolsheviks, both the interventionist and the tsarist armies were ultimately driven back and Soviet power was re-established in the disputed areas.

Chapter III
Stalin and Trotsky

In 1922, Stalin was elected General Secretary of the Party's Central Committee. Lenin had suffered a stroke—he made his last report for the Central Committee in March—and Stalin's election meant he was now the actual leader of the Party.

Lenin's last major act as Party leader had been the introduction of the New Economic Policy (NEP), which had been designed to allow sufficient capitalist economic recovery, under working-class state control, for a pre-socialist base to be laid. By 1924 recovery had reached a point at which plans could be made for ending NEP and establishing this base. This prospect precipitated a controversy with Trotsky and his followers. The controversy was not, as it is often depicted, a personal one between Stalin and Trotsky, but a political controversy about policy between two social groupings in the Party, represented respectively by Stalin and Trotsky. In some of its aspects, it was in fact, a continuation of differences between Trotsky and the Bolsheviks, particularly Lenin, which had begun in 1904.

Leon Trotsky (Lev Davidovitch Bronstein) was, like Stalin, about 10 years younger than Lenin. His father was a landowner in the Ukraine, owning 250 acres and leasing 200 more. (He was restrained from further ownership by the anti-Semitic laws of the time.) The young Trotsky was sent to private schools because few Jews were admitted to the state schools. As a student, he was caught up in the radical ferment in the Ukraine—a mixture of anti-tsarist, nationalist, pro-minority rights, and anti-bourgeois elements—and helped to organize a group of about 200 students and small industry workers—joiners, locksmiths, electricians, seamstresses—in the southern Ukrainian port city of Nikolayev (near Odessa). As a result, he was arrested, imprisoned, and then exiled to Siberia for four years. In 1902, he escaped, and the following year attended the seminal Second Congress of the Russian

Social Democratic Party at which Lenin put forward his concept of the nature of the Party:

> A dispute had arisen in the commission between Martov and me concerning point 1 of that document. We each insisted on different formulae. I proposed that a party member be regarded as one who adheres to the Party programme, gives material support to the Party and belongs to one of the organisations of the Party. Martov, however, thought it sufficient if, in addition to the first two conditions, a member worked under the control of one of the party organisations.[1]

The difference between Lenin's and Martov's views may seem unimportant at first glance, but it was basic. Martov was, in effect, proposing that the Russian Party should be similar to those in the West European capitalist democracies, such as Germany or Austria, namely a loose, largely parliament-oriented party whose members could be active or inactive as they saw fit and endlessly debate party policy. Lenin's insistence that a Party member be active, pay dues, belong to a Party group, and work within the framework of the Party program implied a disciplined Party (ultimately self-discipline in a common cause)—a Party which in current Russian conditions was necessarily revolutionary. The "Party Program" was to be determined at Party Congresses by the elected delegates. Members could, and did, help to form such a program in terms of their own experience but once it was formed, they had to abide by it as a general guide for further activity. Party members should have as much freedom to debate as conditions allowed but not freedom to form factions with diverse programs.

Such a party would necessarily remain comparatively small but it was not to become a sect. On the contrary, its members were to engage in all forms of economic, social, and cultural activity—in trade unions, social groups, women's groups, anti-war groups—and unite on particular issues with other radical political parties. In 1912 the Bolsheviks elected six members of parliament and their newspaper, *Pravda*, had a daily circulation of 40,000. As things turned out, it became apparent that without a close-knit and essentially working-class party with a broad base of activity, Russia could not have advanced beyond bourgeois democracy in 1917.

It was on this issue of the nature of a revolutionary party that not only Martov and the Mensheviks but Trotsky as well split from Lenin and the Bolsheviks. Within a few months of the Congress, Trotsky was condemning Lenin as a Robespierre-like "dictator," under whose aegis "Marx's lion head would have been the first to roll under the guillotine." "I cut myself adrift from both of the leading groups, the Bolsheviks and the Mensheviks," he tells us in his autobiography, and he became, in effect, an independent radical journalist.[2]

In 1905, Trotsky returned to Russia, where he established a radical newspaper, whose circulation he built up to 100,000. When the Petrograd Soviet of some 400 delegates, elected by 200,000 workers, arose, he became its leading member. He did so, however, not on a Party but an individual basis: "Among the Russian comrades, there was no one from whom I could learn anything. On the contrary, I had to assume the position of teacher myself." "Decisions had to be made under fire. I can't help noting here that these decisions came to me quite obviously. I did not turn back to see what others might say, and I very seldom had opportunity to consult anybody; everything had to be done in such a hurry."[3]

To his journalistic talents he now added those of political orator. When the tsar issued a conciliatory manifesto, Trotsky—to the roar of a huge crowd—crumbled it dramatically in his hand: "Citizens! Our strength is in ourselves. With sword in hand we must defend freedom. The Tsar's Manifesto, however, . . . see! it is only a scrap of paper." In view of the fiery nature of his speeches and writings, it is surprising to find that his actual "decisions" as leader of the Soviet were rather on the conservative side. Two days after the tsar's manifesto, he opposed continuance of the general strike which had been the center of the revolution in Petrograd. He was against the Soviet's attempts to enforce the eight hour day, although he supported the demand in itself. When the president of the Soviet was arrested, and a new general strike was proposed, he spoke against it. But when he was arrested and tried, he remained bitterly defiant of tsarist tyranny:

> What we possess is not a national governmental force but an automaton for mass murder. . . . And if you tell me that the pogroms, the arson, the violence . . . represent the form of government of the Russian Empire, then—yes, then I recognize, together with the prosecution, that in October and November we were arming ourselves against the form of government of the Russian Empire.[4]

In 1906, while in prison, Trotsky summarized his views of the "results" of the revolution so far and the "prospects" for the future in a long essay, *Results and Prospects*. "The proletariat," he wrote, "assumes power as a revolutionary representative of the people, as a recognized leader in the fight against absolutism and barbaric feudalism." It will then proceed to "open up a new era, an era of positive legislation, of revolutionary politics." In this era, the proletariat's "claim to be the recognized spokesman of the will of the nation may be endangered." He noted two main "dangers," the first coming from the peasantry:

> Two features of proletarian politics which will inevitably meet with the opposition of the proletariat's allies are collectivism and internationalism. The strong adherence of the peasants to private ownership, the primitiveness of their political conceptions, the limitations of the village horizon, its isolation from world-wide political ties and allegiances, are terrible obstacles in the way of revolutionary proletarian rule.

The second "danger" to the proletariat's union with its "allies" came from its international working-class ties; and the two dangers were linked:

> Left to its own resources, the working class of Russia will inevitably be crushed by the counter-revolution the moment the peasantry turns its back on it. It will have no alternative but to link the fate of its political rule, and, hence, the fate of the whole Russian revolution, with the fate of the socialist revolution in Europe.[5]

Clearly, then, Trotsky did not consider the peasants, with their "primitive" "political conceptions," to be "allies" of the proletariat. By "allies," he must mean the petty bourgeoisie and what was known as the "liberal bourgeoisie." The revolution was to be basically proletarian but with bourgeois and petty bourgeois support, at least in its first phase.

Trotsky believed that Lenin's concept of a "revolutionary-democratic dictatorship of the proletariat and peasantry" was "unrealizable." But he did feel that the workers would "be compelled to carry the class struggle into the villages"—as though it were not there already—and attempt to "find support by setting the poor villagers against the rich." This process, however, would have largely negative results: "The peasantry as a whole will become politically indifferent. The peasant minority will actively oppose proletarian rule." In his autobiography, Trotsky complained that he had been unjustly accused of "ignoring the peasantry," but it is clear that he did not consider them a reliable revolutionary force.[6]

During the 1905 revolution, Trotsky worked with both Bolsheviks and Mensheviks in the Petrograd Soviet. But according to his biographer, Isaac Deutscher, he was considered "the chief Menshevik representative," for "even though he had resigned from the group abroad," he joined with the Mensheviks within Russia. Clearly he still continued to be opposed to the kind of party that Lenin advocated as a revolutionary vehicle. In fact, even with his ties to the (looser) Menshevik organization in Russia he remained, as his autobiography shows, primarily an individualistic revolutionary. It comes as no surprise, then, to find that in the years following the defeat of the 1905 revolution, his opposition to the Bolshevik form of party continued. While Stalin was working out his plans for rebuilding the Party, Trotsky was in Vienna lamenting in his paper, Lenin noted, that "the Party is 'demoralized.'" Unlike some Mensheviks, Trotsky did not advocate "liquidating" the Bolshevik Party but his gloomy and ambivalent position, worked, Lenin believed, toward that end:

> The convinced liquidators state their views bluntly, and it is easy for the workers to detect where they are wrong, whereas the Trotskys deceive the workers, cover up the evil, and make it impossible to expose the evil and to remedy it. Whoever supports Trotsky's puny group supports a policy of lying and of deceiving the workers, a policy of shielding the liquidators.[7]

These views of Trotsky's were integral to a general theory of "permanent revolution," tentatively developed in 1906 and later (1930) elucidated more fully:

> While the traditional view was that the road to the dictatorship of the proletariat led through a long period of democracy, the theory of the permanent revolution established the fact that for backward countries the road to democracy passed through the dictatorship of the proletariat. Thus democracy is not a regime that remains self-sufficient for decades, but is only a direct prelude to the socialist revolution. Each is bound to the other by an unbroken chain.... The socialist revolution begins on national foundations—but cannot be completed on these foundations alone. The maintenance of the proletarian revolution within a national framework can only be a provisional state of affairs.... The way out for it lies only in the victory of the proletariat of the advanced countries. Viewed from this standpoint, a national revolution is not a self-contained whole; it is only a link in the international chain. The international revolution constitutes a permanent process, despite temporary declines and ebbs.

In 1914, in a general attack on Trotsky, Lenin wrote of "his absurdly left 'permanent revolution' theory." Although Lenin does not specify what he means, from the rest of his article it appears that, for one thing, he felt the theory implied skipping the necessary stage of the democratic alliance of the proletariat with the peasantry. Lenin seems to be arguing that Trotsky would substitute a "proletarian dictatorship" for that alliance, jumping ahead to socialism before the groundwork was properly laid for it. Thus, although the theory sounded "left," in application it would lead to disaster. And Lenin may have felt that the same could be said of Trotsky's dependence on revolutionary aid from abroad.[8]

Trotsky's theory is, of course, based ultimately on Marx's "permanent revolution" concept of 1851, but it deviates in at least one major respect from the thinking of Marx (and Lenin) on the subject. Marx and Lenin considered the dictatorship of the proletariat itself to be a democracy, a mass democracy of the proletariat and its allies, a dictatorship only in that it suppresses the still-existing remnants of the old exploiting classes. Trotsky, however, presents it as a dictatorship and nothing else, a dictatorship which is both preceded and followed by "democracy." But what kind of democracy? Bourgeois democracy or proletarian democracy? Although the word for both phenomena is the same, they are clearly very different entities as depicted by Marx and Lenin. Proletarian democracy is the democracy of a non-exploited working mass, bourgeois "democracy" a state with minor concessions for the still economically exploited masses overlying a basic mass oppression. Trotsky, however, uses "democracy" as an undifferentiated abstraction and contrasts it with the dictatorship of the proletariat.

Nor is such non-Marxist language and thinking restricted to Trotsky's theory of permanent revolution. It occurs throughout his works but is especially noticeable whenever he ventures into the realm of general theory. For instance, in his *History of the Russian Revolution*, he discusses what he calls "the law of uneven and combined development"—a "law" not to be found in Marx. Trotsky contrasts the limitations of feudalism with capitalism: "Capitalism means, however, an overcoming of those [feudal] conditions. It prepares and in a certain sense, realizes the universality and permanence of man's development." What "man," of what class (or sex)? What "development"? What is the "universality" and "permanence" which is bestowed upon "man" by a social system of exploitation, oppression, and war, a system which has never embraced all nations, and which, according to Marx, is doomed to destruction after a comparatively short historical existence?

Trotsky writes—here and elsewhere—like a bourgeois historian and a pretentious one at that. And often, as in both the "permanent revolution" theory and the "uneven and combined development" theory, we find concepts which at first reading may sound revolutionary, but on reflection turn out to be rather woolly rhetoric shrouding impractical and even dangerous proposals. What does it mean, for instance, to say that "Each ["democracy"] is bound to the other by an unbroken chain"? Does it mean anything at all? Or similarly with the concept of a "national revolution" being but "a link in the international chain." If this is not simply a truism, it means that a national revolution cannot alone advance to socialism and, hence, is a concept with reactionary implications.[9]

In 1914, when World War I broke out and the socialist parties in Western Europe renounced their previous anti-war declarations and supported "their own" governments, the Bolshevik members of the Russian parliament denounced the war. They were promptly exiled to Siberia. Although the Mensheviks wavered on the issue, Trotsky stood firm and formed a kind of de facto anti-war union with the Bolsheviks. When a mixed group of revolutionary socialists and pacifists met at the Swiss village of Zimmerwald in 1915, he served as an intermediary between the various outlooks and drew up a compromise manifesto:

Never in the history of the world has there been a more urgent, a more noble, a more sublime task, the fulfillment of which must be our common work. No sacrifice is too great, no burden too heavy, to attain this end: the establishment of peace among nations.

Although the manifesto was rather general and did not include the Bolshevik demand to "turn the imperialist war into civil war" it was sufficiently anti-imperialist for Lenin to sign it with a statement of dissent on some issues.[10]

The March 1917 revolution found Trotsky in New York—which he described as a city "of capitalist automatism, its streets a triumph of cubism"— and his return to Russia was held up by detention in Halifax. When he did return in May he supported, in part, the Bolshevik position, declaring to the Petrograd Soviet:

I think that the next step should be the handing over of all power to the Soviet of Workers' and Soldiers' Deputies. Only with authority concentrated in one hand [i.e., in the Soviet] can Russia be saved. Long live the Russian Revolution as the prologue to the world revolution.

Lenin suggested that Trotsky join the Bolsheviks. Instead he started his own newspaper, organized his own group, and proposed that a new revolutionary party be formed. In June, Trotsky had a group of 10 in the national soviet— to the Bolsheviks' 105 and the Mensheviks' 248.

In July, after the workers' demonstration had been drowned in blood by the authorities and a warrant was out for Lenin's arrest, Trotsky joined forces with the Bolsheviks, declaring in an open letter to the provisional government:

> I agree with the main thesis of Lenin, Zinoviev, and Kamenev, have advocated it in the journal *Vpered* and in my public speeches.... The fact that I am not connected with *Pravda* and am not a member of the Bolshevik Party is not due to political differences, but to certain circumstances in our party history which have now lost all significance. ... From all that I have said, it is clear that you cannot logically exclude me from the warrant of arrest which you have made for Lenin, Kamenev, and Zinoviev.

As a result of his position, Trotsky was arrested and was not released until September.

While he was in prison he was elected to the Central Committee of the Bolshevik Party and shortly after his release was elected president of the Petrograd Soviet. In November he played a leading part in the insurrection in Petrograd, as Stalin noted at the time: "All practical work in connection with the organization of the uprising was done under the immediate direction of Comrade Trotsky." Trotsky, however, was clearly able to do this only because he had joined the Bolshevik Party and had its organization at his disposal. If he had remained with his own small group he would have been virtually powerless. And as Stalin also pointed out, he worked not primarily as an individual but under general Party direction. It was the Party leaders, especially Lenin, who decided on the insurrection and outlined the form it would take.[11]

When the revolutionary government was set up, Trotsky was appointed Commissar of Foreign Affairs. As such, one of his first tasks was to negotiate a peace treaty with the German government. On this question a controversy arose in the Bolshevik ranks. Nikolai Bukharin, then the editor of *Pravda* and a member of the Central Committee of the Party, was opposed to a peace treaty, urging a "revolutionary war" against Germany on the grounds that the "Russian revolution will either be saved by the international proletariat or it will perish under the blows of international capital." Lenin, realizing the weakness of the Russian armies after three years of devastating defeats, urged the immediate signing of a treaty. Trotsky, who conducted the actual negotiations with the Germans, hoped, like Bukharin, for a revolution in Western Europe. He advanced the ambiguous proposal "Neither war nor peace," a proposal of which the German government promptly took advantage to continue its advances and seize the Ukraine.

Lenin then insisted on the signing, and commented:

Trotsky's tactics were correct as long as they were aimed at delaying matters; they became incorrect when it was announced that the state of war had been terminated but peace had not been concluded: I proposed quite definitely that peace be concluded. We could not have got anything better than the Brest peace. It is now clear to everybody that we would have realism, supported Lenin:

... if we accept the slogan of a revolutionary war we shall be playing into the hands of imperialism. Trotsky's position cannot be called a position at all. There is no revolutionary movement in the West. There is no evidence of a revolutionary movement. It exists only in potential.... [12]

During the Civil War Trotsky became Commissar of War, and his generalship sometimes ran into opposition in the Party's Central Committee, particularly from Stalin, who held him responsible—among other things—for the initial retreat of the Bolshevik forces before Denikin's armies. In his autobiography Trotsky depicted his leadership as outstanding and claimed that it was recognized as such by Lenin (particularly in an unpublished speech). Whatever his merits as a commander, however, it is clear that he continued to work in his old individualistic style, and he viewed the opposition to him in personal rather than political terms:

It is no wonder that my military work created so many enemies for me. I did not look to the side, I elbowed away those who interfered with military success, or in the haste of the work trod on the toes of the unheeding and was too busy even to apologize. Some people remember such things. The dissatisfied and those whose feelings had been hurt found their way to Stalin or Zinoviev, for these two also nourished hurts. [13]

In late 1920 Lenin came into conflict with Trotsky and Bukharin on the role of the trade unions in Soviet society. Trotsky had argued that in order to increase production, the trade unions should become actual organs of governmental power, have an appointed and not an elected leadership, and control up to two-thirds of the Councils of National Economy. This plan would, Lenin argued, establish a stultifying army-like bureaucracy and, in fact, place top state control in the hands of Trotsky and his group, for they were to do the appointing. "Bureaucratic project-hatching," Lenin termed it. "This is a perfect example of bureaucracy! Trotsky and Krestinsky will select the 'leading personnel' of the trade unions!" Furthermore a plan such as Trotsky's would result in "destroying the need for the Party" and, for this and other reasons, perhaps undermine socialism itself: "be fatal to the Soviet government, for the dictatorship of the proletariat." The episode shows that Trotsky's statement that his past opposition to the Bolsheviks had "lost all significance" as a result of the revolutionary struggle was not true. His old underestimation of the need for a disciplined revolutionary party and its collectivist style of work clearly lay behind his suggestion.[14]

In 1923, when Lenin was ill, Trotsky launched a partly justified attack on growing bureaucracy in the Party—which had disturbed Lenin, too. He also launched an attack on "the opportunistic degeneration of the Old Guard" (i.e., the central leadership)—which was an attempt to split the Party. The following year a major struggle broke out between the Trotskyites and the Party leadership, centering on the possibility of building socialism in one country. "The contradictions," Trotsky wrote, restating his old argument, "inherent in the position of a workers' government functioning in a backward country where the large majority of the population is composed of peasants, can only be liquidated on an international scale, in the arena of a worldwide proletarian revolution." "What," Stalin asked in reply, "is to be done if the world revolution is postponed? What, then, are the prospects for our revolution? Trotsky leaves us with no prospects at all! He sees 'the contradiction ... in the position of a workers' government,' contradictions which 'can only be liquidated ... in the area of a worldwide proletarian revolution.' According to this plan, our revolution is to stew in its own contradictions, and to rot as it stews, while awaiting the advent of the world revolution."

Trotsky, although denying at the time (in rather ambiguous language) that he was against a practical move towards socialism, really was not convinced of its feasibility. This is clear from a comment he made four years later, in 1928, while in exile:

> We have today a "theory" which teaches that it is possible to build socialism completely in one country and that the relations of that country with the capitalist world can be established on the basis of "neutralizing" the world bourgeoisie (Stalin). The necessity to call for a [socialist] United States of Europe falls away, or is at least diminished, if this essentially national-reformist and not revolutionary-internationalist point of view is adopted. But this call is, from our viewpoint, important and vitally necessary because it implies a condemnation of the idea of an isolated socialist development. For the proletariat of every European

country, even more so for the USSR ... it will be most necessary to spread the revolution to neighboring countries and to support insurrections there, arms in hand, not out of any abstract considerations of international solidarity ... but because of those vital considerations which Lenin formulated hundreds of times—namely when he argued that without timely aid from the international revolution, we shall be unable to hold out.[15]

Trotsky's argument is clearly both impractical and dangerous. If the still-weak Soviet republic had in the 1920s attempted intervention in Europe "arms in hand," it would have been overthrown by the capitalist powers; failure to build socialism would have strengthened the internal capitalist forces that had thrived under the NEP and perhaps resulted in the restoration of capitalism. Nor was the Party policy in any sense "reformist." It was aimed not at reforming capitalism but building socialism. And to "call for" a socialist Europe would not have been "revolutionary-internationalism" but simply talking into the wind. The common argument that Trotsky was "internationalist" and Stalin "nationalist" is, then, essentially false. Trotsky's internationalism, like other of his views, sounds very revolutionary. When one penetrates the rhetoric, however, it is seen to be not only impractical but potentially harmful to the cause of socialism. Although Lenin had felt in 1906 that the success of a "socialist revolution" would be "almost hopeless for the Russian proletariat alone," by 1915 he had reversed his position on this point. In the last years of his life he wrote extensively about socialist construction.[16]

A second argument with Trotsky arose on the nature of the Russian revolution. Trotsky, for instance, had written:

The April demonstration, which took a more leftward trend than had been expected, was a kind of scouting expedition which was intended to sound the state of mind of the masses and the relationship of the masses to the majority of the soviets.

Stalin replied:

This naive conception of the political tactics of our party is nothing but a confusion between the ordinary tactics of the military arm and the revolutionary tactics of the bolsheviks.

As a matter of fact, all these demonstrations were the outcome of the spontaneous pressure of the masses who swarmed into the streets in order to demonstrate their indignation against the war....

The political army is not the regular army. The military chief goes to the wars with readymade troops; but the party has to recruit its men during the struggle in the course of the clashes betwixt class and class, slowly, while the masses become aware by their own experience of the truth of the slogans and the correctness of the policy launched by the party.[17]

The difference in viewpoints is that between an individualist revolutionary without firm Party connections and a practical Party worker who had, as part of a collective effort, built a revolutionary movement. Even later when he got into the thick of things, Trotsky showed little sense of the need to build a movement step by step, in consultation with his comrades and guided by organized Party work. This journalist-observer outlook is apparent also in his massive *History of the Russian Revolution*, valuable though it is for its vivid depiction of events.[18]

In 1926 Trotsky and others formed a faction within the Party, known as a "joint opposition." In 1927 this faction issued a platform against what it called "the representatives of the new bourgeoisie" and their "revisionist tendencies"—respectively, the core of the Party leadership and the Party platform of socialist industrialization. One of the key planks in the opposition's platform was the immediate collectivization of agriculture: "transforming a small-scale production into large-scale collective production." Stalin and the other main Bolshevik leaders, although in favor of collectivization, argued that it could not be successfully accomplished until the industrial base had been further built, a base which could, among other things, produce tractors. To attempt mass collectivization too early would, Stalin argued, create "civil war in the countryside" at a time when "peace" was needed there if industrialization was to succeed. The policy being followed was, he stated, one of increasing farm cooperatives and continuing with gradual collectivization.

That Stalin had the Party membership solidly behind him in this controversy with Trotsky and his group is shown by a 1927 Party referendum in which the Trotskyist program was defeated by 725,000 votes to 6,000. In view of Trotsky's contentions, the vote is surprising in showing how tiny the "opposition" forces were in reality. They were but a small—although vehement—faction, disowned by the mass of the Party and fighting for a platform that was obviously impractical and objectively reactionary. To represent the struggle, in 1927 or before, as one between a sinister, maneuvering Stalin and a brilliant, idealistic Trotsky with roughly equal influence within the Party not only smacks more of melodrama than political reality but is a complete misrepresentation. Stalin had the Party membership solidly behind him, and he had it not through maneuvering but because his socialist-construction policies had gained him wide working-class and Party support. In essence, he won because he was right.[19]

During the 1927 conflicts, Trotsky brought up documents written by Lenin in his final illness which showed that Lenin was attempting to oust Stalin as General Secretary of the Party. The most famous of these, Lenin's so-called "testament," had been made known to delegates for the Thirteenth Congress of the Party in 1924:

> Stalin is too rude and this defect, although quite tolerable in our midst and in dealings among us Communists, becomes intolerable in a Secretary-General. That is why I suggest that the comrades think about a way of removing Stalin from that post and appointing another man in his stead who in all other respects differs from Comrade Stalin in having only one advantage, namely, that of being more tolerant, more loyal, more polite and more considerate to the comrades, less capricious, etc.

In another note of the same period (December 1922) Lenin wrote of "Stalin's haste and his infatuation with pure administration." In other notes he expressed worry that the Party was becoming bureaucratic, and in addition to removing Stalin as General Secretary he proposed that the Central Committee add 50 to 100 workers to its ranks and that these "must be mainly workers of a lower stratum than those promoted in the last five years to work in Soviet bodies; they must be people closer to being rank-and-file workers and peasants...." Stalin consequently offered to resign but the Central Committee refused to acccept his resignation.[20]

In 1919 Stalin, then Commissar of Nationalities, was also made Commissar of the Workers' and Peasants' Inspectorate, an organization created by Lenin to have teams of workers and peasants inspect government functioning in order to check corruption and bureaucracy. This method of mass democratic control embodied the essence of Lenin's concept of how a proletarian state should function. The fact that he appointed Stalin as its director shows his faith in him—as he testified in 1922 when Stalin's control of two commissariats was questioned.

> We are [Lenin wrote] solving these problems, and we must have a man to whom any representative of the nationalities may come and discuss matters at length. Where are we to find such a man? I think that even Preobrazhensky could not name anybody else but Comrade Stalin.

The same is true of the Workers' and Peasants' Directorate. The work is gigantic. But to handle the work of investigation properly, we must have a man of authority in charge, otherwise we shall be submerged in petty intrigues.

In 1923, however, shortly after Stalin resigned from the Inspectorate, Lenin launched a forthright attack on it: "Everybody knows that a more badly organized institution than the Workers' and Peasants' Inspection does not exist." Not only was it beset with "the mustiest routine," but it had tried to take bureaucratic shortcuts instead of engaging in patient, mass education:

We must follow the rule: "A smaller number, but better quality." We must follow the rule: "It is better to get good human material in two years, or even in three years, than to work in haste without hope of getting any at all."

Lenin suggested that the Inspectorate unite with the Central Control Commission and that "seventy-five to one hundred workers and peasants" be elected as members of the new organization.[21]

That the Inspectorate could ever have worked, given the state of the inherited bureaucratic apparatus, is doubtful, and the degree of Stalin's responsibility for its failures is not clear. But Lenin's open attack, regardless of his motive, could not but serve to undermine Stalin's authority as General Secretary and hence disrupt the Party.

Another reason for Lenin's dissatisfaction with Stalin was Stalin's handling of a nationalist movement in his native Georgia led by an old Party member, P. G. Mdivani. Stalin felt that Mdivani's group had bourgeois nationalist tendencies. He handled them, as one of them complained, "with the heavy club of the Center's authority." Lenin argued that in matters involving the national question one should always tread carefully, avoiding the "Russian frame of mind," and: "In this case it is better to overdo rather than underdo the concessions and leniency towards the national minorities." He sent a note to Mdivani and others: "I am following your case with all my heart. I am indignant over Ordzhonikidze's rudeness and the connivance of Stalin and Dzerzhinsky. I am preparing for you notes and a speech." He asked Trotsky to intervene and take matters out of Stalin's hands: "It is my earnest request that you should undertake the defence of the Georgian case in the Party [Central Committee]. This case is now under 'persecution' by Stalin and Dzerzhinsky, and I cannot rely on their impartiality."[22]

In December 1926, under attack by Trotsky, Stalin admitted that Lenin had "rebuked me for conducting too severe an organizational policy towards

the Georgian semi-nationalists, semi-Communists of the type of Mdivani."
But he stuck to his original position:

> Subsequent events showed that the "deviationists" were a degenerating
> faction of the most arrant opportunism. Let Trotsky prove that this is not
> so. Lenin was not aware of these facts, and could not be aware of them,
> because he was ill in bed and had no opportunity to follow events.

In the midst of the controversy Stalin may well have recalled some comments he made in 1921 at a conference of Azerbaijan and other non-Russian
communists:

> In the history of the development of Russian communism, the struggle
> against the nationalist deviation never played an important part. Having
> been in the past the ruling nation, the Russians, including the Russian
> Communists, did not suffer national oppression, did not, generally
> speaking, have to deal with nationalist tendencies in their midst, except
> for certain moods in the direction of "dominant-national chauvinism,"
> and therefore did not have to overcome, or hardly had to overcome,
> such tendencies.

Stalin apparently felt that Lenin, as "a Russian Communist," had an insuf-
ficient grasp of the dangers of bourgeois national tendencies among the non-
Russian people of the state. Lenin's position was based on what Stalin
perhaps considered an overly liberal interpretation of the New Economic
Policy in regard to the national republics. For instance, Lenin wrote to the
Georgian and other non-Russian communists in 1921:

> Make the utmost, intense and speedy economic use of the capitalist
> west by means of a policy of concessions and commercial intercourse.
> Oil, manganese, coal (Tkarcheli mines), copper—such is the far from
> complete list of enormous mineral wealth. There is every possibility
> of widely developing a policy of concessions and commercial inter-
> course with foreign countries.

When the union of the soviet republics was first contemplated, Lenin
favored giving "equal basis" governmental power to all republics. Stalin
rejected the suggestion categorically:

> Lenin's correction to paragraph 2, proposing to create along with the
> Central Executive Committee of the Russian Republic, a Central Ex-

ecutive Committee of the Federation, should not, in my opinion, be adopted. The existence of two Central Executive Committees in Moscow, one of which will obviously represent a "lower house" and the other an "upper house," will give us nothing but conflict and debate.[23]

Looking back on events at the time and their subsequent history it appears that Stalin was right and Lenin wrong on these matters, including that of the Mdivani group. They were apparently a bourgeois nationalist faction in the Communist Party of Georgia; in 1928 Mdivani was expelled. Furthermore, even if Lenin had been right, his actions cannot be condoned. If he was in disagreement with Stalin, he should have taken the matter up officially with the Central Committee or Political Bureau and not attempted to undermine the position of the Party Secretary. He seems to have become convinced that Stalin's method of work would harm the Party; but he was also disturbed by Trotsky's "excessive self-assurance" and "non-Bolshevism," both of which he noted in his testament.

Just what Lenin meant by "non-Bolshevism" is not spelled out but it must include Trotsky's long years of opposition to the Bolsheviks—which some certainly held against him—and probably also to his individualistic, non-collectivist style of work. As Lenin had previously strongly supported Stalin, when Stalin was just as "rude" as he was later, his emphasis on Trotsky was perhaps influenced by his illness and his isolation from Party affairs. The sequence of events may be significant: on December 13 and 16 (1922), Lenin suffered further strokes; on December 22, Stalin abused Lenin's wife, Krupskaya, on the telephone for having taken down a letter from Lenin to Trotsky; on December 23, Lenin dictated his "testament"; 10 days later, he added a further note on Stalin. Whatever the reasons for Lenin's behavior, however, subsequent events—including the joint opposition platform—certainly showed that he was seriously wrong in considering Trotsky for General Secretary.[24]

Stalin—"rude,"—sometimes bureaucratic and limited as a Marxist theorist—had a realistic plan for the construction of socialism, and he approached the task with determination, courage, and skill. For all his faults he was the best of the Party leaders available. And this was the opinion of the majority of the Party. Stalin's report and reply to the discussion at the Thirteenth Congress in 1924 show that he had the Party's confidence.

Though he doubtless sometimes felt the ill Lenin troublesome in these final, trying years, there cannot be any doubt of Stalin's general devotion to Lenin or of his admiration of his intellectual depth and political daring, sometimes almost to the point of awe. No doubt Stalin sincerely felt himself to be, as he contended, a "pupil" of Lenin's and believed that he was continuing Lenin's work, both in the construction of socialism and in the realm of political theory. His eulogy, "On the Death of Lenin," is sincere and powerful:

> Scores and indeed hundreds of times in the course of the centuries the labouring people have striven to throw off the oppressors from their backs and to become the masters of their own destiny. But each time, defeated and disgraced, they have been forced to retreat, harbouring in their breasts resentment and humiliation, anger and despair, and lifting up their eyes to an inscrutable heaven where they hoped to find deliverance. The chains of slavery remained intact, or the old chains were replaced by new ones, equally burdensome and degrading. Ours is the only country where the oppressed and downtrodden labouring masses have succeeded in throwing off the rule of the landlords and capitalists and replacing it by the rule of the workers and peasants. You know, comrades, and the whole world now admits it, that this gigantic struggle was led by Comrade Lenin and his Party. The greatness of Lenin lies above all in this, that by creating the Republic of Soviets he gave a practical demonstration to the oppressed masses of the whole world that hope of deliverance is not lost, that the rule of the landlords and capitalists is shortlived, that the kingdom of labour can be created by the efforts of the labouring people themselves, and that the kingdom of labour must be created not in heaven, but on earth.[25]

Chapter IV
Foundations of Leninism

During these years Stalin produced several theoretical works, the most important of which, *Foundations of Leninism* (1924), sold in millions of copies throughout the world. In it he tried to express some of Lenin's basic concepts in compact form. The strengths and weaknesses of the study are clear in the first chapter. Stalin begins with an analysis of Lenin's views of imperialism, the essence of which he sees in the concept of world capitalism being directed (and ultimately being destroyed) by three major "contradictions":

First Contradiction. The conflict between labour and capital. ... Second Contradiction. The conflict between the various financial groups and the different imperialist powers in their competition for control of the sources of raw material, for foreign territory. ... Third Contradiction. The conflict between the small group of dominant "civilised" nations, on the one hand, and the hundreds of millions of persons who make up the colonial and dependent peoples of the world, on the other.

In such passages Stalin performs a service for Lenin which Lenin failed to do for himself, namely to put his general ideas in succinct form. In doing so, he often, as here, adds creatively to Lenin. The three "contradictions" he lists clearly still govern the movement of world capitalism and his discussion of them provides an invaluable framework for understanding world events.

Stalin then goes on to ask why Leninism originated in Russia. He answers that it was because Russia was "the focus of the three great contradictions ... the only land ready to solve the three contradictions by means of revolution."

First of all, every kind of oppression—capitalist, colonial, and military—was rife in tsarist Russia....Secondly, tsarist Russia was a huge reserve force for western imperialism....Not only did it welcome the entry of foreign capital...[but it provided] millions of soldiers to fight the battles of the western imperialists...it was also the agency through which the western imperialists collected from the Russian population the huge sums of interest that were payable upon loans floated in Paris, London, Berlin, and Brussels....Finally, tsarism was the faithful ally of the western imperialists in the partitioning of Turkey, Russia, China, etc.

"The logical deduction," Stalin continues, "is that any one who wanted to strike a blow at tsarism must perforce strike a blow at imperialism....That was why an anti-tsarist revolution could not fail to develop into an anti-imperialist revolution, into a proletarian revolution." As a result of these factors "the Russian communists" could not "confine their activities within the narrow framework of a purely Russian revolution....They had to carry the struggle into the international arena; to lay bare the plague-spots of imperialism....That is why Russia was the birthplace of Leninism."[1]

True, Stalin notes that "every kind of oppression...was rife in tsarist Russia," and notes also—in Lenin's phrase—that "tsarism" was "feudal-militarist imperialism." But he seems rather protective of the old Russia, depicting it as a pawn in the hands of "western imperialism," a "faithful ally" or a "watchdog." Even the exploitation of the Russian people seems to have come largely from Western imperialism, and the revolution which they created was directed first against tsarism and then against "imperialism" (again presumably essentially "western"). In Stalin's view, 1917 was an "anti-imperialist revolution," which he equates with a "proletarian revolution." It was out of this situation that Leninism arose and because of it became a doctrine with international (not merely Russian) application.

This explanation, however, is superficial and confused. Lenin's views did not arise because tsarist Russia was exploited by Western imperialism but because of its basic nature, namely a feudal state with a massive exploited peasantry in which industrial capitalism was developing rapidly, creating both a capitalist class and a working class. Both classes were suppressed by the feudalists and denied political rights until 1907 when the capitalist class received some parliamentary power. The working class bore a double burden of tsarist oppression and capitalist exploitation. Hence the social philosophy of a Russian working-class party had to be revolutionary, in contrast to those in "democratic" Western Europe, which were reformist. And Leninism had special significance for the colonial world because it was a consistent development of Marxism in a nation that had within its borders oppressed nations (such as Georgia).

The fact that the Russian revolution had to go through an anti-feudal stage before it could overthrow capitalism meant that Leninism had to develop an anti-feudal as well as an anti-capitalist strategy. This latter strategy, with its doctrine of soviet power, contained the essence of the anti-capitalist revolution everywhere. The anti-feudal strategy contained elements applicable also in the anti-feudal, anti-imperialist struggles in oppressed nations. Clearly, however, the November revolution was not *basically* an "anti-imperialist revolution" but an anti-capitalist, proletarian revolution even though it contained anti-imperialist elements. And a primarily anti-imperialist revolution (as, for instance, in China in 1911) is, just as clearly, not the same thing as a proletarian revolution. Some of Stalin's old confusions about the nature of the Russian revolution still seem to be present, although in somewhat different form. So, too, do his bourgeois nationalist feelings, feelings which burst out almost vehemently in 1945:

But the defeat of the Russian troops in 1904 during the Russo-Japanese war left bitter memories in the minds of our people. It lay like a black stain upon our country.

Why should there be a "stain"? And who were the "people" who felt it? The defeat was that of a primarily feudal power by a rising capitalist power, a feudal power which had conquered and enslaved other peoples, particularly in Asia, for centuries. How could a Marxist identify in any way with this repressive regime?[2]

A second major weakness of Stalin's study becomes apparent in his treatment of Lenin. "Lenin," he notes at the beginning, "is a Marxist, so of course his philosophy is based upon Marxism." And that is all we hear on the subject. There is no examination of the relationship of Leninism and Marxism. As a result Lenin appears (not without a hint of Russian chauvinism) as a unique phenomenon. To be fair to Stalin, however, we must note that in the opening comments to his *Interview with the First American Labour Delegation in Russia* (1927), he did discuss some of Lenin's roots in Marx and Engels. But *Foundations*, read alone, as it usually was (in study groups, for instance), distorts Lenin's role. Furthermore, even in the *Interview*, there is a down-playing of Marx and Engels: "Clearly Marx and Engels could only guess at the new conditions of the development of capitalism. . . . " It was, however, not a matter of "guessing"—which puts Marx and Engels on a level with bourgeois journalists—but of extending a scientific theory into the future. Although they did not foresee the international interlocking of imperialism, they did anticipate monopoly capitalism, with its polarizations, and Engels in his last years perceived some aspects of the development of imperialism with its drive to war and spur to colonial revolution.[3]

In *Foundations of Leninism*, Stalin writes of problems considered "in former days":

> Where will the revolution begin? In what country can the capitalist front be first broken?
>
> The usual answer was that this would happen where industrial development was most advanced, where the proletariat formed the majority of the population, where the level of civilisation was high, where democracy was thoroughly established.
>
> But, according to Leninist theory, this reasoning is unsound.

Why "the usual answer"? Why "in former days"? Why not name Marx and Engels? Stalin had to indulge in this subterfuge because he was avoiding an examination of Lenin's relations to Marx and Engels. In fact, if we consider 19th century thought, socialist or otherwise, as a whole, the "answer" was by no means "usual." It was specifically that of Marx and Engels. Nor was it a matter of "reasoning" being "unsound." Marx and Engels's reasoning was perfectly sound given the facts as they then were.

The point is that conditions changed and Lenin examined the changed conditions, not, as Stalin implies, that he had superior "reasoning." By failing to show how Lenin actually developed the theories of Marx and Engels, Stalin presents him as a kind of Russian oracle producing "theses." For instance, the third paragraph of the chapter on the dictatorship of the proletariat opens: "Lenin says: 'The fundamental question of the revolution is the question of power.'" There is no discussion of why Lenin said this or in what context. Simply "Lenin says," with the implication that if Lenin said it, it must be true. On the next page, we have two quotations from Lenin, each introduced simply by "Lenin writes," with no explanation of why Lenin wrote the statements or the rationale behind them. One cannot, of course, expect a Marxist to examine every concept of Marx, Engels, or Lenin in every context. Certain fundamentals have been generally accepted, but some statements, especially on specific matters, obviously require explanation. Otherwise we are presented with a string of assertions, with the implication of infallibility—the infallibility of "genius": "Lenin is the greatest of geniuses ... men of his calibre are born once in many centuries." The Marxist view, shared by other social scientists, is that people with Lenin's potential must be born every day, but social circumstances stifle or distort their development. To contend otherwise is to mute the formative effect of social forces on the individual and, hence, to edge toward biological determinism or even plain superstition (the god).[4]

This rather dogmatic method of Stalin's is, as we have seen, present in his early theoretical works, for instance, in *Anarchism or Socialism*. The question is, however, why did it continue? The answer must be that there was a demand for it, and as we survey Russian conditions at the time the source for this demand is clear. The country was just beginning to recover from a devastating civil war; the old order, which had existed for centuries, had been overthrown; a new order, the dictatorship of the proletariat, without past precedent, was being constructed; and the Party was pointing forward to the uncharted seas of socialism. Obviously there was a need for certainty amid so much uncertainty, for intellectual stability in the midst of whirling change. And Stalin supplied the need, a simple statement of the new credo capable of being understood by millions.

Nor was the statement by any means always faulty. Sometimes, indeed, Stalin succeeded in putting Lenin's views more succinctly than Lenin himself, for instance on the developing world revolution:

> As a result, under imperialism, wars become inevitable; and, under imperialism, there must necessarily ensue a coalition between the proletarian revolution in Europe and the colonial revolution in the East, this leading to the formation of a united world-front of the revolution against the world-front of imperialism.

Or on the state and the dictatorship of the proletariat:

> Hitherto, the class State has always been the dictatorship of an exploiting minority over the exploited majority, whereas the dictatorship of the proletariat is the dictatorship of the exploited majority over the exploiting minority.

Nor did Stalin, in spite of his basically practical approach, underestimate the importance of theory, without which practice would have no base. When there began to rise a new generation of "practicals" who felt that action was all and theory irrelevant, and that theory could develop untested by experience, Stalin moved to the offensive:

> The endeavour of "practical" persons to have no truck with "theories" runs counter to the whole spirit of Leninism and is a great danger to our cause. ... But theory becomes the greatest force in the working-

class movement when it is inseparably linked with revolutionary practice: for it, and it alone, can give the movement confidence, guidance,
and understanding of the inner links between events; it alone can enable
those engaged in the practical struggle to understand the whence and
the whither of the working-class movement.

In passages such as these Stalin educated a whole generation of communists
in some of the elements of Leninism even as at the same time he enshrined
a semi-dogmatic approach which is essentially contrary to the spirit of
Marxism but which has continued in some Soviet and other Marxist circles.
So, too, has Stalin's view of Lenin as an unchallengeable oracle—rather
than as a Marxist social scientist.[5]

Chapter V
The Five Year Plan and the Bukharin Opposition

By 1928 the economic incentive supplied by the New Economic Policy had not only stimulated trade and small business but had enabled industry to develop to a point at which a new advance became possible. At the same time the Party began to develop plans for the collectivization of agriculture. In preparation for this, leading Party members, including Stalin, visited various agricultural areas. As a result of these developments, the Central Committee was able in 1929 to launch the first Five Year Plan. The basic emphasis was on the construction of heavy industry: coal, oil, iron, steel, machines—particularly machines that made other machines. Heavy industry was essential for defense and for supplying agricultural tractors and combines. As heavy industry developed, agriculture was to be collectivized. Stalin had put the matter with his usual proletarian bluntness to the Central Committee:

> We must do everything in our power to overtake and surpass the technical development of the more advanced capitalist countries. We have overtaken and surpassed the most advanced capitalist countries in establishing a new political system, the Soviet system. That is all very good, but it is not enough. In order to secure the final triumph of Socialism, we must overtake and surpass these countries also in technique and economic structure. We have got to do that, or be wiped out.
>
> It is impossible endlessly, i.e., for a considerable length of time, to base the Soviet system and Socialist construction on two different foundations, on the foundation of large-scale and highly concentrated Socialist industry, and on the foundation of very fragmentary and

extremely backward small commodity peasant production. Gradually, but systematically and persistently, we must place our agriculture on a new technical basis, the basis of large-scale production, and raise it to the level of socialised industry. Either we succeed in this task, in which case final victory is certain, or we fail in the task, in which case the return to capitalism may become inevitable.

It would be necessary to increase as rapidly as possible the number of collective farms, not by force but (as Lenin had previously advocated) by persuasion and organization: "The solution lies in gradually amalgamating individual small-and-middle-peasant production into large-scale collective and co-operative, entirely voluntary associations, working on the basis of a modern technique, on the basis of tractors and other agricultural machinery." Although the movement was to be "voluntary," peasants entering collectives would have tractors at their disposal and those who did not would not. The plan, however, applied only to the poor and middle peasants. The power of the rich peasants, the kulaks, who had led armed struggles against the government and slaughtered cattle on a mass scale, had to be broken, and this was accomplished in part by deporting many of them to undeveloped regions to begin farming anew.

When some organizers veered from the Party policy of gradualism and tried to skip the stage of cooperatives as preliminary to collectivization, Stalin quickly called a halt:

How could such blockheaded exercises in "collectivisation," such ludicrous attempts to lift oneself by one's own bootstraps—attempts the purpose of which is to ignore classes and the class struggle, but which in practice brings grist to the mill of our class enemies—occur in our midst? They could occur only because of the atmosphere of "easy" and "unexpected" successes that has prevailed on the front of collective farm construction. They could occur only as a result of the blockhead frame of mind prevailing in the ranks of a section of our Party: "We can do anything!" "That's easy!" They could occur only as a result of the fact that certain of our comrades became dizzy with success, and for a while lost clearmindedness and sober vision.[1]

As the Five Year Plan began to unfold, a new opposition group arose within the party, a "right" opposition led by Nikolai Bukharin, Aleksei Rykov, and Mikhail Tomsky. Unlike Trotsky all were old Bolsheviks; and all belonged to the Central Committee and held high public office. Rykov was Chairman of the Council of People's Commissars (the equivalent of

"Premier"), Tomsky was chairman of the All-Union Central Council of Trade Unions, Bukharin was editor of *Pravda* and General Secretary of the Executive Committee of the Communist International. Bukharin, who became the main spokesman for the group, had long been known as a Marxist "theoretician," but one, as Lenin noted in his "testament," with considerable limitations:

> Bukharin is not only a most valuable and major theorist of the party, but his theoretical views may be classified as fully Marxist only with great reserve, for there is something scholastic about him (he has never made a study of dialectics and, I think, never fully understood it).

That Lenin was correct becomes apparent from a reading of Bukharin's works. His *Historical Materialism* is a metaphysical, pedantic work lacking any sense of the interlocking and clashing of economic and social forces, including those of the class struggle. This approach, Lenin pointed out, also dominated Bukharin's *Imperialism and the World Economy* (1918), in which he contends that monopoly has eliminated competition and would abolish capitalist crisis. Lenin characterized this view as "a fable spread by bourgeois economists." In the 1920 dispute with Trotsky and Bukharin on the role of trade unions in a socialist State, Lenin contended that Bukharin's arguments, like Trotsky's, would endanger the Party. He asked "How could Bukharin go so far as to drop into this rupture with communism?" The answer, Lenin thought, lay in part in Bukharin's theoretical limitations and "lifeless and vapid eclecticism," and he issued a warning that turned out to be prophetic: "The more Comrade Bukharin defends his deviation from Communism, which is obviously wrong theoretically and deceptive politically, the more deplorable will be the fruits of this obstinacy."[2]

Bukharin had been an enthusiastic supporter of the New Economic Policy, but, unlike Lenin, he viewed it as a system that would grow of its own accord into socialism and would last for a long historical period: "For many decades we will slowly be growing into socialism through the growth of our state industry, through cooperation, through the increasing influence of our banking system, through a thousand and one intermediate forms." In accordance with this concept, the peasants—including the kulaks—were to move gradually along a peaceful path to an ultimate socialist order:

> The basic network of our cooperative peasant organization will consist of cooperative cells not of a kulak but of a "laboring" type, cells growing into the system of our general state organs and thus becoming links in a single chain of socialist economy. On the other hand, the

kulak cooperative nests will in exactly the same way, through the banks, etc., grow into this same system; but they will be to a certain extent an alien body. . . . What will become of this type of kulak cooperative in the future? . . . If it wants to prosper, it must inevitably be linked . . . with state economic organs.

Bukharin also opposed the industrialization program of the Five Year Plan: "We think that the formula which calls for maximum investment in heavy industry is not quite correct, or rather, quite incorrect." As industrialization proceeded, his opposition, and that of his colleagues deepened: "You can beat your breast, swear allegiance and take an oath to industrialization, and damn all enemies and apostates, but this will not improve matters one bit." So, too, with collectivization. Collectivization was ruining agriculture, creating "a wave of mass discontent" and "a united village front against us"; and Bukharin warned: "Two bells have sounded, the third is next."[3]

Regardless of his intentions, Bukharin's platform, like Trotsky's earlier, would have undermined the construction of socialism. If the NEP had continued for "many decades," capitalism would have become dominant. Without industrialization the Soviet Union would, as Stalin said and subsequent events demonstrated, have been crushed in war; the continuation of individual farms, with their kulak "nests," would in time have undermined proletarian rule. When we examine the platforms of Trotsky and Bukharin, the strength of Stalin, with his stubborn practicality and firm socialist perspective, becomes increasingly obvious.

Once again, Stalin, as General Secretary, gave the answer of the majority of the Central Committee to the new opposition:

Those who support Comrade Bukharin's group hope to persuade the class enemy that he should voluntarily forgo his interests and voluntarily surrender his grain surplus. They hope that the kulak, who has grown, who is able to avoid giving grain by offering other products in its place and who conceals his grain surplus, they hope that this same kulak will give us his grain surplus voluntarily at our collection prices. Have they lost their senses? Is it not obvious that they do not understand the mechanism of the class struggle, that they do not know what classes mean? Do they know with what derision the kulaks treat our people and the Soviet Government at village meetings called to assist the grain collections? Have they heard of facts like this, for instance: one of our agitators in Kazakstan for two hours tried to persuade the holders of grain to surrender that grain for supplying the country. At the end of the talk a kulak stepped forth with his pipe in his mouth and said: "Do us a little dance, young fellow, and I will let you have a couple of poods of grain". ... Try and persuade people like that. Class is class, comrades. You cannot get away from that truth.

As both industrialization and collectivization moved forward, Stalin routed the opposition—and its "two bells" doomsday outlook—with scathing ridicule:

If any difficulty or hitch has appeared anywhere, they already fall into panic lest something may happen. A cockroach somewhere stirs, without having time even to crawl out of its hole, and they are already starting back in terror, and beginning to shout about a catastrophe, about the ruin of the Soviet Government. (General laughter.) We try to calm them, we try to convince them that nothing dangerous has happened as yet, that it is only a cockroach, and there is no need to be afraid. But all in vain. They continue to shout as before: "What cockroach? That's no cockroach, it's a thousand wild beasts! It's not a cockroach, but the abyss, the ruin of the Soviet Government."[4]

In the 1920s Bukharin revived some of the arguments of his book on imperialism. In its monopoly stage, he contended, capitalism in the United States and other nations, was a new kind of capitalism: "All this reflects a peculiar form of state capitalism, where the state power controls and develops capitalism." Capitalism, he wrote: "is again revealing the staggering wonder of technological progress, transforming scientific knowledge . . . into a powerful lever of technological revolution." This "wonder of technological progress," safely under state control, had entered an era of "stabilization," a stabilization which meant that capitalism had overcome the "anarchic nature" which Marx had perceived in it, a stabilization reflecting "deep, internal structural changes." These views were not only a refutation of Marx and Lenin (who saw the state as controlled by monopoly capitalism—not the other way around—and argued that monopoly intensified the contradictions of capitalism) but of the position of the Party. At the Fifteenth Congress of the Party in 1927, Stalin, reporting for the Central Committee, declared: "We have all the symptoms of a most profound crisis and of the growing instability of world capitalism." Furthermore Bukharin's views on imperialism show that underlying his concept of a virtually permanent NEP lay a certain (perhaps unconscious) admiration for capitalism in general.[5]

In 1926 Bukharin became General Secretary of the Executive Committee of the Communist International. At the Sixth Congress of the International in 1928, on the eve of the world capitalist depression, he distributed, without consulting other Party leaders, a series of economic "theses," embodying his "stabilization" and "state capitalism" concepts. The Party leadership, under Stalin, intervened:

> According to Comrade Bukharin's theses it appears that nothing new is taking place at the present moment to unsettle capitalist stabilisation, but that, on the contrary, capitalism is reconstructing itself and that, on the whole, it is maintaining itself more or less securely. It is obvious that the delegation of the C.P.S.U. could not agree with such a characterisation of what is called the Third Period, i.e., the period we are now passing through. ... Accordingly, the delegation of the C.P.S.U. introduced an amendment, which pointed out that capitalist stabilisation is not secure and could not be secure, that it is being shattered, and will be shattered, by the march of events owing to the aggravation of the crisis of world capitalism.

During the course of the struggle against Bukharin, Stalin insightfully discussed the difference between "Rights"—Bukharinites—and "Lefts"—Trotskyists—using as an example the building of the great Dnieprostroy dam. He said, "If, for instance, the Rights say, 'It is a mistake to build Dnieprostroy,' while the 'Lefts,' on the contrary say, 'What is the good of one Dnieprostroy? Give us a Dnieprostroy every year' (laughter), it must be admitted that there is some difference between them." Yet either way they would end up with no Dnieprostroy. "But," Stalin continued, "if the Trotskyist deviation is a 'Left' deviation, does that not mean that the 'Lefts' are more Left than the Leninists? No, it does not. Leninism is the most Left (without quotation marks) tendency in the world working-class movement." In a later succinct comment he noted the basic identity of the right and the "left": "The 'lefts' are in fact Rights who mask their Rightness by Left phrases."[6]

At the time (1928-30), the conflict between Bukharin and the Party majority appeared to be an honest disagreement between leading Party members. Bukharin, although removed from the Political Bureau, retained his seat on the Central Committee and was appointed to the Presidium of the Commissariat of Heavy Industry. In 1934 he was made editor of *Izvestia*. Rykov, removed as premier, was appointed People's Commissar of Posts and Telegraphs; Tomsky, removed from his post in the trade unions, retained his seat on the Central Committee, as did Rykov. All three signed a declaration admitting the errors of their program:

We consider it our duty to state that in this dispute the party and its Central Committee have turned out to be correct. Our views . . . have turned out to be mistaken. Recognizing our mistakes, we will . . . conduct a decisive struggle against all deviations from the party's general line and above all against the right deviation.[7]

Some eight years later, Bukharin and his followers were put on trial, accused of wrecking and of traitorous negotiations, direct or indirect, with the German and Japanese governments. Their trials followed those of "the Trotskyite Center" in 1937 and of the Kamenev-Zinoviev group in 1936.

In order to balance the current denunciations of these trials as frame-ups, we might note the reaction at the time of the U.S. ambassador to the U.S.S.R., Joseph E. Davies, who attended the 1937 and 1938 trials and had himself been a trial lawyer. Davies first attended the trials of the Trotskyite center in January 1937. He reported in a "Strictly Confidential" memo to Cordell Hull, then Secretary of State, that in his opinion, the defendants were guilty as charged. "To have assumed that this proceeding was invented and staged as a project of dramatic political fiction would be to presuppose the creative genius of a Shakespeare and the genius of a Belasco in a stage production."

In 1937, after witnessing the first series of trials, Davies visited Winston Churchill:

Over the coffee, Churchill was interested "in these purge trials." He plied me with questions, I told him the truth as I saw it. It obviously was a great surprise to the diplomatic guests. That sort of talk is not fashionable here, so violent is the prejudice. Churchill has no love for the Communists. He has had some bitter experiences with them. He is, however, fair and judicial minded and wants to know the facts. He is definitely not a "wishful thinker." I gave the facts as interpreted from the Soviet viewpoint and briefly outlined the argument of the government in these cases. Churchill said that I had given him a completely new concept of the situation.

Four other ambassadors confided in Davies that they, too, believed the trials to be genuine and the defendants guilty. But what the ambassadors reported back to their governments and what these governments propagated were different things:

Another diplomat, Minister------, made a most illuminating statement to me yesterday. In discussing the trial he said that the defendants were undoubtedly guilty; that all of us who attended the trial had practically agreed on that; that the outside world, from the press reports, however, seemed to think that the trial was a put-up job (facade, as he called it); that while we knew it was not, it was probably just as well that the outside world should think so.

On the Bukharinite trial, Davies wrote at the time in a letter to his daughter:

All the fundamental weaknesses and vices of human nature—personal ambitions at their worst—are shown up in the proceedings. They disclose the outlines of a plot which came very near to being successful in bringing about the overthrow of this government.

And he wrote in a confidential memo to Cordell Hull:

Notwithstanding a prejudice arising from the confession evidence and a prejudice against a judicial system which affords practically no protection for the accused, after daily observation of the witnesses, their manner of testifying, the unconscious corroborations which developed, and other facts in the course of the trial, together with others of which a judicial notice could be taken, it is my opinion so far as the political defendants are concerned [that] sufficient crimes under Soviet law, among those charged in the indictment, were established by the proof and beyond a reasonable doubt to justify the verdict of guilty of treason.

In the summer of 1941, after the German imperialist attack on the U.S.S.R., Davies commented:

On the train that day, that thought lingered in my mind. It was rather extraordinary, when one stopped to think of it, that in this last Nazi invasion, not a word had appeared of "inside work" back of the Russian lines. There was no so-called "internal aggression" in Russia cooperating with the German High Command. Hitler's march into Prague in 1939 was accompanied by the active military support of Henlein's organizations in Czechoslavakia. The same was true of his invasion of Norway. There were no Sudeten Henleins, no Slovakian Tisos, no Belgian De Grelles, no Norwegian Quislings in the Soviet picture... There were no Fifth Columnists in Russia in 1941—they had shot them. The purge had cleansed the country and rid it of treason.[8]

The most significant and revealing of the trials was that of Bukharin. The basis for Bukharin's opposition, he testified, was his old distrust of rapid industrialization—especially the emphasis on heavy industry—and collectivization. This opposition led Bukharin to slide, to his own dismay, from what he considered legitimate oppositon into anti-socialist activity:

> Psychologically, we, who at one time had advocated Socialist industrialism, began to regard with a shrug of the shoulders, with irony, and then with anger at bottom, our huge, gigantically growing factories as monstrous gluttons which consumed everything, deprived the broad masses of articles of consumption, and represented a certain danger. ... We were ironical about the collective farms ... collective farms were music of the future. What was necessary was to develop rich property owners ... in 1929-30 we pitied the expropriated kulaks, from so-called humanitarian motives.
>
> When all the state machines, when all the means, when all the best forces were flung into the industrialization of the country, into collectivization, we found ourselves, literally in twenty-four hours, on the other shore, we found ourselves with the kulaks, with the counter-revolutionaries, we found ourselves with the capitalist remnants which still existed at the time in the sphere of trade.

At about the same time the Trotskyists—Trotsky himself was in exile—were coming to similar conclusions. "I believed," testified one of their intellectual leaders, Carl Radek, "that the economic offensive was being conducted on too wide a front, that the material forces available (number of tractors, etc.) would not permit of universal collectivization, and that if this general offensive were not slowed down this would, as we defined it by a catch-phrase, 'end like the march on Warsaw.'"[9]

If the Bukharinites were to seriously oppose the Party program, if they really felt the program would destroy socialism by its economic policy and bureaucratic administration, they had to organize and act. Appeals to the Party and the workers had gotten them nowhere and the Bukharinites were, in fact, a comparatively small and isolated group. Therefore the only course open to them was one of fomenting rebellion—especially among the richer peasants—sabotage, wrecking, assassination, and terrorism. As they turned from a political group into a conspiracy, Bukharin testified, moral and psychological disintegration began:

> It was not the naked logic of the struggle that drove us, the counter-revolutionary conspirators, into this stinking underground life, which has been exposed at this trial in all its starkness. This naked logic of the struggle was accompanied by a degeneration of ideas, a degen-

eration of psychology, a degeneration of ourselves, a degeneration of people.... And on this basis, it seems to me probable that every one of us sitting here in the dock suffered from a peculiar duality of mind, an incomplete faith in his counter-revolutionary cause. I will not say that the consciousness of this was absent, but it was incomplete. Hence a certain semi-paralysis of the will, a retardation of reflexes.

National conspiracy turned to international conspiracy. As war loomed closer, the Bukharinites advocated economic deals with the Germans and Japanese whereby they would grant concessions in return for being recognized as the government when, as they and most international observers believed, the U.S.S.R. would go down to inevitable defeat. Bukharin continued:

When the fascists came to power in Germany, exchanges of opinion commenced among the leaders of the counter-revolutionary organizations concerning the possibility of utilizing foreign states in connection with a war situation. Here I must say frankly, and I tell the Court what I precisely remember, that in this major question, which is a very important subject for the Court's consideration and for the determination of the legal sanction, the Trotskyites were outright for territorial concessions, while on the whole the leading circles of the Right counter-revolutionary organization were primarily concerned with concessions, trade agreements, duties, prices, supplies of raw material, fuel, etc.—in short, various concessions of an economic nature.

This policy, however, ran into rather obvious difficulties. The Nazis and Japanese militarists could simply put their "feet on the table and tear up any preliminary agreement." To seize power one would have to work with dissident groups in the Red Army command. And these army leaders—"I was thinking particularly of Tukhachevsky" Bukharin said, "would start out by making short shrift of their allies and so-called inspirers in Napoleonic style." (The Trotskyists, according to Radek, had similar fears: "defeat was inevitable," and so a deal with the Nazis seemed also inevitable, but "if foreign fascism came in" it would have "no need to trouble itself with this crowd of anarchist intellectuals.")[10]

In making his confession, Bukharin asserted, he had never been tortured or drugged:

Repentance is often attributed to diverse and absolutely absurd things like Thibetan powders and the like. I must say of myself that in prison, where I was confined for over a year, I worked, studied, and retained my clarity of mind. ... For three months I refused to say anything. Then I began to testify. Why? Because while in prison I made a revaluation of my entire past. For when you ask yourself: "If you must die, what are you dying for?"—an absolutely black vacuity suddenly rises before you with startling vividness. There was nothing to die for, if one wanted to die unrepented.

That Bukharin would be executed was clear from the previous trials and his was reflected in often-defiant testimony:

VYSHINSKY: And you considered yourself an ideologist?
BUKHARIN: Both an ideologist of a counter-revolutionary coup and a practical man. You, of course, would prefer to hear that I consider myself a spy, but I never considered myself a spy, nor do I now.
VYSHINSKY: It would be more correct if you did.
BUKHARIN: That is your opinion, but my opinion is different.

As one considers Bukharin's evidence, evidence given under the shadow of death—"I am about to finish. I am perhaps speaking for the last time in my life"—it is clear that he told the truth. His honesty is indicated also by other testimony, which spells out in detail the acts to which he refers. The theory that the trials were entirely or mainly fraudulent falls apart in the face of testimony such as Bukharin's and a mass of interlocking evidence given by some 30 witnesses. That evidence, in turn, was supported in the main by the testimony of witnesses at the previous state trials. Even if, as Ambassador Davies suggests, the Soviet prosecutors had had a scriptwriter of Shakespearean genius, they could not have constructed out of whole cloth such a set of complexly integrated events. There were indeed anti-soviet conspiratorial groups. In view of the nature of Russia's revolution and social development, with its widespread assault on capitalist and feudal elements, such groups were inevitable. The indication, as Davies argues, is that the defendants were, on the whole, guilty as charged. In these trials and others, there was evidence of massive and diverse sabotage—in the coal mines, chemical plants, tractor stations, collective farms, the railways. Combined with deliberate economic misplanning and financial fraud, it constituted a concerted effort to destroy the growing socialist state.[11]

The state trials, then, represented the continuation of the political conflicts of the proceding decades in a new form. And behind the political conflicts was, of course, the class struggle. However he may have rationalized his actions, Bukharin, was, in fact, helping the kulaks, the NEP capitalists, and international capital. And so, too, the Trotskyists, as Radek ruefully admitted.

That the myth persists of these trials as an elaborate charade created by inhuman monsters is, in essence, further evidence of the extraordinary scope and depth of anti-Stalin, anti-Soviet defamation. The myth is made to appear believable by appeal to two facts: the defendants confessed their guilt and most of them were executed. There is, however, no evidence that the confessions were exacted by torture or drugs; such a claim was denied by Bukharin and others. The indication is that the defendants confessed because the evidence against them was overwhelming; also, as Bukharin notes, some of them at least had, in spite of their actions, a "duality of mind," a feeling that regardless of their motives, their deeds were morally wrong and would harm their country. Davies certainly had no trouble in believing that the confessions were genuine.

Whether it was necessary to execute most of the defendants or whether imprisonment for all would have served is a question that has to be answered in the light of the then-existing conditions. In a situation of gathering war, with the Italian fascists in Ethiopia, the Japanese militarists invading China, and Hitler supporting Franco and straining for war, the Soviet government obviously decided that a severe counterblow must be struck to stop all efforts to weaken the Soviet state from within. Whatever the decision, however, responsibility for it cannot have been Stalin's alone or even primarily his. The charge that it was stems from the view of Stalin as absolute dictator. But the trials were conducted by the judicial system and although Stalin as Party leader had considerable influence upon that system, he by no means ran it. The trials, we must also remember, came after the new constitution of 1936 with its mass-democratic structures. Furthermore, there was a national outpouring of rage at the time against those who were perceived (correctly) as traitors and saboteurs. The argument that this indignation, which included mass demonstrations, was "rigged" again reflects the automaton picture of Soviet society. No doubt, the Party participated in and helped to organize such demonstrations and other expressions of popular outrage, but it could not have done so had not the feeling itself existed.

In assessing the trials of Bukharin and others we must always be aware of the ferocity and scope of the international class struggle then and now. For the first time in history the masses had seized and held state power— the historic nightmare of the ruling class. From the birth of the new state, the world bourgeoisie was obsessed by a drive to kill it. This drive, inside and outside the U.S.S.R., was reflected, often in subtle ways, in the Soviet intelligentsia. It was aided by the fact that revolutionaries in Russia had long concentrated on the overthrow of feudalism. Some of them, although they would have denied this—as Bukharin certainly would—wavered before the destruction of capitalism and the building of socialism. This was also true, we should note, of Chinese and other revolutionaries. Bukharin does not stand alone on the stage. His case is representative of a general phenomenon.

Chapter VI
Socialism, Democracy and Control

The arguments of the "left" and right opposition groups that their actions were justified because the Party policy was undermining the state are belied by the economic and social record. Between 1928 and 1934 iron production rose from 3 million to 10 million tons, steel from 4 to 9 million, oil from 11 to 24 million. The figures, though stark and simple, have social as well as economic significance. "We inherited from the past," Stalin noted in 1935, "a technically backward, impoverished and ruined country. Ruined by four years of imperialist war, and ruined again by three years of civil war, a country with a semi-literate population, with a low technical level, with isolated industrial islands lost in a sea of dwarf peasant farms." The figures show that this impoverished and largely feudal country was pulling out of the ruins and establishing the economic foundations of socialism. And, as Marx had shown, if the economic foundations are laid—for any society—the social, political, and cultural consequences are immense. Was it any wonder that the Russian people on the whole had trust, admiration, and affection for the Party that had accomplished this, and for its leaders?[1]

In 1933 Stalin could announce that (in the midst of the world capitalist depression) "unemployment has been abolished." The following year he reported on the developing "new village":

The appearance of the countryside has changed even more. The old type of village, with the church in the most prominent place, with the best houses—those of the police officer, the priest, and the kulaks— in the foreground, and the dilapidated huts of the peasants in the background, is beginning to disappear. Its place is being taken by the new type of village, with its public farm buildings, with its clubs, radio, cinemas, schools, libraries and creches; with its tractors, harvester combines, threshing machines and automobiles.

In 1935 he hailed the Stakhanovite movement:

Stakhanov raised the technical standard of output of coal five or six times, if not more. Busygin and Smetanin did the same—one in the sphere of machine-building and the other in the shoe industry.... Life has improved, comrades. Life has become more joyous. And when life is joyous, work goes well. Hence the high rates of output. Hence the heroes and heroines of labor. That, primarily, is the root of the Stakhanov movement.

In 1939 Stalin reported that the iron and steel industry, which had been virtually non-existent in the early 1920s, had made great strides: "In 1938 we produced about 15,000,000 tons of pig iron; Great Britain produced 7,000,000 tons." Agriculture had been mechanized. In 1938 there were 483,500 tractors in use and 153,500 harvester combines—in a previously horse and plow countryside. Wages had doubled, from an annual average of 1,513 rubles in 1933 to 3,447 in 1938. Similar advances had been made in education; in a nation of centuries-old mass illiteracy there were now nearly 34 million "students of all grades"; in higher educational institutions there were 600,000 students; in 1938, 31,300 engineers, 10,600 agricultural specialists, and 35,700 teachers graduated. A new "stratum" of professionals had been born:

Hundreds of thousands of young people coming from the ranks of the working class, the peasantry and the working intelligentsia entered the universities and technical colleges, from which they emerged to reinforce the attenuated ranks of the intelligentsia. They infused fresh blood into it and reanimated it in a new Soviet spirit. They radically changed the whole aspect of the intelligentsia, molding it in their own form and image. The remnants of the old intelligentsia were dissolved in the new Soviet intelligentsia, the intelligentsia of the people.

To run this new industrial society efficiently, authoritative works-managers were needed:

We can no longer tolerate our factories being transformed from productive organisms into parliaments. Our Party and trade union organisations must at length understand that without ensuring one-man management and strict responsibility for work done, we cannot solve the problems of reconstructing industry.

It was necessary also to build up a working-class upper stratum, a skilled, highly paid, permanently located industrial labor force:

> It cannot be tolerated that a rolling mill hand in a steel mill should earn no more than a sweeper. It cannot be tolerated that a locomotive driver on a railway should earn only as much as a copying clerk. . . . In every branch of industry, in every factory, in every department of a factory, there is a leading group of more or less skilled workers who must be first and foremost attached to production if we want to make sure of having a permanent staff of workers. This leading group of workers forms the chief link in production. By attaching them to the factory, or to the department, we attach the whole staff of workers and put an end to the instability of labour power. And how can we manage to attach them to the factory? It can be done by advancing them, by raising their wages, by introducing such a system of payment as will give the skilled worker his due.

As a result of these and other changes, class antagonisms had, he believed, disappeared (1936):

> Unlike bourgeois constitutions, the draft of the new Constitution of the U.S.S.R. proceeds from the fact that there are no longer any antagonistic classes in society; that society consists of two friendly classes, of workers and peasants.

The intelligentsia was also part of this non-antagonistic order:

> The feature that distinguishes Soviet society today from any capitalist society is that it no longer contains antagonistic, hostile classes, that the exploiting classes have been eliminated, while the workers, peasants and intellectuals, who make up Soviet society, live and work in friendly collaboration.[2]

When we consider Stalin's facts and figures, it becomes clear that we are witnessing the most concentrated economic advance ever recorded—greater even than those of the Industrial Revolution. Within 10 years a primarily feudal society had been changed into an industrialized one. And for the first time in history such an advance was due not to capitalism but to socialism.

The point, elementary though it is, requires emphasis for the advance is often represented neutrally as "industrialization." But if it had not been for the fact that the working class controlled the central economy and ran it without the necessity for capitalist profit, such an advance, combining size, swiftness and stability, would not have been possible. On the other hand it is also true that some of the measures Stalin and the Party deemed necessary to achieve this advance contained negative factors.

As early as 1919 Lenin had been worried by the advance of the upper stratum of the workers to virtual power. He felt that the mass of the workers and peasants, brought up under capitalist regimentation or feudal stultification, had insufficient initiative and little Marxist grasp of political realities. "The result of this low cultural level is that the Soviets, which by virtue of their programme are organs of government by the toilers, are in fact organs of government for the toilers, by means of the advanced stratum of the proletariat, but not by means of the toiling masses." And he added: "The Soviet apparatus is accessible to all the toilers in word, but in fact it is far from accessible to all of them, as we all know." Not only did the upper stratum of the working class dominate the soviets, but "hardened bureaucrats" left over from the tsarist government were still in positions of power:

> We dispersed these old bureaucratic elements, shook them up and then began to place them in new posts. The tsarist bureaucrats began to enter the Soviet institutions and practice their bureaucratic methods, they began to assume the colouring of Communists and, for greater success in their careers, to procure membership cards of the Russian Communist Party. And so, having been thrown out of the door, they fly in through the window!

In an effort to counter these various developments, Lenin urged that the Central Committee add to its ranks 50 to 100 "workers of a lower stratum than those who have been promoted in the last five years to work in Soviet bodies." However, Lenin realized that the problem went deeper than this. The basic solution lay in years of patient political and educational work: "But here laws alone are not enough. A vast amount of educational, organisational and cultural work is required, which cannot be done rapidly by legislation and which demands a vast amount of prolonged work."[3]

In 1928 Stalin was troubled by a similar problem:

> Of course, the fact that we have a group of leaders who have risen excessively high and enjoy great prestige is in itself a great achievement

for our Party. Obviously, the direction of a big country would be unthinkable without such an authoritative group of leaders. But the fact that as these leaders rise they get further away from the masses, and the masses begin to look up at them from below and do not venture to criticise them, cannot but give rise to a certain danger of the leaders losing contact with the masses and the masses getting out of touch with the leaders.

A new movement was needed towards democracy within the Party and between the Party and the working class:

It is a question of organising, along the lines of self-criticism and criticism of our shortcomings, the broad public opinion of the Party, the broad public opinion of the working class, as an instrument of keen and vigilant moral control, to which the most authoritative leaders must lend an attentive ear if they want to retain the confidence of the Party and the confidence of the working class.[4]

In the succeeding decade, serious efforts were made to implement this mass democratization policy. Nationwide educational programs raised the "low cultural level" that had troubled Lenin; workers enthusiastically joined the Party in mass campaigns for increased production and, in 1936, in creating a new constitution. Stalin's declaration—"Life has become more joyous"—was not simply rhetoric. It was a fact. But the other tendency noted by Stalin also continued: the "authoritative group of leaders" acquired still more authority.

It has been argued that in these years basic decisions were made in the Political Bureau of the Central Committee, and the Committee itself was bypassed. There may be some truth to this, but it is not the essential truth. In fact, it harbors a distortion of the truth, for it implies a basic dictatorship in a nation which—in 1936—adopted a constitution giving citizens a broader spectrum of rights—not only political but economic—than any in world history. What the U.S.S.R. achieved, was a new form of democracy, a mass democracy, and the fact that mass democracy does not follow all the structures (and charades) of bourgeois democracy does not mean it is not democracy. On the other hand, it is certainly true that in a socialist government— or any government—some decisions, both substantive and executive, must be made by a small top body. Whether that body is responsive to the mass of the population, and has open channels for that response, is the question. In these years this was certainly so in the U.S.S.R. The five-month nationwide discussion of the proposed new constitution, in thousands of meetings of all kinds, reflected a spirit of mass democracy and a genuine admiration for and trust in Stalin and his colleagues. Furthermore, there were frequent meetings of the Central Committee as well as regular Party Conferences and Congresses. As experience has since shown, in socialist states a balance is necessary between mass democracy and strong top leadership. Without such leadership, bourgeois elements tend to surface—as they did in China, Poland, or Yugoslavia—and weaken socialist development.[5]

After the struggles with the "left" and right oppositions, Stalin was keenly aware of such anarchistic dangers and took measures against them. Worker participation in management—although still encouraged—would not be allowed to "transform" factories "from productive organisms into parliaments." "One-man management" was needed, along with worker participation, especially by the "leading group" of "skilled workers," who were to exercise a "vigilant moral control" not only over their fellow workers but over the Party group within each productive unit.

In such policies, Stalin was trying to strike a balance between mass participation and firm leadership, which would provide guidance and structure for such participation. Lenin, as his actions and his plans for socialist development show, was well aware of this need for balance. Lenin was not a liberal or an anarchist, as some of Stalin's opponents seem to imply. If his concept of democratic participation was somewhat broader than Stalin's—and it is not clear that it was, as things developed—this was a matter of degree and not, as had been asserted, basic. Lenin, confronting the problems that the Party faced in these years, could hardly have acted differently than Stalin did.

As we have seen, the "joint opposition" platform of 1927 proclaimed the rise of a "new bourgeoisie" in the U.S.S.R. and, in the succeeding decades, the phrase became general in world anti-soviet circles. But there was no bourgeoisie in any meaningful sense in the U.S.S.R. For there was no economic base for one. What did arise, as does not seem to have been recognized, was a historically new class.

In feudal, slave-commercial, and capitalist societies a group of professionals, along with small capitalists, formed a middle class (or petty bourgeoisie). As capitalism developed, some of these professionals became part of the bourgeoisie. And in capitalist society the middle class was much larger than in other exploitive societies. However, it existed in all of them and its core was formed by the small-business community. With the coming of socialism, this small-business core was eliminated and the total professional group grew into a class in its own right. But this was not simply an expansion of the old professional group, although it had roots there. It was a historically new class, the professional class, called into being by the structural complexity of a planned economy—which had never existed in any civilization—and by the immense social structures which necessarily grew with that economy. If we simply look over the innumerable divisions of the first Five Year Plan, the massive size and intricate interlockings of the economy become apparent. If we then consider the vast structures of social services required in a society in which the whole population was entitled to such services, it becomes apparent that such economic and social systems could not be run by the working class alone; specialists and trained professionals of all kinds were needed in vast numbers in all fields.

Stalin was aware of "the new, Soviet intelligentsia, the intelligentsia of the people," into which the "remnants of the old intelligentsia were dissolved." But he did not consider this new "intelligentsia" to be a class. Soviet "society," he noted in discussing the new Soviet constitution, "consists of two friendly classes, of workers and peasants." However: "The intelligentsia has never been a class, and never can be a class—it was and remains a stratum, which recruits its members from among all classes of society." But the fact that in its formative period the intelligentsia recruited its members from the working class and peasantry (as well as having roots in the old Czarist intelligentsia) did not mean that it could not in time become an integral part of a class. And this, in fact, is what happened. A socialist intelligentsia is indeed a stratum but it is not a free-floating stratum loosely appended to the working class and peasantry. It is a part of the new professional class. It forms the upper stratum of the class: major administrators, scientists and other top professionals. The lower section of the class, which blends into the working class, consists of social workers, teachers, medical and scientific technicians, second-level administrators and so on.[6]

As we read over Stalin's reports, it becomes apparent that he is—whether he was fully aware of it or not—proclaiming the rise of a new ruling political alliance. The center of the alliance was that "leading group of workers" that formed "the chief link in production." Closely associated with them were the works managers, who, under "one-man" control, assumed "strict responsibility for work done." And finally came "the new, Soviet intelligentsia, the intelligentsia of the people," by which Stalin meant essentially engineers, technicians, and economic administrators and planners. However, when we realize that the "intelligentsia" represented part of a class, as did the "leading workers," then the alliance is seen to be basically not a political alliance but a class alliance of the working class as a whole and the professional class as a whole. Under Stalin the working class was the prime force in this alliance. The peasantry was in a subordinate position, possessing political and other rights but not national power or major sociocultural national influence.

As became clear under Khrushchev there was an area of difference of interest between the intelligentsia and the workers, the intelligentsia pushing for less central economic control and more "liberal" views in various fields as well as for personal privileges for themselves. These drives were mitigated both by working-class influence and by pressures within the professional class as a whole, especially its lower echelons. Although the political alliance had considerable executive power, the basic alliance was still social and not political, an alliance of classes. And, as we shall see, when political power under Khrushchev moved too far in a bourgeois direction the working class in time redressed the balance.

As a general historical phenomenon, such class balances, although unusual, are not unique. Ruling-class alliances have existed in various historical situations. In slave-commercial Athens, for instance, an alliance of slave-owning capitalists and feudal landowners ruled for several centuries, not without conflict, of course, but on the whole united. In commercial-capitalist Britain, a similar alliance of landowners and capitalists ruled from the late 17th century into the early 19th. In Athens and Britain, however, both classes were exploiting classes and both were comparatively small. In the U.S.S.R., on the other hand, neither the working class nor the professional class is an exploiting class and both are large classes. They are also divided into two sections, upper and lower, and it is in the upper section of each class that the central political power resides. These upper sections, however, are themselves large. The upper section of the working class embraces almost the whole of the industrial workers.[7]

The rise of the new ruling class alliance did not, however, mean that class struggle had ceased. It was ridiculous for Stalin to declare in 1936 that all class antagonisms had vanished when but six years before he had warned Bukharin that "class was class." He meant that the industrial working class and its professional allies, having broken the back of the kulak resistance, now held undisputed political power and had no major points of contention between them. But this, as events were to reveal, was not entirely true.

These developments must be seen against the background of the great expansion of mass democratic rights embodied in the new constitution of 1936, rights which were not only political but, unlike those in bourgeois-democratic constitutions, also economic: "the right to guaranteed employment," "annual vacations with pay," "free medical services," "free education up to and including the seventh grade."

We might note, as typical, the rights of women: "Women in the U.S.S.R. are accorded equal rights with men in all spheres of economic, government, cultural, political and other public activity. The possibility of exercising these rights is ensured by women being accorded an equal right with men to work, payment for work, rest and leisure, social insurance and education, and by state protection of the interests of mother and child, state aid to mothers of large families and unmarried mothers, maternity leave with full pay, and a provision of a wide network of maternity homes, nurseries, and kindergartens." Further: "Women have the right to elect and be elected on equal terms with men." These gains were not, of course, simply given to women. They had to fight for them. But they fought with Party support and in a situation of emerging socialism. Nevertheless the fact remains that the most dramatic advance—often from feudal bondage—ever made by women was made under Stalin's leadership. And such advances were typical of the whole era.

The political executive power might reside in the hands of the upper strata of the working class and the professional class, but basic political power resided in the masses and their organizations: "The right to nominate candidates is secured to public organizations and societies of the working people. Communist Party organizations, trade unions, cooperatives, youth organizations and cultural societies." These organizations acted only after long and full debate, according to numerous observers and the Soviet press, local and national. Nor was there any major division between the Party and the people. The local Party leaders were everywhere recognized as the leaders of the people. Like the national leaders they were seen as members of a Party which had led the nation from tsarism to socialism. Their power depended upon their ability. Unlike leaders in capitalist countries, they had no base in superior wealth. All candidates for office, men and women alike, received the equal support of their mass organizations. One did not need to be a millionaire or a friend of millionaires to run for office.

In short, the era was one of a mass democratic initiative unparalleled in previous history. This was, of course, not primarily due to Stalin or anyone else but to the general socioeconomic foundation of the (socialist) society, which the people had built—a feat also unparalleled in history. That these obvious facts need to be stressed indicates the degree of distortion that has been created by influential publicists in the capitalist world, who routinely depict the Soviet Communist Party members as petty tyrants. No one, of course, claims that the relationship between Party and non-Party people was idyllic or that there were no conflicts of interest and no corruption. Life does not deal in idylls. But on the whole it was, and is, a warm relationship based on a fundamental coincidence of interest and a general admiration for the hard and often self-sacrificing work of the average Party member.[8]

Chapter VII
Theorist for World Communism

During the years 1924-1938, when he was directing the Party's program for developing socialism, Stalin wrote only one work of a general theoretical nature, a 1938 article on dialectical and historical materialism. This article was included in *History of the Communist Party of the Soviet Union (Bolsheviks)*, which was written under Stalin's direction and was read throughout the world. Furthermore his reports to the Party Congresses and other writings contain important specific theoretical concepts, often presented in the firm, simple style which he exhibited early in his work and turned into an effective medium for mass comprehension.

In 1924, as we have seen, Stalin put forward a theory that the development of world capitalism was determined by three "contradictions": between labor and capital, between imperialist states, between imperialism and the colonial world. In 1930, surveying the total world scene, he added one more contradiction:

> I spoke earlier of the contradictions of world capitalism. But besides these contradictions there is still one more. I mean the contradiction between the capitalist world and the U.S.S.R. True, it is not a contradiction of the internal capitalist type. It is a contradiction between capitalism as a whole and a country building Socialism.

Beset by these contradictions, capitalism had entered a period of "general crisis":

> What does this mean?
> It means first of all that the imperialist war and its aftermath have intensified the decay of capitalism and disturbed its equilibrium, that we are now living in the epoch of wars and revolutions, that capitalism

no longer represents the sole and all-embracing system of world economy, that side by side with the capitalist system of economy there exists the Socialist system, which is growing, which is flourishing, which is resisting the capitalist system, and which by the very fact of its existence is demonstrating the rottenness of capitalism and shaking its foundations.

It means, furthermore, that the imperialist war and the victory of the revolution in the U.S.S.R. have shaken the foundations of imperialism in the colonial and dependent countries, that the prestige of imperialism in these countries has already been undermined, that it is no longer capable of governing in the old way in these countries.

It means, further, that during the war and after it, a young, native capitalism appeared and grew up in the colonial and dependent countries, which competes successfully in the markets with the old capitalist countries, sharpening and complicating the struggle for markets.

In the midst of this general crisis had come the economic crisis:

The basis of the crisis lies in the contradiction between the social character of production and the capitalist form of appropriation of the results of production. This basic contradiction of capitalism is expressed in the contradiction between the colossal growth in the productive capacity of capitalism, calculated to secure the maximum of capitalist profit, and the relative reduction of purchasing power of millions of toilers whose standard of living the capitalists are all the time trying to keep within the limits of the lowest possible minimum. ... The crisis of over-production is the expression of this contradiction in unbridled and destructive forms. If capitalism could adapt production, not to the acquisition of the maximum of profits, but to the systematic improvement of the material conditions of the workers and peasants, then there would be no crisis. But then, also, capitalism would not be capitalism. In order to abolish crises, capitalism must be abolished.[1]

Faced with this dangerous situation, the capitalist governments tried to find a solution in war.

As you see [Stalin wrote in 1934], things are heading toward a new imperialist war as a way out of the present situation.

Of course, there are no grounds for assuming that war can provide a real way out. On the contrary, it is bound to confuse the situation still more. More than that, it is sure to unleash revolution and jeopardise the very existence of capitalism in a number of countries, as happened in the course of the first imperialist war.

Revolutions, however, would not develop spontaneously no matter how great the suffering imposed by crisis or war:

> Some comrades think that, once there is a revolutionary crisis the bourgeoisie is bound to get into a hopeless position, that its end is therefore a foregone conclusion, that the victory of the revolution is thus assured, and that all they have to do is to wait for the fall of the bourgeoisie and to draw up victorious resolutions. That is a profound mistake. The victory of the revolution never comes of itself. It must be prepared for and won. And only a strong proletarian revolutionary party can prepare for and win victory.

Such revolutions when they came would be of two types, those in imperialist countries and those in the colonial or semi-colonial countries; and the two differed in a fundamental way:

> It consists in a strict distinction between revolution in imperialist countries, in countries that oppress other nations, and revolution in colonial and dependent countries, in countries that suffer from imperialist oppression by other states. Revolution in imperialist countries is one thing: there the bourgeoisie is the oppressor of other nations; there it is counter-revolutionary at all stages of the revolution; there the national factor, as a factor in the struggle for emancipation, is absent. Revolution in colonial and dependent countries is another thing: there the imperialist oppression by other states is one of the factors of the revolution; there this oppression cannot but affect the national bourgeoisie also; there the national bourgeoisie, at a certain stage and for a certain period, may support the revolutionary movement of its country against imperialism; there the national factor, as a factor in the struggle for emancipation, is a revolutionary factor.

Ultimately the struggle would come down to one between world capitalism and world socialism:

> It is more than likely that, in the course of the development of the world revolution, there will come into existence—side by side with the foci of imperialism in the various capitalist lands and with the

system of these lands throughout the world—foci of socialism in various Soviet countries, and a system of these foci throughout the world. As the outcome of this development, there will ensue a struggle between the rival systems, and its history will be the history of the world revolution.

By "struggle" here Stalin meant not only war but also social and economic struggle in various forms and stages of development: "the Socialist centre, attracting to itself all the countries gravitating towards Socialism, and the Capitalist centre, attracting to itself all the countries gravitating towards capitalism."

In June 1934 Stalin took time out, as Bernard Shaw noted with some glee, to give H. G. Wells a lesson on the difference between liberalism and Marxism:

> STALIN: Besides, can we lose sight of the fact that in order to transform the world it is necessary to have political power? It seems to me, Mr. Wells, that you greatly underestimate the question of political power, that it entirely drops out of your conception. What can those, even with the best intentions in the world, do if they are unable to raise the question of seizing power, and do not possess power? ... The transformation of the world is a great, complicated and painful process. For this great task a great class is required. Big ships go on long voyages.
>
> WELLS: Yes, but for long voyages a captain and a navigator are required.
>
> STALIN: That is true; but what is first required for a long voyage is a big ship. What is a navigator without a ship? An idle man.
>
> WELLS: The big ship is humanity, not a class.
>
> STALIN: You, Mr. Wells, evidently start out with the assumption that all men are good. I, however, do not forget that there are many wicked men. I do not believe in the goodness of the bourgeoisie.[2]

During the years in which Stalin developed these concepts, he was the leading communist spokesman in the world, and his views formed the basis for communist thinking and action everywhere. Mao Tse-tung and other Chinese communists, for example, grew up on these views and their thinking was largely molded by them. They provided indispensable theoretical guidelines, the predictions they contained were generally accurate, and most are valid today. For instance, the concept of capitalism as being in a condition of "general crisis," not only economic but social, political, and cultural, provides a general historical framework for understanding the present epoch. Capitalist civilization is clearly still in this "general crisis," which is getting worse and which, with ups-and-downs, will continue to get worse until it is superseded by socialism.

The breakdown of colonialism that Stalin predicted has continued until today a direct colonial system is no longer a major factor in the world. Imperialism is, indeed, "no longer capable of governing in the old ways," and capitalist rulers have had to resort to the indirectness of neocolonialism, with reduced political and military controls. The presence of the socialist power in the U.S.S.R. did indeed help to "shake the foundations" of capitalism. It supplied impetus for the Chinese revolution, although that event was, of course, primarily generated by internal forces, and it provided armed power to assist anti-feudal and anti-capitalist revolutions in Eastern Europe following World War II.

The U.S.S.R. remains a powerful anti-monopoly-capitalism world force (as demonstrated in its assistance to the Vietnamese in their revolutionary war against French and U.S. imperialism). If the concept of the "history of world revolution" as essentially a conflict between socialist and imperialist "foci" is somewhat mechanical, it still has a certain basic validity.

Of the two types of revolution noted by Stalin, those in imperialist and those in dependent countries, the second materialized in China, and subsequently in Korea, Indochina, Cuba, Nicaragua, and elsewhere. The first materialized in Czechoslovakia and East Germany, although with some modifications resulting from the intervention of a socialist power. Stalin's analysis—ultimately, of course, with roots in Lenin—forms the basis for two different systems of revolutionary strategy, which we can see developing today throughout the world. In capitalist nations the struggle is essentially one of the working class against the bourgeoisie, in colonial countries one of the working class, peasantry, and capitalist class against feudalism and imperialism. In the first kind of struggle, the working class attempts to rally the mass of the population—women, minorities, farmers, youth, middle class—for a concentrated blow against the capitalist state. In the second, the working class, in alliance with the peasantry, can to some degree share the leadership of the mass movement with the native bourgeoisie in the initial anti-feudal, anti-imperialist phase of the revolution. On this latter situation Stalin reiterated Lenin's warning that the working class must retain independence of action:

> But what does a united front with the national bourgeoisie at the first stage of a colonial revolution mean? Does it mean that Communists must not intensify the struggle of the workers and peasants against the

landlords and the national bourgeoisie, that the proletariat ought to sacrifice its independence, if only to a very slight extent, if only for a very short time? No, it does not mean that. A united front can be of revolutionary significance only where, and only on condition that, it does not prevent the Communist Party from conducting its independent political and organisational work, from organising the proletariat into an independent political force, from rousing the peasantry against the landlords, openly organising a workers' and peasants' revolution, and from preparing in this way the conditions for the hegemony of the proletariat.[3]

Taken as a whole Stalin's comments on world affairs comprise a wide yet unified vision of world development, of a dual, interactive revolution in capitalist and exploited nations functioning as a total historical force which would gradually erode the world capitalist system and replace it with a socialist system. His judgments, measured and responsible, bear the imprint of serious collective thinking. Among his more immediate predictions, that of the coming of World War II proved correct. And his prediction of revolutions following the war—reminiscent of Engels's "last great war dance" projection—also came true in Eastern Europe, China, and Korea. The revolutions in China and Korea followed the anti-feudal, anti-imperialist united-front pattern that he outlined. Stalin apparently would not have considered his general prediction of the worldwide emergence of socialism to be basically affected by the spread of nuclear weapons. When U.S. imperialism threatened the U.S.S.R. with the bomb (after dropping it on Japan) Stalin was quoted in the press at the time as saying that it was a threat designed to frighten those with "weak nerves." Presumably he meant that having been used once, the bomb could not be used again, for the world was aware of its nature. One other factor that can affect in various ways the Marxist-Leninist perspective of world socialist development is the growing global ecological catastrophe, especially the results of carbon dioxide and other atmosphere-warming gases. Of this situation—with its historical irony that the industrial revolution that produced the proletariat and, hence, the possibility of a communist world, has now also produced the means for the destruction of human society—of this Stalin had little or no inkling. This factor, taken in conjunction with nuclear and other weapons of mass destruction, makes the achievement of socialism not only a matter of abolishing economic exploitation and social oppression but of the survival of humanity.

Chapter VIII
World Revolution: China and Eastern Europe

The various charges that have been brought against Stalin in regard to international affairs are perhaps as numerous as those brought against him on the domestic front. The basic image is again that of the reactionary intriguer, this time, however, operating on a world scale, and a point-by-point refutation of the legion of charges serves only to achieve a kind of negative concurrence with the image. What is necessary is to establish the general principles upon which Stalin operated—some of which we have already noted—and to examine some of the major questions in the context of these principles.

While bourgeois publicists assailed Stalin for stirring up world revolution (including the revolution in China), his "left" opponents charged that he tried to hold back revolutionary movements or cut off revolutionary potential. This charge, as we saw, was made by Trotsky in the 1920s; and since then it has been embellished. The essence of it may be found in *Russia, What Next?* by Isaac Deutscher (Trotsky's biographer):

> He certainly did his best to destroy the potentialities for revolution abroad—in the name of the sacred egoism of the Russian revolution. ...He believed that by building up the Soviet "citadel of socialism" he was making the only contribution toward world revolution that could be made at the time.

One of Deutscher's major charges is that Stalin "ordered" ("on Stalin's orders") the Communist Party of China to remain "subservient to the Kuomintang" even when the Kuomintang leadership attacked it.[1]

In considering these matters we might begin with Marx's comment at the conclusion of *The Civil War in France*, written at a time when he and the International Workingmen's Association (of which he was the recognized leader) were accused of having fomented the rebellion that led to the Paris Commune: "The police-tinged bourgeois mind naturally figures to itself the International Workingmen's Association as acting in the manner of a secret conspiracy, its central body ordering, from time to time, explosions in different countries." The Trotskyist position, shared by some liberals and socialists, is in essence that Stalin should have ordered such "explosions," and that he not only failed to do so but prevented their taking place. Revolutions and mass social protest movements, however, as Marx indicates, arise basically from the socioeconomic situation in any particular country, and an outside source cannot initiate them except under unusual circumstances. Conversely, what a socialist country can do to discourage them is also of a limited nature. In trying to ascertain what, in general, can actually be done, we might also return to Marx, to the *Communist Manifesto*: "The Communists fight for the attainment of the momentary interests of the working class; but in the movement of the present they also represent and take care of the future of that movement."[2]

Here we have the essence of Marxist tactics. To proclaim revolution is not to bring about revolution. In fact, to proclaim it at the wrong time can result in disaster. A Marxist must examine a situation to decide what stage of potentially revolutionary development it represents and then use the tactics that seem most likely to advance it to the next stage. Thus in attempting to assist a movement in another country, a communist leader—Lenin, Stalin, or anyone else—must try to determine the nature and stage of the movement and render advice accordingly. If sometimes this advice seems conservative it is not because it is conservative but because it is what is needed at that particular stage of development.

That Stalin did not consider the building of socialism in the U.S.S.R. as the "only" way in which the world revolutionary movement could be assisted is shown by the very existence of the Communist International. Founded by Lenin and led most notably by Georgi Dimitrov, it was strongly supported by Stalin throughout its existence. The leaders of the International, in Moscow, were constantly in touch with communist parties all over the world, having frequent consultations with their leaders, taking promising comrades into Marxist-Leninist schools in the U.S.S.R., and holding periodic international congresses, of which the Seventh Congress in 1935 had the widest representation and world influence. Reports were given to this Congress by communist leaders from all the major capitalist powers, including the U.S., and colonial and semi-colonial countries, including China. The Congress heard reports on how to establish an "anti-imperialist united front" in the colonial and semi-colonial countries. In the main report, Georgi Dimitrov, fresh from the prisons and courts of Nazi Germany, singled out China: "The Chinese Soviets act as a unifying centre in the struggle against the enslavement and partition of China by the imperialists, as a unifying centre which will rally all anti-imperialist forces for the national defence of the Chinese people." This view, as events were to prove, was the right one at the time, suggesting the tactics which advanced the Chinese revolution to a new stage.[3]

The Congress also concentrated on how to establish a "popular front" against fascism in the capitalist countries. At that time, the main objectives were to stop the spread of fascism—which would have destroyed the organizations of the working class in the capitalist countries—and to prevent a world war. Here, too, events proved the view of the need for a popular front to be correct and here, too, the view suggested tactics that advanced the revolutionary process to a new stage. The fascist offensive was stopped through the Popular Front—most dramatically in France—and although the war was not prevented, the struggle against it and against fascism developed progressive social and political movements.

In addition to founding and developing the Communist International, the Soviet government, whenever it could, directly intervened to promote socialist activities. It did so first in Mongolia, before Stalin's ascendancy, and then at the end of World War II, when the Soviet armies, in driving the Nazi armies out of Eastern Europe, helped to establish anti-fascist, anti-capitalist regimes. These actions resulted in a charge that Stalin forced a regimented social order on these countries with "Soviet bayonets" and then used them to build up the economy of the U.S.S.R. at the expense of their own economies and national interests.

Stalin himself, as we have seen in his conflict with Trotsky, was not unaware of the various charges made against him. At a meeting of the Executive Committee of the Communist International in 1926 he stated his own general position and that of the Soviet leadership:

> Whether we are building socialism in alliance with the world proletariat, this the opposition is inclined to doubt. Some of the oppositionists even assert that our Party underestimates the importance of this alliance. And one of them, Kamenev, has even gone so far as to accuse the Party of national-reformism, of replacing the international revolutionary perspective by a national-reformist perspective. That, comrades, is nonsense.... Only in alliance with the world proletariat is it possible to build socialism in our country.
>
> The whole point is how this alliance is to be understood.
>
> When the proletarians of the U.S.S.R. seized power in October

1917, this was assistance to the proletarians of all countries; it was an alliance with them. . . . When the proletarians of Western Europe frustrated intervention against the U.S.S.R., refused to transport arms for the counter-revolutionary generals, set up councils of action and undermined the rear of their capitalists, this was assistance to the proletarians of the U.S.S.R.; it was an alliance of the West-European proletarians with the proletarians of the U.S.S.R. Without this sympathy and this support of the proletarians of the capitalist countries, we could not have won the Civil War. . . . When the proletarians of the U.S.S.R. consolidate their dictatorship, put an end to economic disruption, develop constructive work and achieve successes in the building of socialism, this is support of highest value for the proletarians of all countries, for their struggle against capitalism, their struggle for power; because the existence of the Soviet Republic, its steadfastness, its successes on the front of socialist construction, are factors of the highest value for the world revolution, factors that encourage the proletarians of all countries in their struggle against capitalism. It can scarcely be doubted that the destruction of the Soviet Republic would be followed by the blackest and most savage reaction in all capitalist countries.[4]

Stalin is here attempting to move the subject of proletarian internationalism from the narrow question of how the new proletarian state could assist in developing revolutions abroad to the general perspective of the sociopolitical interrelation between workers in the capitalist world and those in an already proletarian state. To adopt the first outlook is, in effect, to accept the "police-tinged bourgeois" view of a "central" proletarian body "ordering . . . explosions" abroad. Not, of course, that such a state could not assist the proletariat in capitalist states in various ways—and some of these were neither apparent nor possible in 1926—but these ways, Stalin indicates, are usually of an indirect and general nature. In the main they center around the very fact of the existence of the proletarian state. Those who have criticized the U.S.S.R. for failing to intervene "arms in hand" to advance or save a revolution abroad have either urged the impossible or advocated an adventurism which would injure not only the U.S.S.R. but the world proletariat. At the same time, when the U.S.S.R. has been able to intervene directly these same critics condemn the action as unwarranted interference and suppression of "rights."

Stalin, then, viewed the world proletariat as essentially one, its advanced section in the U.S.S.R. moving into socialism, the rest still in capitalist bondage. And he envisaged the alliance between the two sections in a broad sense, not primarily one of political connections but as a historical phenomenon. True, there was no formal "alliance" between the Soviet and the West European workers, but when the workers in Western Europe prevented the spread of intervention following World War I, they were acting in genuine, interactive alliance. So it was too, when workers' delegations from capitalist countries visited the U.S.S.R., bringing and taking away both praise and criticism, and above all understanding. As a result of these delegations, which were encouraged and helped by the Soviet government, thousands of workers visited the U.S.S.R. Furthermore, the government encouraged tourism in general, so that the vision of practical socialism could be spread in capitalist and oppressed nations. It was on one of these tours, in 1934, that I first became aware of the significance of the new workers' state and felt, as did Lincoln Steffens, that "I have seen the future and it works."

Most important of all, of course, although Stalin does not spell it out in his 1926 speech, which was directed at a specific criticism, the U.S.S.R. helped the world proletariat through the International, from whose stage Stalin was then speaking. Nor can the importance of Stalin's final point be exaggerated. The destruction of the U.S.S.R. would indeed have been followed by devastating attacks on the workers, their unions and political parties, in the capitalist world. His position is in essence, then, that a Communist Party, whether in a socialist or capitalist country, must work first to advance the interests of the world proletariat and that a central concern in these interests is the preservation of its developing socialist section. This position can be interpreted as "national-reformist" only if we omit its class character, which forms its essence, and accept the argument that Stalin and the Soviet Party were indeed only trying to reform capitalism, an argument which events soon refuted.

Although in this speech Stalin was concentrating on the relationship of the socialist state with the workers in the capitalist world, at other times he discussed its relationship with the colonial and semi-colonial world. As we have seen, Stalin—like Lenin—regarded the struggle of the proletariat in the capitalist nations and that of the masses in the oppressed nations as essentially one, and linked with the advance of socialism in the U.S.S.R. His position perhaps can best be discussed in relation to his views on China.

When 12 delegates met in Shanghai in the summer of 1921 to found the Chinese Communist Party they represented about 50 communists from small groups, with perhaps another 20 studying in France. Owing to the lack of Marxist roots (and books) in China, none of them had been able to have a Marxist training of the kind that Lenin or the other Bolsheviks had received, beginning in their youth. Some of the delegates, as their later actions indicated, were bourgeois nationalists rather than communists, while others veered toward reformism, and still others wanted only to set up an educational association. Opinion ranged from the extreme right—the working class was "too backwards and stupid" to lead the revolution—to the extreme "left"—the dictatorship of the proletariat was the immediate goal. Ch'en Tu-hsiu, who became secretary, believed that the future lay in the hands of "Mr. Democracy" and "Mr. Science." Another leading figure, Li Ta-chao, placed the main emphasis on the "education of the masses" and argued that "the Chinese revolution would be essentially a peasant revolution." If the delegates succeeded, in founding a Communist Party despite this confusion, it was largely because they were helped by the International, help that came at a time when Chinese society was being churned up by massive anti-feudal, anti-imperialist, and anti-capitalist revolutionary action. This included militant strike movements, especially in Shanghai and Canton, and a few of the delegates, including Mao Tse-tung, had had direct experience with it. In social ferment of this scope, what we might call the practical essentials of Marxist-Leninism can spread with astonishing rapidity and provide general guides to action. Some basic texts began to become available, and the International supplied background material on current events.[5]

Two International representatives, one Russian and one Dutch, came to the founding meeting of the Chinese Party, and the International's hand is visible in the early statements of the Party. A statement of June 1922 notes that although the Party is "the vanguard of the proletariat," its "urgent task" is "to act jointly with the democratic party [the Kuomintang] to establish a united front of democratic revolution." The Kuomintang leader, Sun Yat-sen, agreed to collaborate, but leftist opposition to this policy developed in the Communist Party and the Party issued a second statement a month later emphasizing that this was only a first stage:

> When that stage is reached, the proletariat must launch the struggle of the second phase: (the struggle) for the dictatorship of the proletariat allied to the poor peasants against the bourgeoisie. If the organization and fighting power of the proletariat has been [sufficiently] strengthened, the struggle of this second phase will carry the victory of the democratic revolution to its completion.[6]

When we contrast these documents with the eclectic radicalism that had prevailed previously it is clear that the role of the International was crucial in setting the new Party on the right revolutionary course. Without this initial help the Chinese radical movement might have floundered for years. On the other hand the help would have been of little avail had it not been for the potentially revolutionary situation then existing in China.

The general outlook expressed in the statements did not, of course, originate with the International but reflected the theoretical views of Lenin and Stalin on the particular nature of the revolution in colonial and semi-colonial countries. In a first stage such revolutions centered on an alliance of workers and peasants with those native capitalists who were anti-feudal and anti-imperialist. In a second stage the capitalists would be forced out of the alliance as a democratic mass dictatorship of workers and poor peasants heading for socialism took over. Although this perspective proved to be wrong in some specifics in China, it was basically correct and provided the key to effective political action throughout the revolution.

At the Party's founding meeting Mao was named Hunan secretary, and after the meeting he returned to (his native) Hunan. His first organizing efforts there were among the coal miners of a mining company owned by German capitalists in Anyuan. Within a few months he had organized 7,000 miners and led them in a strike. Next, as he later told Edgar Snow, he turned to the peasantry, 50% of whose produce was taken by the landlord and who paid 30% interest on loans:

Formerly I had not fully realized the degree of class struggle among the peasantry, but after the May 30th Incident [1925], and during the great wave of political activity which followed it, the Hunanese peasantry became very militant.

Within a few months Mao and his associates had "formed more than twenty peasant unions." By 1927 there were 10 million organized peasants in China.[7]

When Sun Yat-sen had agreed to collaborate with the Communist Party his fortunes were at a low ebb and he was in need of Soviet support, but as things improved the Kuomintang established stronger ties with American and British imperialism. Chiang Kai-shek, who had married into the Soong banking family, with its extensive imperialist interests, became leader of the Kuomintang after Sun's death. He launched a military campaign against the feudal national regime in Peking, whose weakening was in the interests of native capitalists, workers, and peasants alike. As Chiang's forces moved north they helped to generate more peasant movements, which were led primarily by the Communist Party. Alarmed by these movements and by militant labor actions in the cities, also led by the Communist Party, Chiang turned his armed forces against his former allies. Some 40,000 workers were slaughtered in Shanghai, Canton, and other cities ("For months the daily rumble of military trucks would be heard, bringing their loads of workers to be shot") and the proletariat was temporarily driven back in disarray. But although thousands of peasants were killed, the Kuomintang was unable to stem the massive peasant tide.

In view of the Kuomintang treachery and the Communist Party defeat in the cities, it has been argued that the Communist International was wrong in its united front policy. Trotsky, for instance, lamented in 1928 that Stalin's "monstrous" policy had "broken the spine of the young Communist Party of China." Events, of course, showed otherwise. The Party not only survived but the united front policy had given the very small Communist Party access to the workers and peasants under the massive Kuomintang Party's control. Mao, for instance, was able to organize the peasants in these years on the scale that he did, not because of his Communist Party membership, but because he was deputy head and actual leader of the Kuomintang's Peasant Movement Training Institute. (At the same time Chou En-lai was deputy head of the political section of the Kuomintang's Military Academy, and other Communist leaders simultaneously occupied leading positions in the Kuomintang.) Largely because of these connections, the Communist Party grew from a small sect to a party of 57,000 within six years. If it had not grown thus, it could not have survived the attack upon it—which, given the existing class forces, would have come anyway, alliance or no alliance—and lived to lead movements that soon resulted in a mass revolutionary base including rural soviets.[8]

The policy of collaboration between the Communist Party and the Kuomintang was not initiated by Stalin but by Lenin. Stalin apparently did not come actively on the China scene until 1925, and when he did he followed the already established policy, with which he agreed. Even after Chiang's attack on the Communist Party, Stalin for a time hoped that the Party could continue an alliance with the left wing of the Kuomintang led by Sun Yat-sen's widow, Ching-ling Soong, among others. However, the left wing folded under pressure and the right became dominant. When this happened, Stalin (like Mao) placed the emphasis on the peasantry—with a mass revolutionary perspective—rather than on a new alliance with bourgeois or petty bourgeois leaders:

Chiang Kai-shek's coup signifies that the revolution has entered the second stage of its development, that a swing has begun away from the revolution of an all-national united front and towards a revolution of the vast masses of the workers and peasants, towards an agrarian revolution, which will strengthen and broaden the struggle against imperialism, against the gentry and the feudal landlords, and against the militarists and Chiang Kai-shek's counter-revolutionary group.

Stalin believed that "in the very near future the entire peasantry of China will go over to the confiscation of the land," and "Therein lies the strength of the Chinese revolution." He supported the peasants' actions. "In a number of areas, such as Hunan, Hupeh, etc., the peasants are already seizing the land, and are setting up their own courts, their own penal organs and their own self-defence bodies." He approved of a Communist International document written before Chiang's attack that urged "converting the peasant committees into actual organs of governmental authority equipped with armed self-defence."

On the other hand, for a time he did not believe that the peasants should set up soviets or that the Communist Party should establish its own Red Army independent of the left Kuomintang, although he emphasized the importance of its independence in general. Just how he felt that peasants' soviets would differ from peasant self-government is not clear, but his argument was that they should be established only in conjunction with workers' soviets: "Soviets of workers' and peasants' deputies will necessarily have to be formed in China at the moment when the victorious agrarian revolution has developed to the full." He had a threefold advance of the revolution in mind: from agrarian to bourgeois-democratic to socialist. Mao, who was not then in charge of the Party, agreed with Stalin's general assessment of the forces involved in the revolution and its general direction, but disagreed on some of these specifics. He established both rural soviets and a communist-led Red Army. That Stalin later agreed with these actions is shown by the fact that the Seventh Congress of the Communist International in 1935 endorsed them.

Once again, we see Stalin's old weakness of dividing revolutions into too-exact stages, not realizing sufficiently—as did Lenin and as Mao found out in China—that they blend into each other. However, as we now look at the direction of the Chinese revolution, it is apparent that Stalin's general emphasis on the working class and the necessity of its alliance with the peasantry was correct. The weakness of the Chinese revolution was its work in the cities, where apparently little organizing of the workers took place. Even after the triumph of the revolution, the workers in general did not seize the factories and many of the former owners were retained. But Stalin's picture was on the whole too structured. Mao's, although wrong in some respects, was more fluid and original: "We should employ our main forces to create rural bases, surround the cities from the countryside and use the bases to expedite nationwide revolutionary upsurge." And this policy was the one that led to victory even though it did not have the effect in the cities that Mao projected.[9]

In spite of his disagreements with some of Stalin's positions in these years, Mao had great admiration for him (while he repudiated Trotsky and Bukharin), and certainly was greatly influenced by his writings, often taking Stalin's general theoretical views as a basis and then developing them. For example, Mao commented in 1930 on the prospects for the Chinese revolution:

> If it is asked whether the revolutionary upsurge will arise soon in China, we can give a definite answer only after studying carefully whether the contradictions leading to the revolutionary upsurge are really developing. Since contradictions are developing internationally between the imperialist countries, between the imperialist countries and their colonies, and between imperialism and the proletariat in these countries, the imperialists feel all the more urgently the need to contend for China. As the imperialists' contention for China intensifies, both the contradiction between the imperialist powers and the whole Chinese nation and the contradiction among the imperialists themselves develop simultaneously in China.

The general concept of the international "contradictions" between imperialist nations themselves, between these nations and their colonies, between capitalists and workers, is based on Stalin's *Foundations of Leninism*, but Mao goes on to apply the concept to China in his own way, picking out the factors which he believed were dividing the ruling classes and driving China toward revolution.

In 1945 when the Communist Party was on the verge of launching revolutionary war and last-minute negotiations were going on with the Kuomintang, Mao issued a warning: "But there are limits to such concessions; the principle is that they must not damage the fundamental interests of the people." The warning was directed partly at Stalin. "Stalin," Mao later declared of the situation at this time, "wanted to prevent China from making revolution, saying that we should not have a civil war and should cooperate with Chiang Kai-shek, otherwise the Chinese nation would perish. But we did not do what he said." This fits in with one of Stalin's "conversations" with Milovan Djilas in 1948:

> True, we, too, can make a mistake! Here when the war with Japan ended, we invited the Chinese comrades to reach an agreement as to how a modus vivendi with Chiang Kai-shek might be found. They

agreed with us in word, but in deed they did it their own way when they got home: they mustered their forces and struck. It has been shown that they were right, and not we.

This position of Stalin's, we should note, was not a new one. It had been the general position of the Chinese Party since its beginning to try to effect a united front with the Kuomintang. And almost up to the opening of the civil war Mao had made overtures to Chiang Kai-shek to try to unite their forces. It was only when it became clear that Chiang was uniting with U.S. imperialism for a concerted drive against the communists that the Chinese Communist Party decided that a revolutionary war presented the only way out. Stalin did not oppose this view because he was opposed to the Chinese revolution as such. That he was not is shown by his release of large amounts of captured Japanese arms and equipment to the Chinese communists in 1945, following the Soviet invasion of Manchuria. He opposed Mao's view presumably because he did not believe that the Chinese communists would win a civil war in which Chiang had superior armaments and numbers. Such, in fact, was the general view at the time. As a communist and a Marxist, however, Stalin should have been able to see further. The fact that he did not reflects both his distance from the scene and, once again, his lack of Marxist imagination, as displayed, for instance, in his failure to perceive that the soviets could be the vehicle for proletarian revolution and his advocacy (until Lenin taught him better) of using them simply as a pressure group against the Provisional government. Again, in 1945 as in 1917, he did not grasp that the situation had changed in a basic way and bold new revolutionary means were needed. However, the conversation with Djilas also shows that Stalin did not conceive of himself as giving "orders" to the Chinese communists but only advice, and that Stalin was not only pleased but rather amused that they had shown him to be wrong. Later Stalin welcomed Mao in Moscow.

In spite of this misjudgment of Stalin's, Mao continued to praise him as a great communist leader although one who had made serious errors. In 1956 he said: "Stalin was a great Marxist-Leninist, yet at the same time a Marxist-Leninist who committed several gross errors without realizing that they were errors." And again, on Stalin's death, in 1953: "Everyone knows that Comrade Stalin had an ardent love for the Chinese people and believed the might of the Chinese revolution to be immeasurable." Mao could believe this, and doubtless did, while at the same time feeling that Stalin was wrong in specifics. Mao, then, did not argue that Stalin had tried to hold back the Chinese revolution at any stage as part of a policy of placing Soviet nationalist interests above international revolutionary ones, as his enemies were contending. He said only that Stalin made mistakes, "without realizing that they were errors," the implication being, perhaps, that he had too narrow a revolutionary vision. Mao felt that Stalin had supported the Chinese revolution unselfishly, and, as he noted in 1950, Stalin rejoiced in its triumph. Stalin also introduced the policy of economic and technical aid to China that was later reversed by Khrushchev. We should note, too, that, as events were to show, Stalin was right in his feeling that insufficient emphasis was being given to the Chinese working class.[10]

In addition to the situation in China, controversy about Stalin's international policies has raged over the rise and development of the "people's democracies" of Eastern Europe.

The common notion in the capitalist world that the countries of Eastern Europe had a kind of regimented socialization thrust upon them by Soviet bayonets is, of course, a myth, again based ultimately on the bourgeois view of the workers as robots. True, as the Soviet armies, in pursuit of the Nazi armies, moved through Eastern Europe, this very action involved the overthrow of the pro-Nazi governments, in, for example, Rumania and Bulgaria. Revolt would have come anyway, however, once the Nazi political power behind those governments crumbled. And it is true also that in some of these nations Soviet representatives later helped—as they should have— to develop socioeconomic bases for socialist construction. The real power and initiative, however, had to come from, and did come from, the peoples of those countries themselves. Furthermore, in two of these nations, Albania and Yugoslavia, the Soviet armies were not directly involved. The revolutions there arose almost entirely from internal actions. In Yugoslavia, for instance, a partisan army of 80,000 was mustered to fight the German invasion; by the end of the war this army had grown to 800,000 and was holding down more German divisions than the combined U.S.-British forces in Italy. Furthermore, Yugoslavia before the war had had a strong Communist Party, with a bloc of deputies in the national parliament. And Czechoslovakia had had powerful Socialist and Communist Parties from the 1920s on.

In short, in many of these countries there had been a considerable socialist-oriented political movement, which, although suppressed by the Nazis, managed to survive and form a core when the Nazi and native reactionary forces were defeated. For instance, in Bulgaria, one of the most economically backward of these countries—a poor, partly feudal nation in contrast to capitalist Czechoslovakia—the Communist Party in 1932 elected 19 of 35 members to the city council of Sofia. When the Nazi dictatorship was overthrown, following the war, an election was held by "direct, secret, and universal suffrage" (according to the *Statesman's Yearbook* for 1955), in which the anti-fascist Fatherland Front of Communist, Socialist, and peasant parties won 364 seats to the opposition's 101. Clearly this movement grew mainly out of the situation within Bulgaria. We might note, too, that in Czechoslovakia in 1946, the Communist Party won 38% of the vote in a national election.[11]

As a result of dislocations from the war, particularly in those economies already at a low, partly feudal level, all possible assistance was needed to move the whole bloc of nations toward socialism. And this the U.S.S.R., although devastated by the war, provided as best it could, giving both economic aid and political assistance; within the bloc the better-off nations, such as Czechoslovakia, aided the weaker ones. In 1949 the whole bloc formed the Council for Mutual Economic Assistance (COMECON). That these efforts soon paid off is clear from the economic figures. For instance, Hungary, which had produced a yearly average of 600,000 tons of steel in the years 1936-38, produced 1,540,000 in 1953. It has, as we have noted, been contended that Stalin used these nations as virtual colonies to supply raw materials for the U.S.S.R. But although the U.S.S.R. certainly needed all the help it could get, there is no evidence of a colonial-like exploitation. On the contrary, the evidence indicates that the U.S.S.R. often gave material and professional aid that it could well have used itself. The relationship in essence was that of the proletarian alliance that Stalin had earlier described, a relationship between a socialist country and a group of countries trying to move toward socialism.[12]

As an example of this relationship, let us take Albania. In 1939, Albania, a tiny nation of 2,000,000 wedged between Greece and Yugoslavia, was invaded by an Italian fascist army of 100,000. The small but militant Albanian Communist Party organized partisans and then moved—as in Yugoslavia—from guerrilla to regular warfare, as arms were captured from the enemy. After a bloody struggle they drove out the Italian invaders, only to be confronted by a Nazi army of 70,000. This army they also defeated, again securing their arms from the enemy. But the cost had been terrible. When the fighting ended, 28,000 Albanians were dead, 52,000 houses had been burned, and almost every bridge in the country destroyed. "Our country," wrote Enver Hoxha, the leader of the Communist Party and the united front government that emerged from the struggle, "was devastated and ruined by the war." "Industry, the mines, and home and foreign trade are either very weak or completely paralyzed." The mines had been put out of action, the oil refineries destroyed.[13]

In this situation, the Albanians, although relying mainly on their own efforts, at first received some help from Yugoslavia, but aid from the U.S.S.R. became of major importance when difficulties developed with Yugoslavia.

And it was forthcoming. In 1947 Albania entered into a trade agreement with the Soviet government. By 1951, 57% of Albania's foreign trade, imports and exports, was with the U.S.S.R. Albania was able to import machinery, chemicals, textiles, and building materials while exporting the products of its mining and oil industries. Soviet assistance was given for the construction of industry in all areas, including oil. And trade agreements were also made through COMECON. Hoxha paid particular tribute to Stalin for this aid (1948): "We owe the extension of our light and heavy industry to the great aid of the Bolshevik Party, to Comrade Stalin and the Soviet state, who helps us unsparingly in this respect as in all other respects." But with the death of Stalin in 1953 and the subsequent rise of Khrushchev, the situation began to change, and Hoxha wrote:

> However, in this field of our relations and contacts with the post-Stalin Soviet leadership, too, we very soon saw the first signs that things were no longer going as before. There was something wrong, there was no longer that former atmosphere, when we would go to Stalin and open our hearts to him without hesitation and he would listen and speak to us just as frankly from his heart, the heart of an internationalist communist. More and more each day, in his successors, instead of communists, we saw hucksters.

The present reactionary anti-Soviet—"the superpowers"—policy of Albania was triggered not by in Stalin but by Khrushchev. And so, too, with the similar Chinese policy.[14]

Hoxha had first met Stalin in July 1947:

> From the beginning he created such a comradely atmosphere that we were very quickly relieved of that natural emotion which we felt when we entered his office, a large room, with a long table for meetings, close to his writing desk. Only a few minutes after exchanging the initial courtesies, we felt as though we were not talking to the great Stalin, but sitting with a comrade, whom we had met before and with whom we had talked many times. I was still young then, and the representative of a small party and country, therefore, in order to create the warmest and most comradely atmosphere for me, Stalin cracked some jokes and then began to speak with affection and great respect about our people, about their militant traditions of the past and their heroism in the National Liberation War. He spoke quietly, calmly and with a characteristic warmth which put me at ease.

A second interview with Hoxha, in November 1949, shows how Stalin worked, a picture very similar to that of the direct, unassuming style Ambassador Davies had noted:

> "We shall help you today and in the future, too," he continued, "therefore we are going to give you more people and more of everything else than we have given you so far. We now have the practical possibilities to give you more because our current five-year plan is going on well."
>
> I thanked Comrade Stalin for the aid they had given and would give us in the future.
>
> "Thank me when you receive the aid," he said smiling, and then asked:
>
> "What do your trains run on—oil or coal?"
>
> "Coal, mainly," I told him, "but the new types of locomotives we have received run on oil."
>
> "Do you process your oil? How is work going on with the refinery?" he asked, continuing the talk.
>
> "We are building a new refinery with Soviet equipment," I said. "Next year we shall install the machinery."
>
> "Do you have coal?"
>
> "We do," I told him, "and geological surveys show that our prospects in this direction are good."
>
> "You must work to discover and extract as much coal as possible," Comrade Stalin advised me. "It is very necessary for the development of industry and the economy in general, therefore give it attention, because it will be difficult for you without it."

Certainly in the relations of the U.S.S.R. with Albania or of Stalin with Hoxha, there is no hint of Soviet exploitation. In fact, just the contrary. The atmosphere in the interviews, as Hoxha indicates, was warm and friendly; Stalin's interest in the Albanian people and their construction of socialism, sincere; and the trade and other economic agreements were of mutual benefit. There is no reason to believe that this was not generally true of Stalin's relationships with the communist leaders of other nations, although, of course, there were exceptions. If Stalin felt—as he did in dealing with Tito, or earlier, the "right" leaders in the German Party—that the actions of leaders would harm both their own movements and that of the proletariat in general, he could be as unyielding and brutally direct as he was friendly and sympathetic to Hoxha, in whom he obviously saw a kindred proletarian spirit, a dedicated communist whose background in an oppressed, colonial nation had been similar to Stalin's own. What has happened is that Stalin's differences with other leaders have been played up, often in a malicious gossip-column style, as by Milovan Djilas, and the basic comradeship pervading these relations has been obscured. That Stalin made mistakes is true, and indeed, inevitable. However, they were not his alone but of the leadership of the International, and there is no evidence that anyone else could have done better. In fact, when we consider Trotsky's narrow leftism and Bukharin's "thesis" that world capitalism had "stabilized" itself—on the brink of the Great Depression—it is clearly fortunate for the world proletariat that in these years the International had Stalin's guiding hand behind it.[15]

Chapter IX
The War Years

On June 22, 1941, a German imperialist army of 3,000,000 crossed the borders of the U.S.S.R. in the greatest military offensive of history. Stalin, who had won the battle for socialist industrialization, now faced the second great challenge of his career. At the time, the German armies appeared to most outside observers to be invincible. In September 1939 they had overrun Poland in a matter of days; in April 1940, they conquered Denmark and Norway; in May, Belgium and Holland; in June, France. Bourgeois "experts" all over the world were taking bets not on whether these armies would conquer the U.S.S.R. but on how long it would take—one month, two, six?

At first it did appear to the superficial observer that the "experts" might be right. Sweeping through the Baltic states, by September the German armies had Leningrad under siege and had captured Kiev; in October, they took Kharkov and Odessa and invaded the Crimea; by November, they were within a hundred miles of Moscow. On October 3, 1940, Hitler triumphantly announced: "The enemy is already broken and will never rise again."

The German imperialist armies, however, would encounter a very different kind of resistance in the U.S.S.R. than they had in Western Europe—as indicated in Stalin's first speech (July 3) after the invasion:

> In areas occupied by the enemy, guerilla units, mounted and [on] foot, must be formed, sabotage groups must be organized to combat enemy units, to foment guerilla warfare everywhere, to blow up bridges and roads, damage telephone and telegraph lines, and set fire to forests, stores, and transports.

The effect of the July 3 speech on the nation was electrifying. As one general remembered: "We suddenly seemed to feel much stronger." Nor did

Stalin attempt to minimize the seriousness of the situation. On November 6, on the eve of the 24th anniversary of the Russian revolution he made a general appraisal:

Today, after four months of war, I must emphatically state that far from having abated, this danger is greater than ever. The enemy has seized a large part of the Ukraine, Byelorussia, Moldavia, Lithuania, Latvia, Estonia, and a number of other regions; he had forced his way into the Donets Basin, hangs like a black cloud over Leningrad, and is threatening our glorious capital, Moscow.

Nevertheless, the Russian army had certain advantages over the Germans, and these would in time prevail:

... as it advances into the interior of our country, the German army is moving farther away from its own German rear, is forced to operate in hostile surroundings, is forced to create a new rear in an alien country, a rear, morever, that is being disrupted by our guerillas.

And he added with the defiant confidence that was to increasingly mark his war speeches: "The German invaders want a war of extermination against the peoples of the U.S.S.R. Well, if the Germans want a war of extermination, they will get it."

The battle for Moscow was massive and savage:

In the bitter Russian winter hundreds of thousands of soldiers stormed backward and forward over the ringing ground as the great armies struggled for a mortal grip. And there, almost within artillery range of the spires of the Kremlin, with victory at its fingertips, the German Army was stopped.[1]

The following summer (1942) the Germans launched a new campaign in the south. Stalin evaluated the situation calmly even though the attack penetrated to Stalingrad:

Apparently the Germans are no longer strong enough to conduct a simultaneous offensive in all three directions, in the South, North, and Centre, as was the case in the early months of the German offensive in the summer of last year.

In November Stalin's confidence was confirmed: "The enemy has been checked at Stalingrad."

A new contempt for the enemy began to enter his speeches (a refreshing antidote to the thinly disguised admiration for Nazi "efficiency" still pervasive in bourgeois films and novels):

> The initiative is now in our hands, and no matter how much Hitler's rusty, ramshackle machine may exert itself, it cannot withstand the pressure of the Red Army.

> Their attempt to chase two hares at once—oil and the encirclement of Moscow—landed the German fascist strategists in difficulties.

> It is no longer the fashion in the enemy camp to talk about a *blitzkrieg*; the noisy chatter about a *blitzkrieg* has given way to despondent lamentations about an inevitably protracted war.

> They have covered Europe with gallows and concentration camps. They have introduced the vile "hostage system." They shoot and hang absolutely innocent citizens whom they take as "hostages" because some German beast was prevented from raping women or robbing civilians. They have converted Europe into a prison of nations.[2]

In February 1943 he announced the turn of the tide: "Today, amidst severe winter conditions, the Red Army is waging an offensive on a front 1,500 kilometres long, and almost everywhere is achieving success."

On May 1:

> During the winter campaign of 1942-43, the Red Army inflicted severe defeats upon the Hitler troops, exterminated an enormous amount of the enemy's man-power and material, surrounded and liquidated two enemy armies at Stalingrad, took over 300,000 men and officers prisoner, and liberated from the German yoke hundreds of Soviet towns and thousands of villages.

In the summer of 1943, just two years after the German imperialist invasion began, the Red Army launched its first summer offensive and began to roll the German forces back all along the line. In the following summer Stalin issued a word of warning (which might have given the British and American imperialists, then on the verge of finally opening a second front, cause for thought):

But our task cannot be confined to that of expelling the enemy troops from our country.... In pursuing the enemy, we must deliver from German bondage our brothers the Poles, the Czechoslovaks and other peoples of Western Europe allied with us who are under the heel of Hitler Germany.[3]

When the war began a State Defense Committee of five was appointed with Stalin in charge. Stalin was also appointed Commander-in-Chief of the Armed Forces. The conduct of the war, then, was primarily in his hands, and, indeed, its conduct from beginning to end bears his stamp—as was recognized by Marshall Zhukov, who worked closely with him throughout: "Stalin mastered the technique of organization of front operations and operations by groups of fronts and guided them with skill, thoroughly understanding complicated strategic questions." His role was also recognized by the Soviet people, and by the end of the war he was regarded as the savior of the nation.

The record shows that the tribute was deserved. Had Stalin not won the fight for industrialization and defeated the Trotskyists and Bukharinites, the U.S.S.R. would have become a Nazi province. Had he not had the foresight to build a metallurgical industry in the Urals, the Red Armies could not have been supplied with arms. Had he not industrialized the economy and introduced mechanized farming, he would have had neither a base for producing arms nor a mass of soldiers trained in the operation of machinery. Had he not signed a nonaggression treaty with Germany, the U.S.S.R. might have been attacked 22 months sooner. Had he not moved the Soviet armies into Poland, the German attack would have begun even closer to Moscow. Had he not subdued General Mannerheim's Finland, Leningrad would have fallen. Had he not ordered the transfer of 1,400 factories from the west to the east, the most massive movement of its kind in history, Russian industry would have received a possibly fatal blow. Had he not built up the army and equipped it with modern arms, it would have been destroyed on the frontiers.

He did not, of course, do these things alone. They were Party decisions and Party actions, and behind the Party throughout was the power, courage, and intelligence of the working class. But Stalin stood at all times as the central, individual directing force, his magnificent courage and calm foresight inspiring the whole nation. When some panic began in Moscow in October 1941 he handled it firmly.[4]

When the Nazi invasion began, Stalin, aided by other Party and army leaders, developed a new strategy for modern warfare. He was able to achieve this primarily because he had a socialist and not a capitalist base from which to operate.

The strategy rested on viewing the war not just from a military point of view but in its total implications. For instance, Stalin immediately named it the Great Patriotic War, not a War for Socialism—as it actually was—for to have done so would have narrowed support for it, both internal and international. He perceived that the war would not be decided by the hitherto successful blitzkreig tactics of the Nazis and their great gains from the shock of the sudden, treacherous onslaught on the U.S.S.R., but by broader factors:

> Now the outcome of the war will be decided not by such a fortuitous element as surprise, but by permanently operating factors: stability of the rear, morale of the army, quantity and quality of divisions, equipment of the army, and organizing ability of the commanding personnel of the army.

Moral and psychological questions were of prime importance:

> The strength of the Red Army lies, primarily, in the fact that it is waging, not a predatory, not an imperialist war, but a Patriotic War, a war of liberation, a just war ... No German soldier can say that he is waging a just war, because he cannot fail to see that he is forced to fight for the plunder and oppression of other peoples. The German soldier has no lofty and noble aim in the war to inspire him and rouse his pride.

The war was to be total, a combination of the regular army, the partisans behind the enemy lines, the workers in the factories. On the battle front the essence of tactics must be mobility: "They [the Red Army commanders] have abandoned stupid and pernicious linear tactics and have firmly adopted the tactics of mobile warfare." This strategy was especially important in combating the blitzkreig tactic of massive tank and air attacks. Militarily, the key to defeating such tactics lay in mobile artillery, both guns and massed rockets:

> The Artillery was the force that ensured the rout by the Red Army of the German troops at Stalingrad and Voronezh, at Kursk and Belgorod, at Kharkov and Kiev, at Vitebsk and Bobruisk, at Leningrad and Minsk, at Jassy and Kishinev.

The unprecedented immensity of the Soviet artillery barrages—turning miles of front into flame—was visible on film at the time and was the wonder of British and U.S. militarists.[5]

From its beginning World War II was a unique kind of war, an imperialist war distorted by the presence of a socialist state, in time becoming a mixed imperialist and anti-socialist war. Although the main imperialist rivals in Europe were the same as in World War I (namely, British and French versus German), the British and French in the pre-World War II years not only allowed the German ruling class to rearm but made great concessions to it. They allowed the German rulers to take Austria, Czechoslovakia, and other territories on the understanding that these new economic and military resources would be used in war against the U.S.S.R. In the first phases of the war the British and French acquiesced in the German conquests of Poland, Denmark, Norway, Belgium, and Holland; and the French ruling class in effect gave its German counterpart a lease on its economic resources for the conquest of the socialist state. The British ruling class split on whether to follow suit but finally decided, with U.S. prodding, that the price was too high. U.S. imperialism saw such concessions as a serious risk, realizing that if German imperialism controlled all of Europe, including the U.S.S.R. and Britain, it would next join forces with Japan and mount a war against the United States.

On the other hand, neither the American imperialists nor the British wished to see the U.S.S.R. victorious. Both hoped that the U.S.S.R. and Germany would mutually exhaust each other and allow British and American imperialist interests to penetrate deep into Europe. Thus they supplied the U.S.S.R. with what they thought was just enough assistance to help it to resist but not conquer the Germans. They delayed opening a second front in the hope of a Soviet-German stalemate, but delayed too long—until the Soviet armies were rolling on to Berlin and seemingly threatened to overrun Europe. The reason for their miscalculation was that they did not understand the special strengths of a socialist state.

Stalin, in spite of later assertions to the contrary, was well aware of all these matters. In March 1939, more than two years before the German invasion of the U.S.S.R., he commented:

Or take Germany, for instance. They let her have Austria, despite the undertaking to defend her independence; they let her have the Sudeten region; they abandoned Czechoslovakia to her fate, thereby violating all their obligations; and then began to lie vociferously in the press about "the weakness of the Russian army," "the demoralization of the Russian air force," and "riots" in the Soviet Union, egging the Germans on to march farther east, promising them easy pickings, and prompting them: "Just start war on the Bolsheviks, and everything will be all right."

Stalin, however, was aware — as were all Marxists at the time — that the British and French ruling classes were split on the issue. Hence the Soviet government offered to honor their treaty with France to come to the aid of Czechoslovakia. This the French government, with Chamberlain's backing, turned down. The Soviet government then (April 1939) offered Britain and France a mutual assistance pact. This, too, was rejected. When it became clear that the right-wing, fanatically anti-Soviet sections of the British and French bourgeoisie were in political control, then, and only then, the Soviet government signed a non-aggression pact with Germany (August 31, 1939). This pact gave the U.S.S.R. a breathing space of almost two years to build up its armed forces for what it saw as an inevitable attack. At the time the pact was stigmatized by some as an alliance. If it had been, Britain would have been conquered and the United States put under seige. Churchill at the time considered the Soviet action as "realistic in a high degree."

When the invasion came and the U.S.S.R., the United States, and Britain became allies, Stalin did all he could to preserve the alliance, no longer, for instance, talking of imperialist powers but distinguishing between "aggressors" and "freedom-loving" states. He was, of course, aware even as he did so of the imperialist and anti-socialist nature of his allies, whose anti-Sovietism—basically anti-proletarianism—had risen to a revealing frenzy in the Soviet-Finnish war of 1939. Even as World War II was winding down and the British were collecting German arms, Churchill ordered such arms to be "stacked" in such a way "that they could easily be issued again to the German soldiers whom we should have to work with if the Soviet advance continues."[6]

The war had scarcely ended when Churchill made his "iron curtain" speech, and Stalin declared that "Mr. Churchill sets out to release war with a race theory, asserting that only English-speaking nations are superior nations, who are called upon to decide the destinies of the entire world." Two years later, in 1948, Stalin stigmatized United States and British policy, saying "What they want is not agreement and co-operation, but talk about agreement and co-operation, so as to put the blame on the U.S.S.R. by preventing agreement and thus to 'prove' that co-operation with the U.S.S.R. is impossible." Nevertheless, Stalin felt that a new imperialist war against the U.S.S.R. was then virtually impossible: "The horrors of the recent war are still too fresh in the memory of the peoples; and public forces favoring peace are too strong for Churchill's pupils in aggression to overpower them and to turn them toward a new war." That he was right is shown by the fact that the war did not occur.[7]

Chapter X
The Last Years

From the end of the war until his death in 1953, Stalin was a revered figure in the U.S.S.R., highly regarded not only as a political leader but as a Marxist theorist. In this latter area he took a leading part in three major discussions: on genetics, on language and "the superstructure," and on the economics of socialism.

In 1946 a controversy on genetic inheritance arose in the U.S.S.R. The generally accepted scientific argument was that characteristics acquired during the life of an organism, such as the muscles of an athlete, are not transmitted to offspring, and that inherited characteristics include only those resulting from a direct change in the germ cells, ova, or spermatozoa, arising from genetic-material accident, chemical change, or radiation. This general position has since been supported by the findings of molecular biology, such as the discovery that genetic change can come about by rearrangements within the units of the nucleic acids. A resurrection of the old and largely discredited argument that "acquired characters" can be inherited was made by Trofim Lysenko, an agronomist, who had produced, like Luther Burbank before him, valuable hybrid forms of plants by cross-breeding and grafting. However, these processes clearly did not—as Lysenko contended—involve the transmission of acquired characters but simply a blending of already existing genetic characteristics. In any case the argument was a scientific one and should have been left to specialists in the biological sciences to settle. Stalin, however, chose to intervene and in 1948 declared support for Lysenko. The opposition was silenced. As a result, Soviet biological science and agriculture were "severely retarded."[1]

Two years later, a new controversy arose, this time about linguistics. Some Russian philologists had argued that language was a part of "the superstructure," and when the question was directed to Stalin, he expounded his theory of "the base" and "the superstructure," a theory which has been widely adopted in Marxist circles (where it is wrongly assumed to stem from Marx) and has caused considerable confusion.

> The base is the economic structure of society at a given stage of its development. The superstructure consists of the political, legal, religious, artistic, and philosophical views of society and the political, legal, and other institutions corresponding to them.
>
> Every base has its own superstructure corresponding to it. The base of the feudal system has its superstructure—its political, legal, and other views and the corresponding institutions; the capitalist base has its own superstructure, and so has the socialist base. If the base changes or is eliminated, then following this its superstructure changes or is eliminated; if a new base arises, then following this a superstructure arises corresponding to it....
>
> The base creates the superstructure precisely in order that it may serve it, that it may actively help it to take shape and consolidate itself, that it may actively strive for the elimination of the old, moribund base and its old superstructure. The superstructure has only to renounce its role of auxiliary, it has only to pass from a position of active defense of its base to one of indifference toward it, to adopt the same attitude to all classes, and it loses its virtue and ceases to be a superstructure.
>
> It is more than one hundred years since Pushkin died. In this period the feudal system and the capitalist system were eliminated in Russia, and the third, a socialist, system has arisen. Hence two bases, with their superstructures, have been eliminated, and a new, socialist base has arisen, with its new superstructure.[2]

The fact is that no such concept as "the superstructure" exists in Marx. The theory was first propounded by Plekhanov—perhaps aided by a faulty formulation by Engels—and then by Bukharin (who included language in "the superstructure" in his *Historical Materialism*). The passage in Marx from which these misconceptions arose can be found in his famed general statement in the Preface to *A Contribution to the Critique of Political Economy* (1859):

> The totality of these production relations constitutes the economic structure of society, the real basis upon which a legal and political superstructure arises and to which definite forms of social consciousness correspond. The mode of production of the material means of life determines, in general, the social, political, and intellectual processes of life. It is not the consciousness of human beings that determines

their existence, but conversely, it is their social existence that determines their consciousness. At a certain stage of their development, the material productive forces of society come into conflict with the existing production relationships, or, what is but a legal expression for the same thing, with the property relationships within which they have hitherto moved. From forms of development of the productive forces these relationships turn into their fetters. A period of social revolution then begins. With the change in the economic foundation, the whole gigantic superstructure is more or less rapidly transformed.

In this passage Marx uses the word superstucture (that is to say, overstructure, as in a building or bridge) twice. He first uses it to refer to political and legal structures, distinguishing between them and certain "forms of social consciousness" or ideas. Both arise from the "economic structures": the political and legal structures directly, and the ideas through class struggle, all, of course, in interaction. In the second use of "superstructure" Marx includes both structures and ideas—"the whole gigantic superstructure." Marx, then, qualifies the term superstructure with the phrases—"legal and political," "the whole gigantic"—and never speaks of "the superstructure" as such. So, too, in all other passages, e.g.: "the superstructure of the modern State edifice"—which is swept away from its "social soil"; "an entire superstucture of distinct and peculiarly formed sentiments...."

Marx is clearly using "superstructure" in a metaphorical way, to indicate the general dependence of the political and cultural aspects of society on their economic (or socioeconomic) foundations. He was not attempting to establish a unique social entity or social-scientific term. This is evident from the fact that he and Engels usually describe the relationships mentioned above without using the term superstructure at all (in contrast to an actual social-scientific term like "surplus value" that is used invariably to describe the phenomenon it represents). As a dialectical thinker, Marx could not have fallen into the abstractionist dogmatism of Stalin's passage. Nor did Lenin. There is no doctrine of "the superstructure" in Lenin. In interpreting Marx's passage for instance, Lenin says only, "Political institutions are a superstructure on the economic foundation," using the term, as Marx sometimes does, as virtually synonomous with the state. (Lenin, of course, also intended to include legal and other state institutions under "political." He is using the word in a broad sense.)[3]

Stalin's arguments are simplistic and mechanistic. If the "feudal ... superstucture" contains the "views" of society then these views must have been "eliminated" when the capitalist "base" and "its own superstructure" arose on the new "base." Actually, as capitalism developed, there was a long period of interlocking class struggle with clashing bourgeois and feudal views, as early represented, for instance, by Paine and Burke. The bourgeois rose as the feudal declined in response to the class struggle. Also, proletarian ideology, although contaminated by bourgeois thinking, took distinct shape and developed its own identity (as in the Chartist movement). The concept of "the base" creating "the superstructure" so that it may "serve it" or of superstructures losing their "virtue" is Aristotelian metaphysics, and has nothing to do with Marxism or objective reality. Even the term "virtue" (essence) is Aristotelian, part of the pseudo-intellectual baggage Stalin picked up in the Tiflis theological seminary.

Stalin's view, however, is not only wrong but harmful, for it obscures the true social relations—particularly, again, those of the class struggle. In the U.S.S.R. and other countries the "superstructure" doctrine was not only frozen into dogma but led to angels-on-the-head-of-a-pin discussions on such questions as whether art and science were "part of the superstructure." The doctrine has also created widespread ideological confusion in China, where it was taken up by Mao and then used by his opponents to help themselves gain power by representing the struggle as an "ideological" one in "the superstructure."

The doctrine of "the superstructure," in short, is a simplistic distortion of Marxism with reactionary implications both theoretical and political. The doctrine—and the thinking behind it—should be abandoned and the areas it covers in class societies should be depicted in the interactive class struggle perspectives of Marx and Lenin. We might note, finally, that there is no "superstructure" theory in Stalin's 1938 treatment of historical materialism. Yet, if it is a basic Marxist theory, how could it have been possible to survey historical development without it? And why did Marxist works in the U.S.S.R. and elsewhere omit it before 1950 and elevate it to supermacy after 1950, and keep it in that exalted status today?[4]

As for the linguistics controversy, if language was not "part of the superstructure," as Stalin contended, where was it? To provide an explanation—for an essentially false question—Stalin evolved a new "category," that of "social phenomena":

> Of course, peculiar to language, as a social phenomenon, is that which is common to all social phenomena, including the base and the superstructure, namely: It serves society in the same manner as society is served by all the other social phenomena, including the base and the superstructure. But this, essentially speaking, exhausts that which is common to and inherent in all social phenomena. Further on, serious distinctions begin between social phenomena.

The point is that social phenomena have, in addition to this common feature, their own specific peculiarities which distinguish them from each other and which are above all important for science. The specific peculiarities of the base consist in that it serves society economically. The specific peculiarities of the superstructure consist in that it serves society by means of political, legal, esthetic, and other ideas and creates for society the corresponding political, legal, and other institutions.[5]

Thus society consists of diverse "social phenomena," such as base, superstructure, and language, all intent upon "serving society." Not only has the class struggle vanished; all struggle, all antagonisms, economic, social, political, cultural, have vanished. Everything—even "the superstructure"—has been devoured by the new omnipresent category of "social phenomena." There is, of course, no theory in Marx, Engels, or Lenin of "social phenomena," either "serving society" or anything else. The concept is not only mechanistic and abstractionist but idealist, for it suggests that abstract "phenomena" and not objective social realities determine historical evolution. There were, as we saw, similar implications in Stalin's passive "rise and fall" theory of social development, first put forward in *Anarchism or Socialism* (1906-1907). And once again the class struggle has disappeared.

In his 1938 essay, *Dialectial and Historical Materialism*, Stalin also discussed past historical development:

In the space of three thousand years three different social systems have been successively superseded in Europe: the primitive communal system, the slave system and feudal system. In the eastern part of Europe, in the U.S.S.R., even four social systems have been superseded (including capitalism).

Stalin's propagation of this view probably explains how the dogma became established in Soviet and other Marxist circles that feudalism arose from a general slave society—a dogma that is still current. Actually, feudalism everywhere, on all continents, grew out of farming society in its later stage. Its basic labor force was peasant, with slave labor used only in industry and commerce — a very small percentage of the whole. Slave-commercial societies were a limited historical aberration—notably in Greece and Rome—resulting from the concentrated commercial wealth of the Mediterranean area. This wealth might have laid some base for commercial-feudal societies there several centuries later, but it had little or no effect elsewhere in Europe and none outside of Europe. Stalin indicates that Russia, which was completely remote from the Roman Empire, had a "slave system" stage. In fact, Russia never had a slave society in any period of its history. Nor did China, where the theory was also taken up and a "slave stage" preceding feudalism was invented by Chinese Marxists.[6]

In 1952 Stalin produced his last general theoretical work, *Economic Problems of Socialism in the U.S.S.R.*, an essay plus answers to correspondents. Much of what Stalin said is abstract, perhaps necessarily so, as he examines an important but neglected subject, namely the difference between economic laws in capitalism and socialism. He argues early in the essay that "the law of value" (that the exchange value of goods is determined by embodied labor power) still has application in a socialist economy and places restraints on planned production.

> Some time ago it was decided to adjust the prices of cotton and grain in the interest of cotton growing to establish more accurate prices for grain sold to the cotton growers, and to raise the prices of cotton delivered to the state. Our business executives and planners submitted a proposal on this score which could not but astound the members of the Central Committee, since it suggested fixing the price of a ton of grain at practically the same level as a ton of cotton, and, moreover, the price of a ton of grain was taken as equivalent to that of a ton of baked bread. In reply to the remarks of members of the Central Committee that the price of a ton of bread must be higher than that of a ton of grain, because of the additional expense of milling and baking, and that cotton was generally much dearer than grain, as was also borne out by their prices in the world market, the authors of the proposal could find nothing coherent to say. The Central Committee was therefore obliged to take the matter into its own hands and to lower the prices of grain and raise the prices of cotton. What would have happened if the proposal of these comrades had received legal force? We should have ruined the cotton growers and would have found ourselves without cotton.

Cotton was "dearer than grain" because more labor is required for its production, and so, too, with baked bread.[7]

Although the "law of value" still exists under socialism, Stalin argues that "surplus value" has been eliminated: "Talk of labor power being a commodity, and of 'hiring' of workers sounds rather absurd now, under our system: as though the working class, which possesses means of production, hires itself and sells its labor power to itself." Even though profit still exists, it is primarily state and not enterprise profit and is non-exploitive:

... profitableness considered from the standpoint of individual plants or industries is beneath all comparison with that higher form of profitableness which we get from our socialist mode of production, which saves us from crises of overproduction and ensures us a continuous expansion of production.

Stalin also discusses the transition from socialism to communism, considering Engels's arguments that in communism the differences between town and country and between physical and mental labor will be eradicated. Stalin's conclusion is that any such fusion will take a long time and go through "a number of stages of economic and cultural re-education." The peasants will continue to produce their "commodities" for many decades; the division between professional and physical workers will similarly continue. The workers and peasants of the U.S.S.R., although differing "from one another in status," are still linked in bonds of "friendship" and "not a trace remains of the former distrust, not to say hatred, of the country for the town." And "the physical workers and the managerial personnel are not enemies but comrades and friends, members of a single collective body of production."

This is clearly only partly true. All was not harmonious, as the power struggle of the mid-1950s was soon to reveal. Although class struggle had mitigated, it had not vanished. Stalin's main emphasis, however, was on the theoretical argument that socialism would continue to exist largely unchanged for longer than Engels apparently thought, and that certain necessary limitations would continue with it.

In spite of these somewhat conservative positions, Stalin's report strongly attacked pro-capitalist tendencies in the U.S.S.R. He came out against the emphasis on individual-concern profit and argued that collective farms would ultimately evolve into socialist state property. He was apparently also, by implication, attacking a tendency to return more of the collective land to private ownership. Nevertheless, although he argued for collective farm property in time becoming "public property" along with industry, he made no proposals that would bring about such a change. In fact he implied that no such change was needed in the immediate future: "Of course, our present relations of production are in a period when they fully conform to the growth of the productive forces and help them to advance at seven-league strides."[8]

Upon Lenin's death, Stalin had been left with a country still struggling to keep its head above water. The U.S.S.R. was a semi-feudal, peasant country with an embryonic socialist sector riddled with capitalism (NEP). Within 15 years, under Stalin's leadership, the country had become socialist and industralized. It is on his role in this process and in World War II that his reputation as a communist leader and historical figure must ultimately rest. During the war he emerged as a truly heroic figure, the embodiment of the will and courage of the workers' state.

Stalin's main weaknesses as a political leader were those noted by Lenin, particularly his tendency to solve problems by organizational rather than mass-education methods, a tendency which had social roots in a soviet society advancing to socialism under pressure from a capitalist world. Stalin, however, did not by any means neglect mass education or mass inititative— as in the campaigns for the five-year plans, for Stakhanovism, and for the new constitution of 1936. The war made necessary a new degree of centralized control but even then there was spontaneous mass initiative in all fields.

Stalin's weaknesses as a Marxist were primarily in the realm of general theory. In philosophy, he confused materialist dialectics and metaphysical abstraction, emphasizing self-generating rise and decline rather than contradiction, and employing a dogmatic rather than a scientific method of reasoning. He obscured the role of economic forces and the class struggle in history by semi-idealist and mechanistic "superstructure" and "social phenomena" theories. Historical development he depicted as determined by growth and decline rather than by the clash of contradictory forces. The "nation" he presented as a monolithic, classless phenomenon of recent origin. The Russian bourgeois-democratic revolution he first saw not as part of a total revolution driving inexorably to socialism but almost as a thing in itself, with a great gulf fixed between it and socialism, or (confusedly) as a prelude to an "anti-imperialist" revolution.

Stalin's emphasis on organizational measures reflected the outlook of the industrial workers as they drove toward socialism in a dangerous situation. In this situation, a theory emphasizing class struggle added to the danger, for it implied a justification of revolt and could have fed the fires of peasant and professional class opposition. It was more practical to emphasize class harmony and depict society as developing under the aegis of a classless "superstructure." On the other hand, the industrial working class as well as its professional allies had to think realistically about practical matters concerning socialist survival, and this necessarily involved Marxist theory— theory, however, of a limited nature.

Stalin, as we have seen, early identified with the industrial working class. A mixture of peasant and working-class background, the petty-bourgeois aspirations of his mother had sent him to a theological seminary where he learned to admire dogmatic logic and unconsciously imbibed idealist concepts. Then he became a radical journalist, teacher, and organizer among the railroad, oil, and marine workers of Tiflis and Baku in an oppressed nation where working-class and capitalist interests coincided to some degree in a fierce nationalist and anti-feudal struggle. He read the Marxist classics and laced them with abstractionist method. He learned how to analyze immediate problems in Marxist terms and was able—sometimes brilliantly—to project this analysis into limited theoretical areas. But when he turned to general theory with no concrete problems to shape his thinking, he slipped easily into idealism and dogmatism. Even with these limitations, however, his general outlook was still basically proletarian—as was his life dedication.

In making an evaluation of Stalin, we must first and foremost keep in mind that he was a Marxist and a proletarian leader; and for Marxists and proletarian leaders, special standards of evaluation are needed. If Stalin had accomplished for the world bourgeoisie what he did for the world proletariat, he would have long been hailed in bourgeois circles as one of the "greats" of all time, not only of the present century. The same general criteria should apply to Stalin's reputation from the Marxist point of view. Stalin advanced the position of the world proletariat and further than any person in history with the exception of Lenin. True, without the base Lenin laid, Stalin could not have built, but using this base he moved about as far as was possible in the existing situation.

In advancing the position of the world working class Stalin also advanced the position of humanity. In doing so he became part of a new kind of historical leader, one who is able to make massive advances for the "many" and not just socio-economic gains for the "few." The first such leader was, of course, Lenin. When Stalin is seen in this perspective it becomes apparent that for all his shortcomings he is far above all exploitive-class leaders. His predecessors are not Caesar or Napoleon but Spartacus and John Ball, Toussaint L'Ouverture and the Communards, and, of course, more directly, Marx and Engels. In short a new class of world leader has emerged, and Stalin is in its highest rank.[9]

Chapter XI
The Khrushchev Report

In his later years, Stalin was virtually worshipped by the Soviet people as the builder of socialism and the savior of the nation. His daughter, Svetlana, tells of a train trip to Georgia:

Here, at the Kutaisi railway station, his Georgian countrymen had given him such a reception that he'd been unable to leave and get into his car. People literally threw themselves under the wheels: They crawled and shouted and threw flowers and carried their children on their shoulders.

On Stalin's death, the U.S.S.R. witnessed an outpouring of mass grief surpassing even that evoked by the death of Lenin. As Harrison Salisbury wrote in *The New York Times*:

Let there be no mistake about it—the news of Premier Stalin's illness is profoundly sad to the ordinary man and woman of Russia. . . . It may be difficult for persons in other lands to grasp, but it is true that to the ordinary Russian the phrases bestowed on Premier Stalin—genius architect, great leader, great teacher—have genuine meaning. Premier Stalin has been to the ordinary Russian a person apart from other humans, a figure of legendary qualities come to life.[1]

Yet, but three short years later Stalin was denounced as a capricious tyrant by Nikita Khrushchev at a secret session of the 20th Congress of the Party. Khrushchev concentrated on the political repressions of 1937–38:

It was determined that of the 139 members and candidates of the party's Central Committee who were elected at the 17th Congress [1934], 98 persons, i.e., 70 percent, were arrested and shot.... The same fate met not only the Central Committee members but also the majority of the delegates to the 17th Party Congress. Of 1,966 delegates with either voting or advisory rights, 1,108 persons were arrested on charges of anti-revolutionary crimes, i.e., decidedly more than a majority. This very fact shows how absurd, wild and contrary to common sense were the charges of counter-revolutionary crimes made out, as we now see, against a majority of participants at the 17th Party Congress.

These arrests were carried out under a special amendment to the Criminal Code introduced in December 1934 relating to "terrorist organizations." Only 10 days were allowed for the investigation of each case, the indictment were presented to the accused person only 24 hours before his trial, defense attorneys were not allowed to be present, and no appeal to a higher court was permitted.[2]

Khrushchev considered these repressions to be rooted in what he called "the cult of the person of Stalin," whereby Stalin had been transformed into a "superman." Stalin himself, Khrushchev charged, aided in building this cult, by such actions as adding sections to his official biography in which he described himself as "the worthy continuer of Lenin's work." However, "people who had worked with Lenin in his life" were executed as "enemies of the Party." And Khrushchev read a letter from Lenin (written shortly before his death) to Stalin in which he threatened to break off relations with Stalin if Stalin did not apologize to Lenin's wife, Krupskaya, for having been rude to her on the telephone. During his latter years Stalin was "sickly suspicious." "He could look at a man and say: 'Why are your eyes so shifty today.'"[3]

Krushchev also attacked Stalin's conduct of the war. He refused, Khrushchev charged, to heed the warnings of Churchill and others that the German armies were about to attack. Industry was not "mobilized properly," the army was poorly armed, Stalin as a strategist was a disaster: "The Soviet army, on the basis of a strategic plan prepared by Stalin long before, used the tactics of so-called 'active defense,' i.e., tactics which, as we know, allowed the Germans to come up to Moscow and Stalingrad." As an example of Stalin's military ineptness, Khrushchev cited the 1942 Russian offensive at Kharhov, which, Khrushchev claimed, led to a serious defeat.[4]

In 1957, the year after Khrushchev's secret speech, Molotov, Kaganovitch and other Party leaders tried to remove Khrushchev as Party Secretary. The Party Presidium voted him out of office, but Khrushchev, aided by Marshal Zhukov, called a special meeting of the Central Committee and, with a display of military power, succeeded in reversing the verdict.[5]

In 1961 at the 22nd Party Congress, Khrushchev renewed his attack on Stalin and broadened it to include the "group of factionalists headed by Molotov, Kaganovitch, and Malenkov," declaring that the "entire Party, the entire people repudiated these renegades, who resisted everything new and tried to revive the pernicious methods which prevailed under the cult of the individual." Molotov had defended Stalin and "tried to justify the actions taken in the period of the personality cult." The execution of a group of army officers just before the war, headed by Marshal Tukhachevsky, was, Khrushchev declared, unjustified and based on documents forged by the German intelligence services. Following the Congress, Stalin's embalmed body was removed from Lenin's tomb, where it had lain next to Lenin's, and was buried in concrete in a deep pit to prevent its ever being removed.[6]

As we review these events, it becomes clear that Khrushchev was not, as he represented himself in his 1956 denunciation of Stalin, a moralist horrified by transgressions against a socialist ideal but the leader in a political struggle for power within the Party between the Khrushchev and Molotov groupings, and this conflict had been going at least since Stalin's death. In 1956, therefore, when Khrushchev denounced Stalin, he did so as the leader of an anti-Stalin faction in the Party. The policies of this faction soon appeared. They were those of liberal, anti-socialist "reforms." Molotov, an old Bolshevik who had worked under tsarist terror, had a long record of devotion to the working class and to socialism. He had supported Stalin's plans for socialist industrialization, and had for many years at Party Congresses, along with Kaganovitch, made the main reports on this subject. The "everything new" that Molotov opposed were Khrushchev's "reforms." In order to win this power struggle with Stalin's followers, Khrushchev had first to destroy the influence and the image of Stalin and break the link between Stalin and Lenin. In spite of these motivations, however, there is clearly some truth to his contentions. The trouble is that it is a fragmented truth divorced from a proper basic perspective.

"I will probably not sin against the truth," Khrushchev declared in his 1956 speech, "when I say that 99 percent of the persons present here heard and knew very little about Stalin before the year 1924, while Lenin was known to all." This is probably true as a statement of an isolated fact but its import distorts the truth. For it omits Stalin's early Party history, his courageous struggles under tsarist terrorism and his long support of Lenin, his leadership of the Party within Russia as head of the Russian Bureau, his founding of *Pravda*, his recognized leadership in the Central Committee where he gave the political report in Lenin's absence in July 1917, his military service during the civil war, his leadership against the Trotskyist opposition. Khrushchev's comment supports by implication the bourgeois caricature of Stalin as a maneuvering upstart.[7]

Khrushchev's treatment of the relations between Stalin and Lenin concentrates on Lenin's growing apprehension of Stalin's bureaucratic methods in 1923. He omits Lenin's earlier admiration for Stalin and his forwarding of Stalin's career in the Party dating back at least to 1912. Nor does he note that Lenin's later attacks on Stalin were made when Lenin was ill and cut off from Party activity, and that even then, in his "testament," he considered Stalin to be one of the outstanding Party leaders, his faults not those of "non-Bolshevism"—as with Trotsky—but of an over-bureaucratic method of work and personal "rudeness." The fact that people who had "worked with Lenin" were executed means little unless we know who the people were and why they were executed. The fact that people worked with Lenin does not mean that they were pro-socialist, as witness Kamenev and Zinoviev, both of whom Lenin condemned in his "testament."

To attribute all the ills of Soviet society to the "cult of the person of Stalin" (or anyone else) is not only non-Marxist but reflects a simplistic bourgeois concept of history. There was, indeed, such a cult, but it was primarily an effect and not a cause. It arose originally from the Soviet people's need for certainty amid uncertainty and their virtual worship of Stalin as the architect of socialism and the leader of the war against German imperialism. Stalin, however, was not an egocentric individualist—as Khrushchev implies—but a disciplined communist who, like all such communists, subordinated personal interests to those of the Party. In 1937, before he had met Stalin, U.S. Ambassador Joseph Davies reported to the Secretary of State: "He is generally considered to be a clean-living, modest, retiring, single-purposed man, with a one-track mind, devoted to communism and the elevation of the proletariat." On meeting Stalin these impressions were reinforced: "His demeanor is kindly, his manner almost deprecatingly simple, his personality and expression of reserve strength and poise very marked. . . . He gave me the impression of being sincerely modest." "Free of affectation and mannerisms," wrote Marshall Zhukov, "he won the heart of everyone he talked to. His visitors were invariably struck by his candour and his uninhibited manner of speaking, and impressed by his ability to express his thoughts clearly, his inborn analytical turn of mind, his erudition and retentive memory." "He never tolerated any luxury in clothing, furniture, or his life in general."

Enver Hoxha, then fresh from leading the Albanian revolution, meeting Stalin in the 1940s, had the same impression: a "modest, kindly, wise man" who "loved the Soviet people wholeheartedly . . . his heart and mind worked for them." Svetlana tells us that her father used to let his salary checks pile up unused on his desk and that he hated public adulation. Applause for his speeches at a Party Congress he would accept as directed at the Party leadership and not at himself as a person. The development of the "cult" was not his doing:

> As we pulled in at the various stations, we'd go for a stroll along the platforms. My father would walk as far as the engine, giving greetings to the railway workers as he went. You couldn't see a single passenger. It was a special train, and no one was allowed on the platform. It was a sinister, sad, and depressing sight. Who ever thought up such a thing? Who had contrived all these stratagems? Not he. It was a system of which he himself was a prisoner....[8]

If Stalin later in some ways encouraged the "cult" it was not out of personal vanity but because he felt it was helpful for the advancement of socialism. Certain attacks on Stalin could become—as Khrushchev was to demonstrate—attacks on socialism; and strengthening the image of Stalin as the embodiment of the Soviet will assisted both the war struggle and rebuilding after the war.

During the war a small top leadership group was needed. With this group, however, as Zhukov noted, Stalin worked collectively. "Today, after Stalin's death," he writes, apparently answering Khrushchev, "the idea is current that he never heeded anybody's advice and decided questions of military policy all by himself. I can't agree with it. When the person reporting knew what he was talking about he would listen and I know of cases when he reconsidered his own opinions and decisions. This was the case with many operations." "As a rule the General Headquarters worked in an orderly, business-like manner. Everyone had a chance to state his opinion...He [Stalin] listened attentively to anybody speaking to the point."

After the war, however, Stalin continued to rule through a small group (in the form of the Secretariat of the Central Committee). There were no Party Congresses or Central Committee meetings called between 1939 and 1952. This certainly seems unjustified and dictatorial. No explanation has been presented. It does not mean, however, as has been asserted, that the Soviet system as a whole had been transformed into a political dictatorship. There were still trade-union meetings, Party branch meetings, local and other governmental meetings, and so on, all with a great deal of autonomy, as the Party leadership rallied the masses for the immense task of rebuilding a shattered nation, a task which they could have accomplished only with wide popular support.[8]

Even if Khrushchev was not Marxist enough to perceive the class forces behind the "cult" and associated phenomena, he could have at least noted that it was not a matter involving only Stalin and a few others, but the Party leadership in general, including Khrushchev himself, who at the 18th Congress in 1939 had declared:

> Despite all the hectic activity of the capitalist spy organizations, despite all the efforts of the public enemies I have mentioned, we are advancing victoriously to communism. Under the leadership of the great Bolshevik Party, under the leadership of Comrade Stalin, the working class and the people as a whole have broken the enemies' resistance, swept them to destruction and are continuing their victorious advance to communism.[9]

Khrushchev's charge that Stalin did not prepare properly for the war was also repudiated by Zhukov: "the country's defence was managed correctly in its basic and principal features ... between 1939 and the middle of 1941 the people and Party exerted particular effort...." Stalin's prewar speeches show that he was under no delusions about Nazi intentions. He knew the attack would come sooner or later and that he was simply buying time in signing the nonagression treaty. As for Churchill's warnings, Stalin perhaps suspected that Churchill wanted to involve the U.S.S.R. in the war prematurely. In the reports of Marshal Voroshilov and others to the 18th Party Congress in March 1939, we get the impression of intensive war preparation. Voroshilov, for instance, reported on the superior power of the Soviet artillery units over the German (and this was borne out during the war). When we consider the massive power the Nazis and their allies had mustered for the attack, Khrushchev's contention that better preparation could have stopped them nearer the borders seems baseless and is in fact, denied by Zhukov: "even this optimum situation would not have given us a chance to parry the enemy's thrusts completely and to bar their deep penetration into our territory." The Red Army, then largely inexperienced, apparently had no choice but to retreat, and the German armies could only have been defeated after their lines of communication had been extended. As to Stalin's tactics at Kharhov, Khrushchev could have been right. The offensive was perhaps premature, but it is easier to perceive such things after the event than before. That Stalin committed errors was inevitable, but the overall fact remains that the war was won and the Red Army offensive was a masterpiece of military strategy. And Stalin, as Khrushchev's Kharkov story itself shows, and as Zhukov spelled out in detail, was in supreme command.

Khrushchev's charge that Marshal Tukhachevsky and his group were executed on the basis of forged German documents is an echo of similar bourgeois press charges. There seems to be no evidence for the existence of such documents, and it would have been senseless for the Soviet government to execute these officers without substantial evidence of treachery. They were tried by a military court and no records of the trial have been released.[10]

Since Khruschev's denunciation of the political repressions of the late 1930s, a veritable deluge of "exposés" have appeared, from Solzhenitsyn's "Gulag" books to Robert Conquest's *The Great Terror* and Roy A. Medvedev's *Let History Judge*. All these works are anti-Soviet, often fanatically, but some of the material (in memoirs, for instance) in them must have validity. However, as the Soviet government has released no statistics, all figures on the number of arrests, imprisonments, and executions are based on indirect calculations, indeed sometimes, upon pure conjecture. Medvedev, for instance, claims that "on the most cautious estimates, four to five million people were subjected to repression" and that between 400,000 and 500,000 were executed, but he does not give the basis for his "cautious estimates." That they were indeed cautious, however, is apparent when we turn to Conquest's *The Great Terror*. Conquest agrees with an estimate— based on a budget of the Commissariat for Internal Affairs, which was said to have been found by the Nazis—of 7,000,000 prisoners in labor camps for 1940. Merle Fainsod in his *How Russia Is Ruled* calculates that number at 3,500,000 based on the same data. But this so-called "secret" document offered no numbers of prisoners, and given the extent of the Commissariat's jurisdiction—which included everything from militia to fire stations—calculating numbers of camp prisoners on the basis of its general budget is problematic to say the least.

Conquest's next estimate is 13.5 million camp prisoners. This figure is based on "a discrepancy between the aggregate payroll for the whole economy and the total wage bill" derived from "official labour statistics," part of which discrepancy is "accounted for by the Army." This kind of negative estimating is clearly mostly speculation. Conquest's next estimate is based on a general census study: "Again, the author of the most authoritative study of the Soviet population (Lorimer) was puzzled by a residue of 6,790,000 unaccounted for in terms of unemployment, pensions, Army, etc., plus 1.25 million labelled 'social group not indicated.'" On this basis, Conquest calculates the number of people in prison camps at 10 million. It is not, however, at all clear that the discrepancy in these figures represents prisoners.

Then come calculations based on individual "prisoners' reports": 8-12 million. Finally, on executions, Conquest reports: "It will be seen that no exact estimate of total executions can be given, but that the number was most probably something around a million." This figure is even more speculative than those on numbers in prison camps, since Commissariat for Internal Affairs budgets, payroll discrepancies, and census statistics give no basis for statistics on executions. The figure of one million is based mainly on prisoners' reports and calculations by former Internal Affairs officers, neither of whom would be likely to give objective estimates and most or all of whom can have known only a segment of the total operation.[11]

Until the Soviet government releases figures—if it has them—the controversy on numbers will continue. All that we can say on the present evidence is that an unusually large number of men—very few women seem to have been involved—appear to have been in labor camps at the time for one reason or another, and that an unknown number of those arrested were executed.

In addition to those executed, a large number were said to have died in the labor camps from malnutrition and ill-treatment. Conquest argues that 90% of those imprisoned in the labor camps perished. But this does not make any sense for the camps were, after all, labor camps—lumbering, road building, canal construction, mining, farming, and so on—and there would be no point in having 90% of the workers perish if the state wanted to get the work done. No doubt some people died in the camps, as in any prison camp, but again, the numbers will remain speculative unless statistics become available.[12]

But the question of numbers, however, of imprisonments or deaths, is not the essential question. The basic issues are those of motivation and guilt. Why were these people arrested? What had they done? Why was the penal code amended to secure swift arrest and imprisonment? The underlying, indeed sometimes outspoken thesis of Khrushchev, Medvedev, Conquest, and others is that of a sadistic persecution of innocent people by an insane dictator. But this view smacks more of sensationalist journalism than of social analysis. Moreover, Stalin alone could not have initiated the prosecutions. Even if the whole Party leadership was not involved, the central leadership certainly was. At the time, this inner core of leaders included Molotov, Kaganovitch, Zhdanov, Voroshilov, and Manuilsky. Thus, if the professional anti-Stalinists are to be believed, we are confronted with not one insane dictator but a group of insane dictators. When we consider the records of these men, their years of heroic revolutionary work and their determined struggle for socialist industrialization, it is clear that, mistaken or not, they must have believed they were acting in the face of a threat to socialism. They were all responsible and serious men, not men who would persecute for the sake of persecution or who would lightly endorse executions.

In the 1930s, as we have seen, the spread of industrialization and collectivization brought about a socialist state with a broad spectrum of social and political rights. As we would expect from such a state, the legal and prison systems that it established were essentially just and nonpunitive. In fact, they were praised and admired by liberal attorneys and penologists throughout the world. People's Courts, in which ordinary citizens sat with a professional judge on the bench, tried 80% of all cases, and legal services could be obtained free of charge. As a desirable alternative to prisons, "agricultural and industrial labor colonies" were established where some prisoners brought their families and where they were allowed to marry. The basic objective of the system was rehabilitation, not just in words, as in capitalist states, but in reality, as was dramatically shown, for instance, in the film *Road to Life*, depicting the regeneration of teenage criminals. One of the most extensive industrial camp projects was the building of the Baltic-White Sea Canal by prisoners, a vast enterprise whose three chief engineers were former "wreckers." At the completion of the project, 300 prisoners received scholarships, 12,000 were freed, and 59,000 had their sentences reduced. Such was the normal course of working-class justice in the U.S.S.R. Therefore, if changes were made in some aspects of the system, there must have been reasons for it.[13]

As we look over the history of the 1920s and 1930s in the U.S.S.R., one of these reasons quickly becomes apparent, namely massive sabotage—in the mines, on the railways, in factories, in agriculture, in economic planning, in government. A picture of the extent of this sabotage emerged only in the trials of the various opposition leaders between 1936 and 1938, which also revealed that sabotage was linked with plans for the destruction of the Soviet Union in war. These public trials of the "opposition" leaders, however, had revealed only the tip of the iceberg. They indicated the existence of followers everywhere—wrecking machinery, making the wrong parts, sending materials to the wrong places, poisoning farm animals, starting pit fires in mines, planning railway sabotage to build up to the immobilization of the railways in the coming war. Nor was the sabotage only physical. Economic plans were deliberately distorted, government documents lost, statistics faked—actions which could cause widespread disruption in a planned economy. Furthermore, this sabotage, which appears to have been the most massive in history, was coordinated with Nazi and Japanese war plans and with terrorism. Sergei Kirov, the popular head of the Party in Leningrad, was assassinated, and terrorist plans seem to have been afoot to assassinate the whole top Party leadership.

To assert, then, that most of those arrested were innocent "victims" is patently absurd. If the leaders were guilty—and the evidence, as we have seen, indicates that they were—, their followers on the whole must have been guilty also. When the workers began to realize the nature of the situation—the assassination of Kirov in particular evoked angry demonstrations and petitions—they demanded action. The Party, which until then had actually been lagging behind events, began wide investigations and amended the penal code in order to move forward swiftly in a situation of threatening war.

Who was under investigation? We know comparatively few names but Medvedev notes the following groups: "jurists," "educational administrators," "scholars," "biologists," "technical intelligentsia," "designers in the garments industry," "executives, chief engineers, plant managers," "painters, actors, musicians, architects and film people," "military commanders." If to these we add kulaks, largely engaged in agricultural sabotage, it appears that the opposition to the dictatorship of the proletariat came, as we might expect, primarily from the upper professionals and the wealthier peasants. This group of professionals engaged in sabotage—economic, political, or cultural—and other anti-socialist activities, may have been large, but apparently, from the continuing efficient functioning of the nation, they constituted but a small proportion of the population or of the professional class.[14]

Nevertheless, it seems clear that a number of pro-socialist people were imprisoned and some of them were executed. This process was noted, with some alarm, by Andrei Zhdanov at the 18th Congress of the Party in 1939:

> Changing his tactics, the enemy fastened on the question of vigilance and made capital out of it, endeavouring under a mask of hypocritical talk about vigilance to victimize as many honest Communists as possible with the object of fostering mutual distrust and disorganizing our ranks.
>
> The slandering of honest people under the guise of "vigilance" is at the present time the most widespread method used to mask and screen hostile activities.

The enemies of the workers' state had penetrated the Party, the State police and the judicial system, and, as we might expect, made use of the situation to get rid of pro-socialist people in every field. They were able to do this because in their fear and anger the working class and the Party discarded the normal Soviet judicial procedures.

Zhdanov's report was given in 1939. Even if we assume that the confusion sown by anti-Soviet elements was greater than he indicates, and more "honest communists" were "victimized" than he implies, it seems difficult to believe that Khrushchev's figures are correct. According to Khrushchev, Zhdanov was addressing a body—the Party Congress—more than half of whose members had been arrested in 1937 and 1938 and 70% of whose Central Committee had been executed. But there is no indication in Zhdanov's speech or the proceedings of the Congress of anything of this magnitude having taken place. The essential spirit of the Congress was one of exaltation in socialist progress. Molotov opened the Congress with the words: "Comrades: Our Party has come to the present Congress crowned with victories historic in their importance." And he continued: "We have, in the main, brought to completion an entire epoch in our developmental work so that we can now enter upon a new epoch, the epoch of gradual transition from socialism to communism." The Congress does not at all give the impression of a demoralized group. Quite the contrary. The positive note struck by Molotov was the dominant note. Is it possible, then, in view of the obviously high morale of the Congress and its support for the Party leadership, that Khrushchev's figures are correct? They could only be correct if there was a general conviction in the Party that the vast majority of those who had been condemned were guilty and that their actions had threatened the life of the (socialist) nation.[15]

Lenin in 1918 wrote in his *Letter to American Workers*:

The English bourgeoisie have forgotten their 1649, the French their 1793. The terror was just and legitimate when it was applied by the bourgeoisie for its own advantage against the feudal lords. The terror became monstrous and criminal when the workers and poor peasants dared to apply it to the bourgeoisie. /

Lenin was referring to the repression which he and the Party were beginning against the Socialist Revolutionaries and others who had tried to overthrow the Bolshevik government. At the time, Lenin opposed a move to abolish the death penalty and approved the repression waged by the state police (Cheka). Felix Dzerzhinsky, head of the Cheka, commented at the time: "The Cheka must defend the revolution and conquer the enemy even if its sword falls occasionally on the neck of the innocent." Nor is there, in fact, any way to avoid injustice once a massive repression begins whatever its social roots.[16]

The repression in Stalin's time was not in essence different from that in Lenin's. It was simply on a larger scale; and it was on a larger scale because the enemies of socialism were more numerous and better organized. That the repression had been basically directed at those engaged in anti-socialist actions, was, Stalin contended, shown by the fact that reactionaries everywhere immediately took up the cry of "injustice" and condemned the U.S.S.R. out of hand (as they had also in Lenin's day):

To listen to these foreign drivelers one would think that if the spies, murderers and wreckers had been left at liberty to wreck, murder and spy without let or hindrance, the Soviet organizations would have been far sounder and stronger. Are not these gentlemen giving themselves away too soon by so insolently defending the cause of spies, murderers and wreckers?

As the present century has amply and bloodily demonstrated, wherever the working class moves toward power, the bourgeoisie will work to destroy it by every means at its disposal, war, terrorism, massacre, counterrevolution, sabotage, subversion, lies. If a working class in power is not able to thwart these attempts it will be defeated and socialism destroyed.

In the Paris Commune of 1870, the working class was unaware of the savagery of a bourgeoisie driving to regain power, even enlisting help from its enemies; and 30,000 corpses were piled in the streets of Paris. The Russian workers almost fell into the same trap. The evidence at the public trials had shown that some of the accused had been in contact with foreign governments for a number of years, yet it was not until 1937 that this contact became known. What was the explanation? It lay first, Stalin argued, in "an underestimation of the power and purpose of the mechanism of the bourgeois states surrounding us and of their espionage organs, which endeavor to take advantage of people's weaknesses, their vanity, their slackness of will, to enmesh them in their espionage nets and use them to surround the organs of the Soviet state." It lay, second, in "an underestimation of the role and significance of the mechanism of our socialist state and of its intelligence service, by an underestimation of this intelligence service, by the twaddle that an intelligence service in a Soviet state is an unimportant trifle."[17]

That Stalin was right in the first explanation was indicated when the German imperialist armies crashed across the border, eloquently testifying to the fact that the hatred of the imperialist powers for the U.S.S.R. had been continuous and relentless, a hatred which compelled them to get agents in the Soviet system at all costs. That Stalin was right in his second explanation, a neglect of the Soviet intelligence system, was clear from the penetration of this system by enemy agents and the initial slowness and limited range of its investigations.

The anti-Soviet commentators and Khrushchev give the impression of an all-encompassing "terror" which virtually paralyzed Soviet life. But this was clearly false. Industrial production increased at a rapid rate between 1936 and 1940, the life of the average Soviet citizen went on much as before, for some it even took a special swing upward:

... during the period under review the party succeeded in promoting to leading state and party posts over five hundred thousand young Bolsheviks, members of the party and people standing close to the party, over twenty percent of whom were women.

The Party, which Khrushchev depicted as decimated by purges, appears to have been active and healthy. According to Zhdanov in his report to the 18th Congress, more than 50% of the Party members were between 31 and 35 years of age, and "over two million members and candidate members attended the discussion at Party meetings" in preparation for the Congress, and "about one million comrades took part in the discussions at these meetings." The reports at the Congress by Stalin, Molotov, Kaganovitch, and others are all mainly concerned with positive planning, socialist construction, and cultural progress (between 1933 and 1938 more than 20,000 new schools were built).[18]

Finally, if Soviet society had been so shaken by the trials and purges and so corrupted as Khrushchev, Conquest and Medvedev imply, the U.S.S.R. could not have won the war. Only a basically sound society could have achieved such a feat, a feat which required national cooperation, initiative, and morale.[19]

In spite of all the Party's efforts, the bourgeois corruption which bred treachery still continued in Soviet society. Stalin perceived it and was troubled by it. When Svetlana was transferred from Moscow to Kuibyshev during the war, a private school was set up for her and the children of other government officials—as she reported to her father:

"What? A special school" I saw that he was getting angrier by the minute. "Ah, you"—he was trying to find a word that wasn't too improper—"Ah, you damned caste! Just think! The government and the people from Moscow came and they give them their own school."

And she adds:

He was quite right. It was a caste, a caste of bigwigs from the capital that had come to Kuibyshev. Half the population had to be evicted to make room for all these families, who were used to a comfortable life and felt cramped in modest provincial apartments.

But it was too late to do anything about it. The caste was already in existence, and it lived by laws of its own.

In his last work, *Problems of Socialism in the U.S.S.R.*, Stalin directed his fire at the growth of anti-socialist economic tendencies. But, as Svetlana noted, "it was too late." The tendencies continued.[20]

It is in the light of this growing anti-socialist influence that we have to view Khrushchev's "secret speech." The speech has nothing to do with Marxism. It does not examine the class or even the political forces behind events but is a superficial, essentially bourgeois narrative centered around a personal vilification of Stalin. Moreover it was a reactionary document, applauded by the world bourgeoisie and serving to split the world communist community.

This bourgeois-type outlook is clear in the policies associated with Khrushchev and his group both before and after their seizure of executive political power (which they were perhaps able to do because of the decimation of the working class in the war). They extended private plots and privately owned farm animals, dismantled much of the central economic planning system, gave factory directors more power, elevated profit as a major incentive to production, favored consumer goods over capital goods, and allowed a cultural "thaw," the essentially bourgeois nature of which is made clear in Ilya Ehrenberg's autobiographical writings and other works, indeed in Ehrenberg himself. In foreign policy, a tendency to appease imperialism was followed by an irresponsible swing in the other direction by exporting nuclear missiles to Cuba (to balance the U.S. missiles near the Soviet border in Turkey).

Nevertheless, socialism did not disappear, as some seem to think. No capitalist corporations arose to exploit the working mass. Mainly, the economy was still centrally planned and it developed at a steady pace without economic crises or unemployment. Medical services, education, and social services of all kinds—including nurseries for the children of working mothers—remained free and open to all; the costs of housing and transportation remained minimal.

There was, then, no seizure of power by an anti-socialist class. Apparently, what happened was political power shifted in the ruling alliance between the industrial working class and the "new, Soviet intelligentsia"—engineers, scientists, economic planners, government bureaucrats, and other professionals, plus perhaps Ukrainian and other "nationalists." Part of this intelligentsia, as Stalin realized, had solidified into a "caste," which sought special privileges. Although the caste continued its alliance with the proletariat after Stalin's death, it pursued further extension of these privileges and gained further executive political power. It achieved this power with the rise of Khrushchev. In 1955, only 14% of the deputies to the Supreme

Soviet were workers. In 1956, only 32% of the Party members were workers and 50% of all members came from the professional class.

The zig-zag instability of a regime yielding to professional class plus peasant and bourgeois-nationalist influence was vividly revealed in the Cuban missile crisis, and Khrushchev was forced from office. Under his successor, Leonid Brezhnev, the trend toward the decentralization of the economy was retarded, foreign policy became firmer, and the Czechoslovakian "intelligentsia" and its international capitalist supporters were thwarted in a bid for power. A tougher attitude was adopted toward the so-called "dissidents" (mostly professionals who seek the restoration of capitalism, or, in the case of Solzhenitsyn, of feudalism). The central political power had shifted back to the industrial workers and the class alliance with the professionals (necessarily) continued but on a more balanced basis. In 1972, 42% of the deputies to the Supreme Soviet were workers, and in 1976, 41% of Party members were workers. The working class is clearly the basic force that forwards the socialist elements in the society and retards anti-socialist movements. The workers not only have central power but exert pressure through local and national elections (39% of local Soviet deputies were workers in 1972), through their unions, through worker-manager meetings, through Communist Party branches and local committees, through the "comrades courts," and through letters to the press (in 1970 *Izvestia* handled 500,000 letters).[21]

There has been considerable debate over whether the U.S.S.R. today can correctly be called a socialist state, and its critics have pointed to such apparently unsocialist factors as high salaries and other privileges for a section of the professional class, the use of the profit motive to increase production, the use of economic incentives such as bonuses, and the large area of private farming still in existence. These factors must, however, be seen within an overall framework of state ownership of the means of production, distribution, communication and finance, the dominance of collective and state farms, the existence of a mass-democratic system, which—bourgeois critics to the contrary—is much more extensive than capitalist "democracy" and ensures a primarily working-class control over the economy. Furthermore, that society, if it covered the earth, would result in a world permanently at peace. The answer to those who deny the U.S.S.R. socialist status is that they do not recognize socialism when they see it.

When we consider the problems faced by socialism in the U.S.S.R., the wonder is not that there are still inequalities, but how egalitarian the society on the whole has become, as illustrated, for instance, in such a study as Victor and Ellen Perlo's *Dynamic Stability: The Soviet Economy Today.* The Perlos found a basically working-class mass-democratic society everywhere.

Socialist industrialization has continued and can advance — as the present regime recognizes — at a faster pace if technoligcal and social reforms are achieved. The capitalists of the world, we might note, have no delusions about the U.S.S.R. being capitalist but have attempted by war, economic discrimination, subversion, and sabotage to destroy it since its birth and now threaten it with nuclear annihilation. Capitalists, in fact, consider it "communist" — not being interested in evolutionary historical distinctions — and the leading state in a "communist bloc."

The other "bloc" states are also basically socialist, although with varying degrees of socialist development. They range from Albania (which has great mineral resources and underwent a deep transformation in a revolutionary war), Czechoslovakia and the German Democratic Republic (both of which had capitalist industrial foundations) to the other East European states (which arose from largely feudal societies). So too with the east Asian socialist nations, all of which were largely feudal and — along with Cuba, Nicaragua, and Ethiopia — had been plundered by imperialism. Taken together, these nations represent the central historical movement of the present century, a movement unqiue in history, signifying what Marx and Engels said it would: the beginning of the movement of humanity from 5,000 years of exploitation and oppression to a world communist community. Without these nations, the world would be dominated by monopoly capitalism and there would be little hope of averting nuclear war or global ecological devastation.

These advances are all connected, directly or indirectly, with Stalin. Stalin's armies paved the way for revolution in Eastern Europe and assisted it in China. Once the foundations of socialism were established under his leadership in the U.S.S.R., a model was given to the world, for socialism, although differing in specifics and in different countries, is — like feudalism or captialism — necessaily everywhere the same in its general nature. In omitting or distorting this historial background, the detractors of Stalin produce a shallow and false picture. Some of the attacks on Stalin arise, it is true, from honest disagreement with his view and methods, but mostly they are basically anti-Soviet, often sweepingly and dangerously so.

Like their predecessors the present Soviet leaders have made no serious attempt to evaluate Stalin — or Khruschev. To do so would perhaps require a deeper examination of social and historical forces than they wish to attempt. Yet in failing to do so they are playing into the hands of the anti-Sovieteers.

In trying to evaluate all these matters it is important to keep general historical perspectives in mind. When the Bolsheviks seized power in November 1917 this was the first time in history that a group with scientific understanding of the historical process had taken power and went on to change society by consciously utilizing these processes. The wonder, then is not that they made mistakes but that they made so few and that on the whole they succeeded. Their laboratory was society and their units were not atoms or molecules but social groups, most importantly, social classes. They elevated social classes that had been at the bottom to the top and forced those that had been at the top to the bottom. This produced a primal scream of rage from the top classes in the rest of the world and this scream was transmuted in complex forms into massive distortion. Khrushchev's Report, whatever gobbets of fact it contains, is essentially a reflection of this distortion.

Appendix I
Portrait of Stalin by
Marshal Zhukov

(From *The Memoirs of Marshal Zhukov*, New York, 1971, pp. 279–285. The *Memoirs* were first published in the U.S.S.R. in 1969.)

All the events I have been describing since my return to Moscow from the South-Western Front I saw from the viewpoint of Chief of Staff and it was in this role that I participated in them, sharing the responsibilities, the bitterness of setbacks, and the joy of infrequent victories with the ranking commanders of many arms and services.

And here I feel it would be appropriate to say a few words about the work of the General Headquarters and Stalin himself.

In July 1941 the Politbureau of the Central Committee of the All-Union Communist Party (Bolsheviks) decreed a reorganization of the Armed Forces' strategic command system. On July 10 the State Committee for Defence reorganized the General Headquarters of the High Command into the General Headquarters of the Supreme Command. The General Headquarters was composed of J. V. Stalin (Chairman), V. M. Molotov, Marshal S. K. Timoshenko, S. M. Budenny, K. Ye. Vorshilov, B. M. Shaposhnikov and General G. K. Zhukov. On July 19, J. V. Stalin was appointed People's Commissar for Defence and on August 8—Supreme Commander-in-Chief of the USSR Armed Forces. Thenceforth the supreme body of the strategic leadership was named—General Headquarters of the Supreme Command.

The population and the Army in the field were favourably impressed by Stalin's nomination for he enjoyed great authority in the country and abroad. . . .

The General Staff was the General Headquarters' sole executive apparatus. The General Headquarters' orders and instructions were normally issued through the General Staff. Stalin's study in the Kremlin was, in fact, a place where General Headquarters' decisions were taken and directives for the Fronts adopted.

The study was a rather light, spacious room. The walls were panelled with stained oak. A long table stood in the room, covered with a green cloth. There were portraits of Marx, Engels and Lenin. Portraits of Suvorov and Kutuzov were hung during the war. There was hard-seated furniture and no unnecessary things. There was a huge globe in the adjacent room. A table stood nearby. The walls were hung with maps of the world.

Down the study, near the wall, was his desk on which there always lay a heap of documents, papers and maps. On the desk were also radio-frequency and extension telephones, and a pile of sharpened pencils. He used to write down notes in blue pencil. He wrote fast and in a bold hand, but fairly legibly.

One could enter his study through Poskrebyshev's room and then the small premises occupied by the chief of Stalin's personal security team. Behind the study was a lounge and a signal room with Baudot and other means of communications used by Poskrebyshev to connect Stalin with the front commanders and General Headquarters' representatives at the fronts.

There was a big table on which members of the General Staff and General Headquarters spread out maps and reported on the situation at the fronts. They stood while they reported; sometimes they used notes. As Stalin listened to a report he paced the room in big strides, waddling somewhat. From time to time he would come up to the table and, bending over, scrutinize a map. Or he would go to his desk, take up a pack of tobacco, tear it up and slowly fill his pipe.

The General Headquarters was mainly concerned with elaborating and assigning strategic missions to the troops, allocating forces and *matériel* to the Fronts and strategically important sectors, planning and directing combat actions both of the Army and the Navy. General Headquarters reserves played an important role; fresh units were constantly being raised and replenished. The Supreme Command employed them as a potent weapon to reinforce our forces operating against most important objectives and in decisive operations.

Conferences to project strategic policies were normally held in the presence of the Members of the State Committee for Defense. Also summoned were top officers of the General Staff, Chief of the Air Force, Chief of Ordnance, Chief of the Armour and Automotive Service, Chief of Rear Services, heads of some of the Defence Commissariat departments. Front commanders were summoned whenever matters within their province came up for discussion, mostly in planning an operation. Sometimes aircraft, tank and artillery designers were invited too.

As a rule, the General Headquarters worked in an orderly, business-like manner. Everyone had a chance to state his opinion.

Stalin was equally stern to everybody and rather formal. He listened attentively to anybody speaking to the point.

Incidentally, I know from my war experience that one could safely bring up matters unlikely to please Stalin, argue them out and firmly carry the point. Those who assert it was not so are wrong.

The General Staff was the General Headquarters' executive organ. At the outset of the war the staff officers and myself worked round the clock collating often conflicting data supplied by the Fronts and working out urgent recommendations for the General Headquarters. The General Staff functions immediately grew immeasurably more complex; the volume of work expanded sharply; much of what was satisfactory in peace-time, became totally unacceptable now. Reorganization was proceeding rapidly but we could not manage all at once.

Accurate intelligence reports and information on the Soviet and enemy forces' dispositions would come through to us at irregular intervals, day and night, which made it difficult for us in good time to make considered recommendations regarding provision of a front with equipment and ammunition, and write the most important directives on the instructions of the Supreme Command within mere hours and sometimes even minutes.

It was impossible to go to Stalin without being perfectly familiar with the situation plotted on the map and to report tentative or (which was worse) exaggerated information. Stalin would not tolerate hit-or-miss answers, he demanded utmost accuracy and clarity.

Stalin seemed to have a knack of detecting weak spots in reports and documents. He immediately laid them open and severely reprimanded those responsible for inaccuracies. He had a tenacious memory, perfectly remembered whatever was said and would not miss a chance to give a severe dressing-down. That is why we drafted staff documents as best we possibly could under the circumstances.

In a most trying situation at the front, at a time when the country's life was being regeared to serve the war effort, the General Staff personnel immediately got down to business and worked creatively under extreme strain, which was much to the credit of the General Staff leadership.

Later on, till the end of the war, I never once lost contact whether personally or officially with the General Staff, which largely aided me at the front in planning and conducting major operations. The General Staff personnel efficiently trained fresh contingents; it was sufficiently skilled and quick in working out draft directives and orders of the Supreme Command; it strictly enforced the State Defence Committee's instructions, directed the work of the main headquarters of the Arms and Services and approached the General Headquarters with matters of strategic importance.

Stalin based his judgments of crucial issues on the reports furnished by General Headquarters representatives, whom he would send to the Fronts for on-the-spot assessment of the situation and consultations with respective commanders, on conclusions made at the General Headquarters and suggestions by Front commanders and on special reports.

After 1940, when I served as Chief of Staff of the Red Army and later, during the war, as Deputy Supreme Commander-in-Chief, I had occasion to get to know Stalin closely.

Stalin's outer appearance has been described on more than one occasion. Though slight in stature and undistinguished in outward appearance, Stalin was nevertheless an imposing figure. Free of affectation and mannerisms, he won the heart of everyone he talked with. His visitors were invariably struck by his candour and his uninhibited manner of speaking, and impressed by his ability to express his thoughts clearly, his inborn analytical turn of mind, his erudition and retentive memory, all of which made even old hands and big shots brace themselves and be "on the alert."

Stalin did not like to remain seated during a conversation. He used to pace the room slowly, stopping now and then, coming up close to the person he was talking with and looking him straight in the face. His gaze was clear, tenacious, and seemed to envelop and pierce through the visitor.

Stalin spoke softly, clearly shaping his phrases, almost without gesticulation. He used to hold his pipe, though not lighted at times, and stroke his moustache with the mouthpiece.

He spoke Russian with a Georgian accent, but flawlessly. In his speech he often used figures of speech, similies, metaphors.

One seldom saw him laughing; and when he laughed he did so quietly, as though to himself. But he had a sense of humour, and appreciated sharp wit and a good joke.

Stalin had excellent eyesight. He never used glasses in reading. As a rule, he wrote by hand. He read widely and was extensively knowledgeable in many different fields.

His tremendous capacity for work, his ability quickly to grasp the meaning of a book, his tenacious memory—all these enabled him to master, during one day, a tremendous amount of factual data, which could be coped with only by a very gifted man.

It is hard to say which of his character traits was predominant.

Many-sided and gifted as Stalin was, his disposition could not be called even. He was a man of strong will, reserved, fervent and impetuous.

Ordinarily calm and sober-minded he sometimes lost his temper, and objectivity failed him. He virtually changed before one's eyes—he grew pale, a bitter expression came to his eyes and his gaze became heavy and spiteful. I knew of few daredevils who could hold out against Stalin's anger and parry the blow.

Stalin had a rather singular daily schedule: he worked mainly in the late hours of the evening and at night, hardly ever rising before noon. He worked a lot, 12–15 hours at a stretch. Adapting themselves to Stalin's schedule, the Central Committee of the Party, the Council of People's Commissars, the Commissariats and the major government and planning bodies would likewise keep working until late at night. Such a routine exhausted people.

Many political, military and other issues of nation-wide importance were debated and decided upon not at official meetings of the Central Committee Politbureau or its Secretariat, but at night, over dinner at Stalin's apartment or his summer cottage, usually attended by those members of the Politbureau who were most closely associated with Stalin. And it was there, during those customarily very modest dinners, that Stalin would parcel out instructions to members of the Politbureau or to People's Commissars who were invited whenever something within their jurisdiction was discussed. The Chief of Staff was sometimes invited to participate in these functions together with the Defence Commissar.

Before the war it was hard for me to judge of Stalin's knowledge or abilities in military science, in problems of tactics and strategy, since the topics discussed in Stalin's presence (at least whenever I had occasion to be in attendance) mainly related to problems of organization, mobilization or material and technical supply.

I can only repeat that Stalin devoted a good deal of attention to problems of armament and *matériel*. He frequently met with chief aircraft, artillery and tank designers whom he would question in great detail about the progress achieved in designing the various types of equipment in our country and abroad. To give him his due, it must be said that he was fairly well versed in the characteristics of the basic types of armament.

Stalin urged the chief designers and managers of munitions plants (many of whom he knew personally) to produce new models of aircraft, tanks, guns and other major *matériel* within established time-limits and to make sure their quality should be not only on a par with foreign-made models but even superior to them.

Without Stalin's approval not a single item of armament or *matériel* was either adopted or discarded—and this certainly curtailed the initiative of the Commissar for Defence and his deputies responsible for the armament of the Red Army.

Before and especially after the war an outstanding role was attributed to Stalin in creating the Armed Forces, elaborating the fundamentals of Soviet military science and major doctrines of strategy, and even operational art.

Is it true that Stalin really was an outstanding military thinker, a major contributor to the development of the Armed Forces and an expert in tactical and strategic principles?

From the military standpoint I have studied Stalin most thoroughly, for I entered the war together with him and together with him I ended it.

Stalin mastered the technique of the organization of front operations and operations by groups of fronts and guided them with skill, thoroughly understanding complicated strategic questions. He displayed his ability as Commander-in-Chief beginning with Stalingrad.

In guiding the armed struggle as a whole, Stalin was assisted by his natural intelligence and profound intuition. He had a knack of grasping the main link in the strategic situation so as to organize opposition to the enemy and conduct a major offensive operation. He was certainly a worthy Supreme Commander.

Of course, Stalin had no knowledge of all the details with which the troops and all command echelons had to deal meticulously in order to prepare an operation properly by a front or a group of fronts. For that matter, this was something he didn't really need to know.

In these cases he would naturally consult the members of the General Headquarters, General Staff, and experts in artillery, tank, air and naval operations, and on problems of logistics and supply.

To Stalin is usually ascribed a number of fundamental innovations such as elaborating the methods of artillery offensive action, the winning of air supremacy, methods of encircling the enemy, the splitting of surrounded groups and their demolition by parts, etc.

All these paramount problems of the art of war are the fruits of battles with the enemy, the fruits of profound thinking, the fruits of the experience of a big team of leading military leaders and the troops themselves.

Here Stalin's merit lies in the fact that he correctly appraised the advice offered by the military experts and then in summarised form—in instructions, directives and regulations—immediately circulated them among the troops for practical guidance.

As regards the material and technical organization of operations, the build-up of strategic reserves, the organization of production of *matériel* and troop supplies, Stalin did prove himself to be an outstanding organizer. And it would be unfair if we, the Soviet people, failed to pay tribute to him for it.

Appendix II
Dialectical Materialism: Stalin and After

In 1938, when the *History of the Communist Party of the Soviet Union* was being prepared under his general direction, Stalin contributed a section on dialectical and historical materialism, which was also issued as a separate work. It was read in millions of copies throughout the world and is still in print in many countries, including the U.S. In the dialectical materialism section, Stalin gives the impression that he is presenting the ideas of Marx, Engels, and Lenin in compact and newly organized form. And at a first reading this may appear to be so. But a closer examination reveals that it is not, and incidentially provides an interesting challenge in disentangling Marxist from non-Marxist concepts.

Stalin begins as follows:

> Dialectical materialism is the world outlook of the Marxist-Leninist party. It is called dialectical materialism because its approach to the phenomena of nature, its method of studying and apprehending them, is *dialectical,* while its interpretation of the phenomena of nature, its conception of these phenomena, its theory, is *materialistic.*
>
> Historical materialism is the extension of the principles of dialectical materialism to the study of social life, an application of the principles of dialectical materialism to the phenomena of the life of society, to the study of society and of its history.[1]

Marx and Engels did not believe that they were formulating the "world outlook" of a political party but of a class, namely the industrial working class, a view already inherent in the class although not in cohesive form. They believed also that this view contained general truths about nature and society which would hold good in a future communist society long after the working class and its party had vanished.

In his second sentence Stalin makes a distinction between "dialectical" and "materialistic" in which he restricts the first to "method" and the second to "interpretation." The concept of "dialectical" as primarily a "method," that is to say a form of thought or logic, continues throughout the essay. Dialectical materialism, however, is called dialectical not primarily because of its "method" of reasoning but because the dialectical process is inherent in nature and society. The "method" of dialectical materialism and its "interpretation" are at the same time dialectical and materialist. As Marx noted, a dialectical materialist has first of all to work scientifically. His first step is not to apply a "method" of thought but to gather and test his data: "to appropriate the material in detail, to analyse its different forms of development, to trace out their inner connexion." Stalin, unlike Marx (or Lenin), places the dialectical "method" first and materialistic "interpretation" second. And he does so throughout the essay.[2]

"Historical materialism is the extension of the principles of dialectical materialism to the study of social life." Historical materialism, however, has its own roots and its own being. It was not conceived as (nor is it) an extension of a set of "principles"; rather, it arose from participation in and analysis of the class struggle and other social phenomena. True, the processes of society, like those of nature, proceed by the continuous resolution of interactive opposing forces. This arises, however, not from "principles" but from the fact that people and society evolved from nature, which is inherently dialectical: people from animals, society from animal society, directly from simian to hominid to human.

Furthermore, Stalin uses "historical materialism" in a broad sense not implied in Marx or Engels. It refers only to the historical aspects of society, not all its aspects. Stalin's error has been continued in Soviet writings. The actual contrast is between Marxism and dialectical materialism, the first primarily reflecting society, the second primarily the relation of people to nature.

As the essay continues, the Aristotelian, metaphysical approach—metaphysical in the sense of boxed-in categorical thinking—implied in these paragraphs becomes more marked. For example:

> The dialectical method therefore requires that phenomena should be considered not only from the standpoint of their interconnection and interdependence, but also from the standpoint of their movement, their change, their development, their coming into being and going out of being.

Or, further: "interconnection and interdependence of phenomena, as established by the dialectical method. . . ." But that the phenomena of nature and society are dialectical in how they change was not primarily "established" by "dialectical method" but by scientific investigation ("Nature," Engels noted, "is the test of dialectics") and by social struggle and analysis, ultimately, as Marx and Lenin emphasized, by "practice." Of course, after practice has disclosed sufficient such phenomena, we can make generalizations which aid us in perceiving other specific dialectical processes. The basic element involved, however, is not a "method" of thought but activity and testing. True, Stalin does discuss these matters later in the essay—"our knowledge of the laws of nature, tested by experiment and practice"—but by this time he has already established the priority of "method." We might note also that when Lenin discussed these matters in his encyclopedia article on Marx, he discussed "Philosophical Materialism" first, and "Dialectics" second, thus emphasizing, as did Marx, the primacy of materialism in the dialectical materialist complex.

In discussing the questions of epistemology ("knowing"), Stalin writes:

> Further, if nature, being, the material world, is primary, and mind, thought, is secondary, derivative; if the material world represents objective reality existing independently of the mind of men, while the mind is a reflection of objective reality, it follows that the material life of society, its being, is also primary, and its spiritual life secondary, derivative, and that the material life of society is an objective reality existing independently of the will of men, while the spiritual life of society is a reflection of this objective reality, a reflection of being.[3]

Once again, "practice" is omitted, and mind is presented as a passive "reflection" of external reality—exactly the approach that Marx attacked and denied:

> The chief defect of all hitherto existing materialism—that of Feuerbach included—is that the object, reality, sensuousness, is conceived only in the form of the *object* or *contemplation* but not as *human sensuous activity, practice,* not subjectively.

Not only, then, does Stalin here omit practice as the basic way of ascertaining truth but he lacks any sense of the active interaction of matter, body, the senses, and mind, or of the connection of this living complex with a struggle to "change the world." This static view of "mind as mirror here, matter as object there" leads to another exercise in formal logic: if nature is primary and mind derivative then it "follows" that society is primary and its "spiritual life" derivative. But the one does not "follow" from the other at all. Stalin has, in fact, proposed a false question, that is to say, one dealing with non-existent entities. Let us again return to Marx: "It is not the consciousness of human beings that determines their existence, but, conversely, it is their social existence that determines their consciousness." There is nothing in Marx about nature and society as entities separately "reflected" by mind. His concept is that of "sensuous" human beings in struggle producing forms of consciousness that interact with both nature and society.[4]

In examining "the principal features of the Marxist dialectical method," which Stalin discusses first ("The principal features of the Marxist dialectic method are as follows"), he lists and discusses them presumably in their order of importance. First is that "any phenomenon can be understood and explained if considered in its inseparable connections with surrounding phenomena." Second is that nature is in a "state of continuous movement and change, of continuous renewal and development, where something is always arising and developing, and something always disintegrating and dying away." Third is that qualitative changes arise from quantitative changes. And finally:

Contrary to metaphysics, dialectics holds that internal contradictions are inherent in all things and phenomena of nature, for they all have their negative and positive sides, a past and a future, something dying away and something developing; and that the struggle between these opposites, the struggle between the old and the new, between that which is dying away and that which is being born, between that which is disappearing and that which is developing, constitutes the internal content of the process of development, the internal content of the transformation of quantitative change into qualitative changes.

Not only does Stalin place contradiction last but his treatment of it is the opposite of Marx's or Lenin's: "The splitting of a single whole and the cognition of its contradictory parts ... is the essence ... of dialectics." "This aspect of dialectics," Lenin added, "usually receives inadequate attention." For Stalin, contradiction is not "the essence," and it is fuzzily blended with other phenomena. "Internal contradictions" certainly have "positive and negative sides" but this cannot simply be equated with the fact that they have "a past and a future, something dying away and something developing." Or, as Stalin put it earlier in the essay: "coming into being and going out of being." To imply that the essence of development can lie in the rise of the new and decline of the old blurs the essential picture (of "contradictory parts") and leaves unsettled the question of what causes the rise and fall, thus opening the way for an idealist, Hegelian interpretation. The reactionary implications of this view come out clearly when Stalin, in the historical materialism section of his essay, applies it to society:

> There are different kinds of social ideas and theories. There are old ideas and theories which have outlived their day and which serve the interests of the moribund forces of society. Their significance lies in the fact that they hamper the development, the progress of society. Then there are new and advanced ideas and theories which serve the interests of the advanced forces of society.

There is of course nothing in Marx, Engels or Lenin about "old ideas" that have "outlived their day" or about "new and advanced ideas." According to Marx and Engels, ideas—in this context—are, and can only be, class ideas. The ideas change as the classes change in response to economic and social developments. Ideas do not "advance" or grow "old" of their own accord or live a life of their own, hastening like servants to "serve" or "hamper" nebulous "social forces."

The same non-Marxist outlook is continued in the next paragraph: "New social ideas and theories arise precisely because they are necessary to society, because it is impossible to carry out the urgent tasks of development of the material life of society without their organizing, mobilizing and transforming action." "Necessary" for what class, originating in what class? The ideas of Hitler were certainly "new" ideas and they were certainly "necessary" for monopoly capitalist domination; the ideas of the German Communist Party were also "new" ideas and were necessary if the German working class was to advance to socialism. To say that either set of ideas was "necessary" for an abstract "society" obscures both the class struggle and the social roots of ideas in it and in the underlying economic forces.[5]

Stalin, then, although listing contradiction among the "laws" of dialectics, fails to give it the central position it occupies in Marx and Lenin, treats it primarily as a "method" of thought, and takes the heart out of it. In fact, the picture of development which emerges from Stalin's treatment is, in spite of his nod to "contradiction," essentially that which Lenin condemned as "lifeless, pale and dry" in his well-known notebook note *On the Question of Dialectics:*

> Development is the "struggle" of opposites. The two basic (or two possible? or two historically observable?) conceptions of development

(evolution) are: development as decrease and increase, as repetition, and development as a unity of opposites (the division of a unity into mutually exclusive opposites and their reciprocal relation).

In the first conception of motion, *self*-movement, its driving force, its source, its motive, remains in the shade (or this source is made *external—God, subject, etc.) In the second conception the chief attention is directed precisely to knowledge of the source* of "*self*"-movement.

The first conception is lifeless, pale and dry. The second is living. The second *alone* furnishes the key to the "self-movement" of everything existing; it alone furnishes the key to the "leaps," to the "break in continuity," to the "transformation into the opposite," to the destruction of the old and the emergence of the new.

As we look over the laws of dialectics that Stalin lists, "the negation of the negation" is conspicuous by its absence. There is, it seems to me, justification for Stalin's skepticism. Engels's examples (via Hegel) of plant-seeds-plants and so on, as indicating a development to a "higher level" with something of the old retained, seem only to embody a regular quantitative-qualitative-quantitative change sequence. Engel's general efforts to show that such examples do embody change to a higher level are unconvincing. (We end up with more plants but not better plants.) But if Stalin had come to the conclusion that the law of the negation of the negation was invalid he should have explained why and not silently dropped it. Furthermore, in doing so he is not only repudiating Marx and Engels but Lenin: "A development that repeats, as it were, the stages already passed, but repeats them in a different way, on a higher plane (negation of negation)." Since Lenin's comments appear in his well-known encyclopedia essay on Marx, Stalin is, then, implicitly indicating that Lenin was wrong, and that this would be understood by his Soviet, Marxist readers. It is also typical of Stalin's dogmatic method that he does not examine the problems at issue but simply implies a new dogma.[6]

As we read Stalin's essay it becomes evident not only that he is often wrong in content but that his style is not like Lenin's one of a revolutionary bent on change; but of a philosophical lecturer. When we note that the essay was written in 1938 we might attribute these and other characteristics to the fact that by then Stalin had been long in power and had lost his revolutionary edge, but his 1906 article, "Anarchism or Socialism," has the same approach. And when he revised this article in 1946 for publication in his *Works*, he changed comparatively little. At the beginning of the article he writes: "Why is this system called dialectical materialism? Because its method is dialectical, and its theory is materialistic." Contradiction is not only muted but non-existent: "Life is in continual motion, and therefore life must be viewed in its motion, in its destruction and creation." "Consequently, everything in nature must be regarded from the point of view of movement, development. And this means that the spirit of dialectics permeates the whole of present-day science."

We can see also the germs of the future confusion of subjective and objective: "the ideal and the material are two different forms of the same phenomenon." What phenomenon? Again: "According to Marx's materialism, consciousness and being, mind and matter, are two different forms of the same phenomenon, which, broadly speaking, is called nature." In the 1946 revision Stalin changed this to "is called nature or society," which only adds to the confusion. There is nothing in Marx or Engels about matter and mind being forms of nature (or society). On the contrary, nature is a manifestation of matter, inorganic and organic, the human mind an evolutionary development from organic matter, and society a product of nature and humanity. To posit some third force as basic to both mind and matter, whether one calls it nature or something else, is not materialism but idealism, ultimately, perhaps, a derivative of Aristotle's "prime mover" and reminiscent of William James's view (noted with approval by Bertrand Russell) that "the fundamental stuff of the world is neither mental nor material, but something simpler and more fundamental" (i.e. God). And whatever Stalin's hypothetical basic "phenomenon" is, it cannot be *both* nature and society.[7]

In the 1946 version Stalin added a new comment: "If we can call the material side, the external conditions, being, and other phenomena of the same kind, the *content,* then we can call the ideal side, consciousness and other phenomena of the same kind, the *form.*" Stalin, as his next paragraph indicates, is apparently basing these statements on Marx's distinction in his 1859 general statement between the economic and other "structures" of society in periods of "social revolution" and the "ideological forms, in which human beings become conscious of this conflict and fight it out to an issue." For "ideological forms" Stalin substitutes "ideological form"; and the distinction is crucial. Marx was using "forms" here not in the philosophical sense of the difference between content and form but in the everyday sense of the word, meaning "kinds" or "types," a sense which includes both form and content. He lists them: "legal, political, religious, aesthetic or philosophic." By "form," however, Stalin does intend the philosophical sense, "pure form," as in the Aristotelian "categories," a concept that Marx made fun of in *The Poverty of Philosophy:*

It is surprising that, if you let drop little by little all that constitutes the individuality of a house, making an abstraction first of the materials of which it is composed, then of the form that distinguishes it, you end up with nothing but a body; that, if you make an abstraction of the limits of this body, you soon have nothing but a space—that if, finally, you make an abstraction of the dimensions of this space, there is absolutely nothing left but pure quantity, the logical category?[8]

Apparently Stalin is saying that matter is the content of reality, mind its form. When we add this concept to those of mind as a passive reflector of objective reality, and both mind and matter as separate emanations from an undefined "nature," it becomes apparent that Stalin's outlook is idealist, that is to say, essentially theological. Furthermore, his "method" is based on the Aristotelian concept that so long as abstractions are "logical," they provide the path to truth. This underlying assumption of the primacy of "pure logic" is clearly present in Stalin's thought when he is expounding "dialectical method." Unlike Lenin, Stalin tended to lose direction when he was not reasoning about a particular event or problem, and his under- lying idealism shows through. In this ideal realm he sets up his logically derived abstractions and then makes "deductions" from them. In his political thinking, on the other hand, he works as Marx did, first marshaling his facts and then pursuing their interconnections.

It is the idealist essence of Stalin's philosophy that accounts for some of its other nonmaterialist characteristics, for instance, his seeing dialectics as a "method" and examing this "method" first instead of first examining materialism. So, too, with his conception of historical materialism as a kind of logical derivative of dialectical materialism. His abstractionist, Aristo- telian "method" doubtless had cultural roots in his schooling at the theo- logical seminary in Tiflis.

In spite of the idealist base for his philosophical outlook, however, it would be wrong to simply tag Stalin as an idealist in general, a charge he would have vehemently denied—and with some reason. He was strongly anti-clerical from his Georgia days on, and in some areas, as we have noted, he reasoned materialistically. What his thinking shows is that idealist influ- ences penetrate the working class in various ways, affecting even strong proletarian revolutionaries.

AFTER STALIN

With the rise of Nikita Khrushchev to power in the years following the death of Stalin in 1953, Stalin's philosophical views were presumably repudiated along with his social views. However, much of Stalin's approach to dialectical materialism was, in fact, retained, and some of his successors in the philosophical field strayed even further from Marx, Engels, and Lenin than he did. Their views were embodied in, for instance, *The Fundamentals of Marxist-Leninist Philosophy* (1974), the production of a group of prominent Soviet philosophers and bearing something of an official stamp.

When we turn to *The Fundamentals of Marxist-Leninist Philosophy* we note that the "laws" of dialectics are treated in the same order as in Stalin: the law of "universal connection and development" comes first, then "the transformation of quantity into quality," and only then "the law of the unity and struggle of opposites," which both Marx and Lenin emphasized as central. *The Fundamentals of Marxist-Leninists Philosophy* differs from Stalin in restoring "the law of the negation of the negation" (in last place); it is, however, silently restored without examination of its omission by Stalin or his implied repudiation of Lenin.

This arrangement, from "development" to "opposites," naturally affects, as with Stalin, the general interpretation of dialectical materialism. Development is seen, as in Stalin, as resulting from "connection and interdependence, the interaction of phenomena," as though interaction in itself somehow explained development. Then the authors, omitting Lenin's comment on contradiction as the essence of dialectics *(On the Nature of Dialectics)*, indicate that Lenin, in his encyclopedia article on Marx, found the "most essential features of dialectics" in "interdependence" and "connection." They neglect to note that before he mentioned "interdependence" in the article, Lenin spoke of "inner impulses for development, imparted by the contradiction, the conflict of different forces and tendencies reacting on a given body or inside a given phenomenon."[9]

"Dialectics," the Soviet authors write, "the most complete, comprehensive and profound theory of development, is the heart and soul of Marxism-Leninism, its theoretical foundation." But as Marx indicated, a Marxist cannot speak simply of "dialectics." He must make clear that he means "scientific" or "rational" dialectics and emphasize its grounding in materialism. Nor is materialist dialectical process, as Marx and Engels saw it, primarily a "theory" but part of objective reality. It is only derivatively a "theory": "the ideal is nothing else than the material world reflected by the human mind, and translated into forms of thought." And as a "theory," it is not a theory of "development." There is no "development" inherent in nature. There is only change, some of which, by chance interactions, assumes developmental sequence. The interactions of opposite elements, such as negative and positive atomic charges, produce complexity. To assert "development" as inherent in nature is idealist, an echo of the theologians' "purpose." So, too, is to assert "development" as the "heart and soul" of dialectical materialism or of "Marxism-Leninism." The essence of both is the interpenetration of opposites, as in nature itself. Other elements, too, must be considered in trying to ascertain the essence of materialist dialectical thinking. Dialectical thinking is, as Marx interpreted it, an integral part of materialist thinking in general, including, for instance, the scientific analysis of data, the penetration beyond appearance into "their inner connection," and, as Lenin in particular emphasized, the avoidance of "one-sidedness" in thinking.

Nor are the flaws inherent in the statement by the Soviet authors about dialectics incidental. They underlie the whole book: a confusion of objective and subjective, a separation (as in Stalin) of dialectics from its materialist base, a narrow and metaphysical concept of dialectical reasoning, and, finally (as also in Stalin), the implication that "historical materialism" — by which they mean Marxism—is a derivative of a philosophical theory and not a body of knowledge, social and natural, arrived at basically by struggle and testing.

Although the Soviet authors quote Lenin in the beginning of their discussion of quantity and quality as saying that development results from the "unity of opposites," they ignore this statement in their treatment:

> The distinguishing feature of the dialectical conception of development lies in the understanding of development not as a simple quantitative change (increase or decrease) of what exists, but as a process of disappearance, destruction of the old and emergence of the new. This process is demonstrated in the law of the transformation of quantitative changes into qualitative changes and vice versa. To find out what this law is all about we must examine a number of categories such as property, quantity, quality and measure.

Here, as in Stalin, the emphasis is on the "destruction of the old and emergence of the new" instead of, as in Marx or Lenin, on contradiction or the "struggle" of opposites. Hence the creation of new qualities by quantitative means is actually based, in spite of the authors' disclaimer, on "increase or decrease," the concept that Lenin specifically repudiated and saw as having theological implications.[10]

We might note also the implied primacy of "law" over "process." The process of the decline of the old and the rise of the new is "demonstrated" in the "law," and not by science. And law here is clearly used in a subjective sense, a law of thought, for otherwise, the statement would be redundant: an objective process is "demonstrated" in an objective process. But clearly, as Marx, Engels, and Lenin saw things, process was primary and law a reflection of it. Processes would exist with or without these laws.

Similarly, there is nothing in Marx, Engels, or Lenin about quantity and quality being "categories." They are characteristics of objective process that the human mind turns into laws. The laws are basically verified by practice and not by examining abstract categories—an approach stemming not from Marx or Engels but from Aristotle and Kant.

What of "property" and "measure"? That different things have different properties is obvious, and the reasons for these differences lie in atomic, molecular, and other arrangements. There is no such "category" as "property" in Marx, Engels, or Lenin, a "category" which shows us what the "law" of the change from quantity to quality is "all about."

The "category" "measure" is discussed as follows:

> Thus, the quality of things is inseparably linked with a certain quantity. This connection and interdependence of quality and quantity is called the measure of a thing. The category of measure expresses the kind of relationship between the quality and quantity of an object that obtains when its quality is based on a definite quantity, and the latter is the quantity of a definite quality. It is the changes in such interrelationships, changes of measure, that explain the mechanism of development. Hence development should be understood not as motion within certain fixed and immutable limits, but as replacement of the old by the new, as an eternal and ceaseless process of renewal of what exists.[11]

Even without close examination, this statement by its very style and manner of thought—again derived from Stalin—obviously has nothing in common with expositions of dialectical materialism by Marx, Engels, or Lenin. Whereas they are concretely analytical, this is abstract and academic, and the style is one of philosophers writing for philosophers, not of Marxists writing for the people. Once more it places category first and objective process second, and views development as essentially "replacement of the old by the new," here going beyond Stalin into a mystical exaltation of "eternal" "renewal." Further the reasoning is redundant and circular: the relationship between quantity and quality is "measure"; "measure" (and not the objective process of the struggle of opposites) explains "the mechanism of development" embodied in the quantity-quality change.

As one reads *The Fundamentals of Marxist-Leninist Philosophy* it becomes apparent that all aspects of dialectical materialism are included in one place or another, so that the authors can always point triumphantly to this fact in answer to criticism. Thus they do discuss the "law of the unity and struggle of opposites." But what is the nature of the treatment? What aspects are considered as basic and what as secondary or derivative? Although the "law of the unity and struggle of opposites" is given its own section, this—as we have noted and also as in Stalin—comes after interaction and quantity-quality have been treated and is presented as a self-motivating process. As a result, the struggle of opposites has in effect already been robbed of its central, initiating position. Furthermore, the treatment of this struggle is characterized by the same subjective and metaphysical outlook as were these previous "laws," for example:

But the interdependence of opposites is only one of the specific features of dialectical contradiction. Another of its vital aspects is mutual negation. Because the two aspects of the whole are opposites they are not only interconnected but also mutually exclusive and mutually repellent. This factor is expressed in the concept of the struggle of opposites.

"Mutual negation" does not appear in Marx, Engels, or Lenin, and if it exists at all it could only represent circular motion. And this is indicated also in the concept of the two "aspects" of a contradiction being "mutually exclusive." If they are mutually exclusive they cannot interact and not even circular movement would be possible. The concept of things being at once mutually exclusive and interdependent reminds one of Marx's comment on the "gifted" Proudhon "playing" with dialectics in order to make "brilliant paradoxes." All this reasoning, we might also note, is kept in the abstract. No examples are given here or generally in the exposition of these matters. And in the conclusion that this "factor" is "expressed" in a "concept," we are back with idealism.[12]

Stalin, as we saw, simply banished without explanation the negation of the negation. The authors of the *Fundamentals* restore it but within a basically Hegelian framework:

Development is, in fact, a chain of dialectical negations, each of which not only rejects the previous links, but also preserves all that is positive in them, thus concentrating more and more in the further, higher links, the richness of development as a whole. The infinity of development lies not in the infinite arithmetical addition of one unit to another, but in the emergence of new and higher forms which create within themselves the preconditions for further development.

As with quantity and quality, the negation of the negation is treated in isolation from contradiction. "Development" becomes a kind of god which "preserves" the "positive" and creates "new and higher forms" in "infinity." Certainly Aristotle as the proponent of divine "ends" would not have objected, nor perhaps even Plato; and Hegel would have rejoiced to see the restoration of his self-developing Absolute.[13]

Following the chapter on "the dialectical laws" in the *Fundamentals* comes one entitled "Categories of Materialist Dialectics" with special sections on the following categories: The Individual, Particular and Universal, Cause and Effect, Necessity and Chance, Possibility and Reality, Form and Content, and Essence and Appearance. And to these we have to add quantity and quality and property and measure.

The concept of categories was introduced into philosophy by Aristotle, who proposed 10 categories or modes of thought, including quality and quantity, into which Being could be divided and then reasoned about. Although Descartes, Locke, Leibniz, and Hume to some degree used these forms of thought, they did not do so formally, nor did they think in terms of a system of categories. The concept of a system of categories was reintroduced into philosophy by Kant as part of his attempt to shore up what was left of epistemology after Hume's skeptical sweep. Kant expounded a system of 12 categories, including cause and effect, existence and non-existence, possibility and impossibility, necessity and chance, which he viewed not as reflections of reality but as emanations from the mind's internal nature. Beyond the categories was the always unknowable "thing in itself." Hegel, although deploring the rigidity of Kant's categories, accepted the notion that they were not reflections of objective reality but forms of thought inherent in the human mind via the divine mind of the Absolute.

The attitude of Marx and Engels toward categories is succinctly revealed in Marx's comment on Proudhon: "Instead of conceiving the economic categories as theoretical expressions of historical relations of production, corresponding to a particular stage of development of material production, he garbles them into preexisting, eternal ideas." And we have already noted Marx's sarcastic comment on "pure quantity" as a "logical category." Whatever categories of thought may be developed must, Marx contended, have a basis in objective reality. They must not be constructs in terms of which reality is viewed. Actually, however, there is little about categories in Marx and Engels. They seldom use the term but usually speak simply of ideas or concepts, theories or hypotheses. Engels writes of "identity and difference—necessity and change—cause and effect," and discusses them in various places, but he does not systematize them and makes no distinction between them and other general concepts. Furthermore, his emphasis is on the fluidity of concepts, reflecting the fluidity of objective reality. There is no chapter or section headed "Categories" in *Anti-Dühring* with its full treatment of dialectical materialism. Nor is there in Lenin's *Materialism and Empirio-criticism*. In the *Philosophical Notebooks* Lenin discussed some categories because he was following Hegel's exposition but he does not consider them as comprising a "system." Like Marx he emphasizes their basis in reality. "If," he asked, "everything develops, does not that apply also to the most general concepts and categories of thought?"—a question which he answered in the affirmative. Lenin, again like Marx or Engels, noted but few categories, considering them to be the same as fluid "general concepts" which were helpful in "cognizing the world." He emphasized that they "have to be derived" from objective reality "and not taken arbitrarily or mechanically," not established "by exposition" but by scientific "proofs." Categories can become, he warned, following Hegel, "instruments or error and sophistry."[14]

In Stalin's 1938 essay, which he intended as a condensed account of the views of Marx, Engels, and Lenin, there is no mention of the categories of dialectical materialism; nor was there in other works on dialectical materialism at the time, for instance in David Guest's *A Textbook of Dialectical Materialism* (1939). The concept of categories as a major aspect of dialectical materialism apparently first achieved prominence in *The Fundamentals of Marxist Philosophy* in 1958. By the time of *The Fundamentals of Marxist-Leninist Philosophy* in 1974, they had grown into a veritable philosophical army.

In addition to the 13 categories listed above, there are others:

> In the previous chapters we have examined several philosophical categories, for example, matter, motion, space, time, the finite and the infinite, consciousness, quantity, quality, measure, and contradiction.

To which if we add "property" we have a total of 25 categories. And there are another 16 similar entities which appear to be granted a kind of semi-category status:

> Universality and difference are the relationship of the object to itself and to other things, characterising the stability and variability, equality and inequality, similarity and dissimilarity, identity and non-identity, imitability and inimitability, continuity and discontinuity of its properties, connections, relationships and tendencies of development.

The importance of the "categories" can scarcely be exaggerated. They form the pathway to truth, transcending science:

> The general concepts of every science also play a methodological role. The categories of dialectics differ from the general concepts of the specialised sciences, however, in that the latter are applicable only to a certain sphere of thinking, while philosophical categories, as methodological principles, permeate the whole tissue of scientific thought, all fields of knowledge. They make it possible to give a true reflection of the extremely complex, contradictory processes of material and intellectual life. The categories of philosophy, constantly accumulating the results of the development of the specialised sciences, thus enrich their own content . . . A person must master the categories in the course of his individual development in order to possess capacity for theoretical thought. . . . Categories are so interconnected that they can be understood only as elements in a definite system of categories.[15]

That general scientific concepts or theories, such as "the conservation of energy," are valid and necessary is obvious. But, as Engels pointed out, as science develops, the abstractions of "philosophy" will no longer be needed—particularly, he would doubtless have agreed, in the form of a "system of categories." In fact one wonders how Marx, Engels, and Lenin got along without "mastering" this immense "system," for, as we have seen, there is very little about categories in any of them; somewhat more in Lenin than in Marx or Engels but certainly nothing approaching this vast intellectual structure with its apparently infinite capacity for "enriching" itself out of its own substance.

The authors of *The Fundamentals of Marxist-Leninist Philosophy* seem uneasily aware of the problem for although they title the chapter "Categories of Materialist Dialectics," within the chapter they refer to them as "the categories of philosophy." What philosophy? Representing, Marx might have asked, what class? We might note also some earlier statements: "Dialectics, like philosophical science, is concerned with universal laws." What is "philosophical science"? How is it connected with "dialectics"? What "dialectics," Hegelian or Marxist? "According to the general laws of knowledge we must first investigate the qualitative differences between things. . . ." What are these "general laws of knowledge"? What is their connection with dialectical materialism? Or again: "The categories of possibility and reality occupy an important place in the well-stocked armoury of modern theoretical thinking." The "armoury of modern theoretical thinking" is certainly "well-stocked," especially in capitalist nations, but the categories under discussion—possibility and reality—are not particularly "modern." They are derived from Kant ("possibility and impossibility") via Aristotle ("potentiality and actuality").[16]

Perhaps the "modern" authors of the *Fundamentals* have advanced beyond Marx, Engels, and Lenin? Certainly there would be nothing wrong with this. Marxism must grow. Lenin developed the philosophical and other ideas of Marx and Engels. However, if the authors have performed a similar service for Lenin as well as for Marx and Engels surely this should have been noted and the reasons for it given. It is certainly true, as Lenin noted, that an awareness of some categories—or, more simply, general concepts—and of their tested correspondence to objective reality is basic to generalized comprehension. But the exposition of a "system" of 25 categories mostly unmentioned by Marx, Engels, or Lenin as basic to dialectical materialism and dialectical thinking is on the very face of it suspect, aside from the subjective nature of these particular categories and the dominant position which they occupy. Although, for instance, it is admitted that the views of science "also play a methodical role" this is clearly subordinate to that played by the categories. It is primarily the categories which "make it possible to give a true reflection" of reality. The path to truth now lies not in struggle or practice but in the philosophical study of abstractions. So extensive is the domain of the categories, in fact, that not only Marxist but all thinking is to be enclosed in abstractionist ideological boxes.

The categories seem to have devoured almost everything, even the "laws" of "dialectics": "Thus, the law of the unity and struggle of opposites is expressed through the categories of opposition, contradiction, etc." To omit mention of the actual "'struggle' of opposites" and refer only to the "law" which reflects it, and then to subordinate the law to a category shows that, as before, we are back not with Marx but with Kant. In fact the whole "system" of categories is basically Kantian (viewing the world through a series of mental constructs). True, the authors claim that their categories, unlike Kant's, are based on objective reality, but they do not demonstrate this by example or scientific reference, and in practice they use the categories as Kant does, as impositions on reality.

Once again the "system" moves into idealism: "... the system of interacting individual things where each thing is poured into the 'cup' of the universal, revives it and partakes of its reviving juices." "Essence is expressed ... in these manifestations." "Essence" or the "'cup' of the universal" has become, in effect, a God, Plato's One or Hegel's Absolute.[17]

Following the chapter on categories come two chapters on epistemology (knowing) of which the following statements may be taken as representative. "Thus in the process of proof knowledge does not go beyond its own sphere, but remains, as it were, confined within itself. This is what has given rise to the idea of the existence of *formal* criteria of truth, when truth is established by collating one set of knowledge with another." "But knowledge that lays down laws must contain within itself both necessity and universality." "All real knowledge takes the form of judgements or systems of judgement."[18]

True, there are throughout the chapters references to science and practice and objective reality. It soon becomes clear, however, that the authors regard knowledge, like the categories, as essentially a kind of self-generating and inviolate absolute, "confined within itself," which "lays down" its own "laws." Truth is established not basically by practice but by rubbing one set of absolutes against another. Knowledge is not even primarily knowledge of objective reality but of "systems of judgment."

All this, including "the categories," of course, goes beyond Stalin but its Aristotelian approach, dogmatic method, and basic idealism make it the kind of thing that Stalin began. Furthermore, as we have noted, the authors of the *Fundamentals* take—albeit stealthily—many of their basic concepts from Stalin. The *Fundamentals* was published in 1974. Since then little, if any, advance has taken place, at least so far as one can judge from popular works available in English translation. For instance, in two recent works, *Fundamentals of Dialectics* (Moscow, 1981) by Yu. A. Kharin and *Marxist-Leninist Philosophy* (Moscow, 1978) by A. P. Sheptulin although the authors put more stress on contradiction, give some scientific examples to support their conclusions, and reduce the number of categories, the categories are still present and still dominant. Concepts are silently added that are not to be found in Marx, Engels, or Lenin. In this, too, we see the heritage of Stalin, namely the general method of stating propositions without first establishing their objective base and then forcing reality into them. Both books are (necessarily) obscurantist in style, indistinguishable from bourgeois academic pretension.[19]

On the other hand, it should be noted that the writings of Soviet scientists—at least to judge by the essays in *Lenin and Modern Natural Science* (Moscow, 1978)—are often concrete and stimulating. The same is true of Soviet political analysis, which is in general realistic and dialectical. Presumably the difference is due in part to the fact that the scientists and political leaders are perforce thinking in concrete terms and generalizing from them, whereas the philosophers have no such disciplining focus but dwell in the realm of what they call "theoretical thought." But the problem must go deeper than this. What is involved is both the penetration into the Soviet intelligentsia of bourgeois influence and a constricting proletarian fear that if free debate is allowed a flood of anti-socialist ideas will be released.

Perhaps so; but surely Soviet socialism has now reached a point at which it could be safely absorbed. It is clearly time for a re-examination of philosophical method, for a return to the scientific spirit of inquiry of Marx, Engels, and Lenin, and a renunciation of the idealist and dogmatic underpinnings derived at least in part from Stalin. Otherwise no real development of theoretical questions can take place, and philosophy will be unable to descend from its celestial towers into the streets. What soviet philosophy is at present saying, in effect, is that dialectical materialism—with its esoteric mazes and "system" of "categories"—can only be fully comprehended by "philosophers." Hence, it cuts the mass of the population off from dialectical materialism and spreads confusion along with idealism.

NOTES

Chapter I

1. Karl Marx and Frederick Engels, *Correspondence, 1846–1895* (London, 1934), p. 437 (April 23, 1885); *Encyclopedia Britannica*, 11th ed., 1911, "Russia"; *Historical Statistics of the United States, 1789–1945*, Bureau of the Census, Washington, D.C.; Shepard Bancroft Clough and Charles Woolsey Cole, *Economic History of Europe* (New York, 1952), p. 579; *Encyclopedia Britannica*, 14th ed., "Russia."

2. Adam B. Ulam, *Stalin: The Man and His Era* (New York, 1973), p. 58; Robert C. Tucker, *Stalin as Revolutionary, 1879–1929* (London, 1973), p. 83; Isaac Deutscher, *Stalin: A Political Biography* New York, 1967), p. 15. *The Encyclopedia Britannica*, 11th ed., 1911, notes that Tiflis had, among other attractions, "an astronomical and physical observatory." Stalin worked in this observatory for a time after leaving the seminary (E. Yaroslavsky, *Landmarks in the Life of Stalin*, Moscow, 1940, p. 23). The Georgian oil industry was largely owned by the Rothschild and Nobel firms (Ulam, p. 43). In 1904, Baku refined half the world's oil (ibid., p. 58).

3. Robert Payne, *The Rise and Fall of Stalin* (New York, 1965), p. 48. For a later version of part of the poem, see ibid., p. 49. Yaroslavsky, p. 12. For an examination of the political symbolism of Shelley's *Prometheus Unbound*, see Kenneth Neill Cameron, *Shelley: The Golden Years* (Cambridge, Mass, 1974), pp. 475–564. Deutscher's and Payne's biographies embody hostile caricatures of Stalin but are useful for factual or background material.

4. J. V. Stalin, *Works* (hereinafter referred to as *Works* without author's name) (Moscow, XIII, 1952–55), 115-16; Yaroslavsky, pp. 14, 13; Payne, p. 274.

5. V. I. Lenin, *Selected Works* (New York, n.d.), I, 390, 444, 452-53.

6. *Works*, VIII, 183; *History of the Communist Party of the Soviet Union (Bolsheviks), Short Course* (New York, 1939), p. 21; N. Popov, *Outline History of the Communist Party of the Soviet Union*, (New York, n.d.), I, 52; *Works*, I, 20-21.

7. L. Beria, *On the History of the Bolshevik Organizations in Transcaucasia*, 1935 (New York, n.d.), p. 29; Tucker, pp. 79-82, 132-33.

8. *Works*, I, 29; *History, C.P.S.U.*, p. 39, 58, 79-80, 84; quoted in Beria, pp. 80-81 (see also, *Works*, I, 272-73 for a different and less effective translation). The *Encyclopedia Britannica*, 1911, noted for Batum: "In the winter of 1905-1906, Batum was in the hands of the revolutionists, and a 'reign of terror' lasted for several weeks."

9. *Works*, VIII, 183; Leon Trotsky, *The Russian Revolution*, ed. F. W. Dupee (New York, 1959), p. 215; *Works*, VI, 56. Kamenev (Lev Borisovich Rosenfeld), Trotsky's brother-in-law, joined Lenin abroad in 1902. He was tried and shot as a traitor in 1936. "Whenever I went to see him [Lenin] abroad—in 1906, 1907, 1912 and 1913—I saw piles of letters he had received from practical Party workers in Russia, and he was always better informed than those who stayed in Russia." *Works*, XIII, 123.

Sverdlov was a well-read Marxist, whose annotated copy of *Capital* accompanied him in exile and prison. See K. Sverdlova, *Yakov Sverdlov* (Moscow, 1981), p. 42.

The reports by Molotov and the others at various Party Congresses show them to have been intelligent and knowledgeable with a basic Marxist understanding. Before Stalin returned from exile following the March 1917 revolution, Molotov, then a young worker, was in charge of the Russian Bureau of the Party. The Bureau's analysis showed a good, Marxist grasp of the situation, anticipating in some respects Lenin's views propagated in April. The Bureau described the Provisional Government as "a class government of the bourgeoisie and the large landlords" and described the policy of pressuring that government for concessions as "a palliative measure incapable of achieving its purpose, viz., control over the realization of the fundamental demands of the revolutionary democracy." Popov, *Outline History, C.P.S.U.*, I, 252.

10. Ordzhonikidze, quoted in Deutscher, *Stalin*, p. 100; *Works*, II, 171-72, 151, 160. Stalin's views on "god-building" and other matters were not just a following of Lenin but often independently developed. Lenin in these years by no means had the authority that he did later. For instance, in 1910 Stalin wrote: "The plan for a bloc reveals the hand of Lenin—he is a shrewd fellow, and knows a thing or two. But this does not mean that any kind of bloc is good" *(Works*, II, 215). Lenin is a "shrewd fellow," not an oracular leader. Although Stalin regarded him with admiration and affection, at times he differed with his policies. See, for example, *Works*, II, 170-73.

11. *Works*, II, 202, 204; V, 132.

12. Beria, pp. 134-35; letter in *The Alliluvev Memoirs*, trans., ed. David Tutaev (New York, 1968), p. 139. On the editing and cutting of these memoirs, see Svetlana Alliluyeva, *Twenty Letters to a Friend* (New York, 1967), p. 37. On the horrors of life in Siberian exile, see *Sverdlov*, pp. 53-61. Sverdlov lived in "a narrow room, three paces across and seven long" with a "plank bed" and a "dim, kerosene lamp" and was constantly harassed by the police.

13. Karl Marx, "Address to the Communist League," *Handbook of Marxism*, ed. Emile Burns (New York, 1935), pp. 67, 64. The *Handbook* translation—by Max Beer, first published in *The Labour Monthly*—seems preferable to that in Marx and Engels, *Selected Works* (Moscow, 1973), I, 175-85.

14. Lenin, *Selected Works*, "Lecture on the 1905 Revolution," III, 4.

15. *Works*, II, 64-65, 61; I, 234-235, xviii-xix.

16. Lenin, *Selected Works*, III, 82, 145, (see also pp. 82, 110, 124).

17. *Works*, I, 300-01. Lenin, *Collected Works* (Moscow, 1970), XXXVIII, 360.

18. *Works*, I, 319. On the whole, however, Stalin's article is clearly written and contains some interesting passages. See, for instance, pp. 317-18 (on the class consciousness of a "shoemaker"—perhaps suggested by Stalin's father), pp. 332-33 (on capitalist expansion), and p. 344 (on capitalist democracy).

19. Joseph Stalin, *Marxism and the National and Colonial Question* (New York, 1934), pp. 8, 13. See, for instance, p. 17, on class factors:

> But the policy of national repression is dangerous to the cause of the proletariat also on another account. It diverts the attention of large strata of the population from social questions, questions of the class struggle, to national questions, questions "common" to the proletariat and the bourgeoisie. And this creates a favourable soil for lying propaganda regarding "harmony of interests," for glossing over the class interests of the proletariat and for the intellectual enslavement of the workers.

Stalin wrote the essay in January 1913 *(Works, II, 437)*. See also Stalin's 1904 essay: *The Social-Democratic View of the National Question (Works, I, 31-62)*.

Chapter II

1. Leon Trotsky, *The History of the Russian Revolution*, trans. Max Eastman (Ann Arbor, Michigan, 1964), p. 109; Michael T. Florinsky, *Russia: A History and Interpretation* (New York, 1953), II, 1381-1386; James H. Meisel, Edward S. Kozera, *Materials for the Study of the Soviet System* (Ann Arbor, Michigan), p. 1.

2. Lenin, *Selected Works*, VI, 23.

3. Joseph Stalin, *The October Revolution* (New York, 1934), pp. 75-76; *Works*, III, 2, 8, 45; Tucker, p. 168. In his book, *The Stalin School of Falsification*, 1937 (New York, 1972), p. 239, Trotsky published (from notes taken at the time) Stalin's report to an All Russian Conference of Party Workers, March 28, 1917, in which Stalin declared:

> The only organ capable of taking power is the Soviet of Workers' and Soldiers' Deputies on an All-Russian scale. We, on the other hand, must bide our time until the moment when the time comes, when the events have matured, and until then we must organize the center—the Soviet of Workers' and Soldiers' Deputies—and strengthen it. Therein lies the task of the moment.

"It is not," he noted, "to our advantage at present to force events, hastening the process of repelling the bourgeois layers, who will in the future inevitably withdraw from us" (p. 238). The speech again demonstrates, although this was not Trotsky's intention in publishing it, that Stalin was cautiously moving toward the position that Lenin later put forward in Petrograd (and that was, indeed, being expressed at the time in his writings sent to the Party from Geneva).

As we have noted, Molotov and others were also moving toward the position Lenin later put forward and were dubious of the policy of pressuring the Provisional Government. They did not, however, as did Lenin, see the Soviets as the actual state form for the proletarian dictatorship and socialism. And this—the key point—was indeed a difficult thing to grasp. Even Sverdlov, one of the best of the Bolsheviks in Russia, did not at first understand it. As his wife comments on his position in April before the April Conference: "His views were neither totally clear nor completely accurate, and it was hard for him to formulate the concept of Soviets as a governmental form through which the dictatorship of the proletariat would operate" *(Sverdlov*, p. 81). After Lenin presented his views to the Conference, however, Sverdlov, like Stalin, supported him. The evolution of Stalin's views, then, was apparently characteristic of the Bolshevik leadership.

4. Lenin, *Selected Works*, VI, 171, 173-74. Lenin hid with the Alliluyev family in a room where Stalin had often stayed and where Stalin visited him. Stalin later married Nadezhda Sergeyevna Alliluyev. *(Alliluyev Memoirs*, pp. 189-98). Lenin soon left for the safety of Finland, his beard shaved off (Stalin acting as barber, according to Anna Alliluyev; ibid., p. 198).

5. *Works*, III, 189, 191; *October Revolution*, p. 81. See also *Works*, IV, 330; "Smiling and glancing at us slyly, he said, 'Yes, it seems you were right.'"

6. *Works*, III, 190-200; Lenin, *Selected Works*, V, 141; Joseph Stalin, *Leninism*, English trans. Eden and Cedar Paul (London, 1932), I, 215; *Works*, VIII, 184. The delegate who wished to postpone the revolution in Russia until Western Europe also went socialist was E. A. Preobrazhensky; his position was supported by Bukharin (Deutscher, *Stalin*, p. 153), who later collaborated with him on *The ABC of Communism*.

7. Florinsky, II, 1418; James Bunyan, H. H. Fisher, *The Bolshevik Revolution, 1917–1918, Documents and Materials* (Stanford, California, 1934), p. 13; Lenin, "The Elections to the Constituent Assembly . . .," Dec. 29, 1919, *Selected Works*, VI, 464; W. H. Chamberlin, *The Russian Revolution* (New York, 1935), I, 185-86; *History, C.P.S.U.*, p. 196.

8. *The Bolsheviks and the October Revolution: Minutes of the Central Committee of the Russian Social-Democratic Labour Party (Bolsheviks), August 1917— February 1918* (London, 1974), pp. 76, 58, 104.

9. *Works*, III, 279, 293; *October Revolution* pp. 82-83; *Works*, III, 393, 395.

10. *Bolsheviks and the October Revolution*, p. 109; *History, C.P.S.U.*, p. 208; John Reed, *Ten Days That Shook the World* (New York, 1934), p. 126.

11. N. K. Krupskaya, *Reminiscences of Lenin* (New York, 1975), p. 347:

No one who has not lived through the revolution can have any idea of its solemn grandeur. Red banners, a guard of honor of Kronstadt sailors, searchlights from the Peter and Paul Fortress lighting up the way from the Finland Station to the Krzesinska Mansion, armoured cars, files of working men and women guarding the road.

The Krzesinska Mansion of the tsar had been taken over by the Petrograd Bolshevik Committee.

12. George Vernadsky, *A History of Russia* (New Haven, 1961), pp. 310-13; *Outline History, C.P.S.U.*, II, 80; *Works*, IV, 190, 279. For a concise account of Stalin's role in the civil war see Ian Grey, *Stalin: Man of History* (London, 1982), Chapter 20. Grey, although seeing people and events in personal, psychological terms, sifts evidence carefully and tries to give a balanced picture of Stalin. Alex de Jonge's *Stalin and the Shaping of the Soviet Union* (New York, 1986), on the other hand, is openly hostile to Stalin and the Soviet Union and makes little attempt to evaluate its sources.

Chapter III

1. Robert Payne, *The Life and Death of Trotsky* (New York, 1977), p. 9; Ronald Segal, *Leon Trotsky, A Biography* (New York, 1979), p. 14; Isaac Deutscher, *The Prophet Armed, Trotsky: 1897–1921* (New York, 1954; reprinted 1980), p. 30; Segal, p. 27; Lenin, *Selected Works*, II, 373. The biographies by Deutscher, Payne, and Segal give the main facts on Trotsky's life and political activities, supplementing Trotsky's autobiography, *My Life* (New York, 1930). They are particularly useful for the excerpts they give from works, particularly Trotsky's early works, and documents that are otherwise somewhat difficult to find, at least in English. Of the three, Deutscher is the most sympathetic toward Trotsky. Deutscher (p. 56) states that the pseudonym "Trotsky" came from the name of one of the young Trotsky's jailers when he was in prison in Odessa.

2. *History, C.P.S.U.*, pp. 155, 149; Segal, p. 50; Trotsky, *My Life*, p. 184.

3. Deutscher, *Trotsky*, p. 126; Payne, *Trotsky*, p. 106; Deutscher, *Trotsky*, pp. 126-31; Trotsky, *My Life*, p. 184; Segal, p. 71.

4. Deutscher, *Trotsky*, pp. 129, 131-32, 135, 139-40, 143, 168.

5. Payne, *Trotsky*, p. 114; Segal, p. 75.

6. Segal, p. 76; Payne, *Trotsky*, pp. 115, 222.

7. Deutscher, *Trotsky*, p. 131; V. I. Lenin, *Against Trotskyism* (Moscow, 1972), p. 72. See also Deutscher, *Trotsky, pp. 194-97. Against Trotskyism* is a selection from Lenin's writings on Trotsky.

8. Leon Trotsky, *The Age of Permanent Revolution* (New York, 1973), pp. 64, 65; *Against Trotskyism*, p. 103.

9. Trotsky, *Permanent Revolution*, p. 84.

10. Ibid., p. 83.

11. *My Life*, p. 270; *Permanent Revolution*, 97, 98, 99; Deutscher, *Trotsky*, pp. 286, 287; Stalin, *The October Revolution*, pp. 30, 70-71.

12. Stephen F. Cohen, *Bukharin and the Bolshevik Revolution* (New York, 1975), p. 66; *Against Trotskyism*, p. 149; *Works*, IV, 28.

13. *My Life*, pp. 447, 446.

14. Lenin, *The Trade Unions . . .* and *Once Again on the Trade Unions . . . Selected Works*, IX, 59, 26, 35, 55.

15. Stalin, *Leninism*, I, 188; Trotsky, *Permanent Revolution*, pp. 147-48 (punctuation dots in text). See also Deutscher, p. 158.

16. Lenin, *Selected Works*, III, 135.

17. *Leninism*, I, 199, 200.

18. We might note that Trotsky's account of the conflict within the Party in his autobiography reads like gothic fiction:

> Lenin was laid up at Gorki; I was in the Kremlin. The epigones were widening the circle of the conspiracy. At first they proceeded cautiously and insinuatively, adding to their praise ever larger doses of poison. (Trotsky, *My Life*, p. 498.)

The Epigonoi were the (inferior) sons of the Seven Heroes of Thebes (in Aeschylus's play *Seven Against Thebes*) who later razed the city. Hence, the word came to mean inferior imitators. Thus by "epigones"—which he used regularly—Trotsky means that the successors of Lenin were inferior and destructive.

19. Leon Trotsky, *The Challenge of the Left Opposition* (1923–25), ed. Naomi Allen (New York, 1975), pp. 31-32; *Works*, X, 203; Popov, *Outline History, C.P.S.U.*, II, 323.

20. V. I. Lenin, *Collected Works*, XXXVI, 596, 606, 597. What Lenin had in mind in "more loyal" is not clear. Stalin's loyalty, indeed, devotion both to Lenin and the Party was unquestionable as was his loyalty to the cause of socialism. Lenin was perhaps referring to the fact that Stalin was deviating from some of Lenin's views on certain issues. Stalin apparently referred (rather jocularly) to Lenin's characterization of him as "rude" in his report to the 14th Congress of the C.P.S.U. in 1925: "Yes, Comrades, I am a plain-spoken and rather rough sort of fellow. I don't deny it" *(Leninism*, I, 444). See also *Works*, X, 180-181.

21. Payne, *Stalin*, p. 278; Lenin, *Selected Works*, IX. 390, 396, 389, 383.

22. Tucker, p. 257; Lenin, *Collected Works*, XXXVI, 606, 609; XLV, 608, 607. Sergo Ordzhonikidze was in Georgia representing the Central Committee. He and Mdivani clashed. See Grey, *Stalin*, pp. 167-169.

23. *Works*, IX, 69; V, 2; Lenin, *Selected Works*, IX, 204; Payne, *Stalin*, pp. 286-87. For Stalin's account of the Mdivani group events, see *Works*, V, 233-39.

24. Lenin, *Collected Works*, XLV, 606-08, 757-58.

25. *Works*, VI, 48-49.

Chapter IV

1. Stalin, *Leninism*, I, 81-82, 83, 84-85.

2. J. Stalin, *On the Great Patriotic War of the Soviet Union* (Calcutta, 1975), p. 172.

3. *Leninism*, I, 79; *Leninism*, II, (1933), 43-48, 44. See, for example, Engels's Preface to Sigismund Borkheim's *Zur Erinnerung fur die Mordspatrioten 1806-1807* (1887) on the coming European capitalist war and succeeding revolutions, in Marx, Engels, *Correspondence*, pp. 456-57, his letter to Frederich Sorge, Jan. 7, 1888 (ibid., pp. 455-56) on the same subject, and his letter to Karl Kautsky, Sept. 12, 1882 (ibid., p. 399) on the coming colonial and proletarian revolutions.

4. *Leninism*, I, 101, 110, 111; *Works*, VI, 35. Modern science has also indicated that there are inherited bases for individual differences but their direction and development are determined by social factors.

5. *Leninism*, I, 99, 115, 94

Chapter V

1. Stalin, *History*, *CPSU*, pp. 286-289; Grey, *Stalin*, pp. 224-225; *Leninism*, II, 152-53, 156, 131, 270, 285 ("Dizzy With Success").

2. Lenin, *Collected Works*, XXXVI, 595; Cohen, *Bukharin*, p. 35; Lenin, *Selected Works*, IX, 36, 67, 79. The more we read of the views and policies of many of the Party leaders who lived abroad prior to the revolution—Kamenev, Zinoviev, Bukharin, and others—the more it becomes clear that they were really not Marxist (proletarian) revolutionaries but petty bourgeois revolutionaries with fragmented Marxist views. It was the combination of Lenin's clear Marxist vision with the Marxist class consciousness, discipline, and organizational skills of the so-called "practicals" that provided the basic revolutionary leadership.

3. Cohen, *Bukharin*, pp. 147, 198, 245, 296, 290.

4. *Leninism*, II, 236-37, 415.

5. Cohen, *Bukharin*, p. 255; *Works*, X, 291.

6. *Leninism*, II, 175, 191-92; *Works*, XIII, 370.

7. Cohen, *Bukharin*, p. 335; *Report of the Court Proceedings in the Case of the Anti-Soviet "Bloc of Rights and Trotskyites"* (Moscow, 1938), pp. 380, 381.

8. Joseph E. Davies, *Mission to Moscow* (New York, 1941), pp. 43, 150, 70-71, 72, 82, 113, 269, 271-72, 273, 280. Evidence was presented at the trials to show that one of the defendants, Gregori Pyatakov, had gone from Berlin to visit Trotsky in Norway, but according to Norwegian authorities, no planes landed at

the time at the designated airport (Robert Conquest, *The Great Terror* (New York, 1973), pp. 236-37). This apparently fraudulent piece of testimony has been used for the charge that all the testimony was fraudulent. The distinguish British jurist (King's Counsel), D.N. Pritt, in *The Zinoviev Trial* (London, 1936) also concluded that the trials were fair and the defendants guilty. So, too, Sir Bernard Pares, a leading authority on the U.S.S.R., and the U.S. journalist, Walter Duranty, who wrote extensively on the U.S.S.R.

9. *Proceedings, Rights and Trotskyites*, p. 380; *Report of the Court Proceedings in the Case of the Anti-Soviet Trotskyite Centre* (Moscow, 1937), p. 84.

10. *Proceedings, Rights and Trotskyites*, pp. 775-76, 429-430, 431; *Proceedings, Trotskyite Centre*, p. 125.

11. *Proceedings, Rights and Trotskyites*, pp. 777, 432, 778.

Chapter VI

1. *National Economy of the U.S.S.R.: Statistical Returns* (Moscow, 1957), pp. 58, 59; Joseph Stalin, *Leninism: Selected Writings* (New York, 1942), p. 361.

2. *Works*, XIII, 200, 342; *Leninism: Selected*, pp. 371, 337, 337, 340, 451, 455, 456-57, 476; *Leninism*, II, 376, 430; *Leninism: Selected*, pp. 388, 458.

3. Lenin, *Selected Works*, VIII, 353, 349, 353; *Collected Works*, XXXVI, 597; *Selected Works*, VIII, 349.

4. *Works*, XI, 34, 35. See Charles Bettelheim, *Class Struggles in the U.S.S.R.: Second Period, 1923-1930* (New York, 1979), p. 440 for a Party resolution against bureaucracy at the time.

5. Bettelheim, p. 459; *Materials for the Study of the Soviet System*, eds. James A Meisel, Edward S. Kozera (Ann Arbor, Michigan, 1953), pp. 242-66.

6. *Leninism: Selections*, pp. 476, 388, 397.

7. Despite frequent claims of a large number of upper professionals and others earning fabulous sums in the U.S.S.R., the available statistics show a generally balanced range of earnings; about what we would expect in a socialist society as defined by Marx or Lenin. According to Victor and Ellen Perlo in their book *Dynamic Stability: The Soviet Economy Today* (New York, 1980), p. 177, "The range of wages and salaries from the minimum to the maximum is about 10 to 1 — from 70 rubles to 700 rubles a month." The "comparable range in the United States" they estimate at "about 250 to 1." According to Al Szymanski, in the mid 1960s an average worker's wage was 100 rubles a month, a few leading professionals — apparently mostly in the arts — were earning 1,500 a month, top government officials 600, works' managers 190-400. (Al Szymanski, "Socialism or Capitalism in the U.S.S.R.," *Science and Society*, XLI, Fall 1977, p. 342.) In assessing these figures we have to remember that housing, schooling, medical care, social service, and transportation costs are minimal or non-existent. See also Michael Goldfield and Melvin Rothenberg, *The Myth of Capitalism Reborn* (San Francisco, 1980), pp. 42, 53, 54, on salary scales, etc.

8. *The Soviet System*, pp. 261-62, 263, 265. See William M. Mandel, *Soviet*

Women (New York, 1975), pp. 74-77 and Stalin's speeches in *The Woman Question: Selections From the Writings of Karl Marx, Frederick Engels, V. I. Lenin, Joseph Stalin* (New York, 1951).

As we consider Stalin's accomplishments in these years—his leadership in industrialization and collectivization, in defeating the "left" and right anti-socialist oppositions, in championing the new constitution—it is disturbing to note that he has been virtually written out of Soviet history, for instance in *History of the U.S.S.R.: The Era of Socialism* (Moscow, 1982). In Chapter Four, "Building the Economic Foundations of a Socialist Economy (1926-1932)," Stalin is barely mentioned. The first five-year plan was drawn up and accomplished by "the Party," the "Party Congress," or the "Party Plenum." Stalin is mentioned only as the author of the brief article "Dizzy With Success" (p. 276). He is mentioned as one of those who struggled against the Trotskyites, but that he led this struggle is not noted. His name appears tenth (p. 246) in a list of 11. That he led or even participated in the struggle against Bukharin (p. 259) and the right opposition is not noted. In regard to the constitution, it is simply noted (p. 321) that: "The main report of the Constitutional Commission was given by its chairman J. V. Stalin." Yet it is noted later that the 20th Congress, at which Khrushchev denounced Stalin, passed a resolution acknowledging "the great services performed to the Party and the country by J. V. Stalin" (446). What services? The previous 400-odd pages have not mentioned anything of consequence. The 20th Congress also performed a "thorough criticism of the personality cult"—which seems to endorse Khrushchev's denunciations; yet Khrushchev is not mentioned either.

It is clear to anyone who knows how a Communist Party functions that its General Secretary has great power and initiative. Hence, Stalin must have played a special initiating and leading role in all the events of those years. And this was acknowledged by the press, the Party, and Soviet historians at the time. The present Soviet attitude is clearly a historical and biographical distortion. Stalin is similarly written out of the current version of the *History of the C.P.S.U.* All this is unfortunately in line with the current bourgeois picture of Stalin and supports anti-Sovietism.

Chapter VII

1. *Leninism*, II. 320, 314-15, 312-13.
2. *Works*, XII, 300, 304; X, 11; *Leninism*, I, 215, 71; Joseph Stalin, H. G. Wells, *Marxism vs. Liberalism, An Interview* (New York, 1950), pp. 13-14.
3. *Works*, X, 17.

Chapter VIII

1. Isaac Deutscher, *Russia, What Next?*(New York, 1953), pp. 95, 94.

2. Karl Marx and Frederick Engels, *Selected Works* (Moscow, 1969), II, 241; I, 136.

3. Georgi Dimitrov, *Report, VII Congress of the Communist International* (Moscow, 1939), p. 173.

4. *Works*, IX, 143-45.

5. Jerome Ch'en, *Mao and the Chinese Revolution* (New York, 1965), pp. 70-73, 173; Han Suyin, *The Morning Deluge: Mao Tse-tung and the Chinese Revolution, 1893–1954* (Boston, 1972), pp. 90-94, 61; Stuart Schram, *Mao Tse-tung* (Penguin Books, 1970), p. 38.

6. *Essential Works of Chinese Communism* (revised edition), ed. Winberg Chai (New York, 1972), pp. 26, 27.

7. *Morning Deluge*, pp. 95-102; Edgar Snow, *Red Star Over China*, 1938 (New York, 1968), p. 159; Ch'en, *Mao*, pp. 105, 109; *Chairman Mao Talks to the People*, ed. Stuart Schram (New York, 1974), p. 219.

8. *Morning Deluge*, p. 154; Leon Trotsky, *Criticism of the Draft Program of the Communist International*, 1928, *The Age of Permanent Revolution* (New York, 1973), p. 246; Schram, *Mao Tse-tung*, pp. 76, 77, 85, 89.

9. *Works*, IX, 229, 263-64; X, 21; IX, 269. Mao Tse-tung, *Selected Works*, IV (New York, 1956), 178. Both Mao's and Stalin's emphasis on the peasantry was ignored at the time by the Chinese Party's central leadership (in Shanghai), of which Mao was not then a member. See *Morning Deluge*, pp. 130-31. Mao, however, did not emphasise the need for organizing the workers.

10. Mao, *Selected Works*, II, 51; ibid., I, 120. Mao, *Selected Works*, IV (Peking, 1969), 49; *Chairman Mao Talks to the People,*, p. 191; Schram, *Mao Tse-tung*, pp. 286, 284; Mao, June 6, 1950, *Selected Works*, V (Peking, 1977), 33. Milovan Djilas in *Conversations With Stalin* (New York, 1962), p. 182. See also V. Dedier, *Tito Speaks* (London, 1953) p. 331.

11. Ramadan Marmal Marmullaku, *Albania and the Albanians* (London, 1975), p. 12, quoting Winston Churchill: "These guerilla forces are containing as many German divisions as are the British and American armies put together." *The Statesman's Yearbook*, 1955 (London, 1955), p. 842; ibid. (1971-1972), p. 833; F. Lee Benns, *European History Since 1870* (New York, 1955), p. 597. In East Germany, incredible though it may seem, remnants of the Communist Party and Social Democratic Party survived Nazi persecution and united to form one party. For an interesting picture of these events, see Margrit Pittman, *Encounters in Democracy* (New York, 1981), pp. 27-49.

12. Benns, p. 859. See, for instance, Pittman, pp. 51-58 for a brief account of Soviet economic relations with East Germany.

13. Stefanaq Pollo and Arben Puto, *The History of Albania* (Boston, 1981), pp. 224-39; William Ash, *Pickaxe and Rifle* (London, 1974), p. 78, Enver Hoxha, *Selected Works* (Tirana, 1974), I, 451.

14. Peter R. Prifti, *Socialist Albania Since 1944: Domestic and Foreign Developments* (Cambridge, Mass.), p. 74; Hoxha, *Selected Works*, II, 9-11; Enver Hoxha, *The Khrushchevites: Memoirs* (Tirana, 1980), p. 62.

15. Enver Hoxha, *With Stalin: Memoirs* (Tirana, 1979), pp. 56, 150-51. Djilas, *Conversations*, p. 152, writes of Stalin in 1948: "There was something both tragic and ugly in his senility." But there is no hint of senility in Hoxha's accounts of his meetings with Stalin in 1949, 1950, and 1951. In fact, quite the opposite. Stalin appears as sharp-minded and logical (as he does also in Marshall Zhukov's *Memoirs*). In another place (p. 106) Djilas refers to Stalin as an "ungainly dwarf" whose "armies and marshals, heavy with fat and medals, and drunk with vodka and victory, had already trampled half of Europe under foot." One can hardly expect objectivity from Djilas. Hence, an account (p. 143) he gives of Stalin's agreeing that Yugoslavia should "swallow" Albania and putting his fingers in his mouth to illustrate his meaning is hard to believe or at least to take literally. Nicolas C. Pano in *The People's Republic of Albania* (Baltimore, 1968), p. 80, concludes that Stalin and Molotov, who was also present, "were obviously toying with him (Djilas)." In the light of the subsequent letters of the Communist Party of the Soviet Union denouncing the Yugoslav leadership as right opportunist it appears that Pano is right. However, it is no doubt true that earlier, before the direction of the Yugoslav Party became clear, Stalin and the Soviet Party felt that the close cooperation established after the war between Albania and Yugoslavia should continue. See Hoxha, *Selected Works*, I, 702-08. For another example of Stalin's sardonic humor see Grey, *Stalin*, p. 388 (Stalin's teasing Churchill that after the war 50,000 German officers would be executed).

Chapter IX

1. Vernadsky, *History of Russia*, p. 430; Stalin, *Great Patriotic War*, pp. 12, 16, 19-20, 25; Grey, *Stalin*, p. 329 (quoting General I. I. Fedyuninsky); Vernadsky, p. 430.

2. Stalin, *Great Patriotic War*, pp. 54, 67, 37, 56, 83, 64.

3. Ibid., pp. 75, 81, 124-25.

4. *The Memoirs of Marshal Zhukov* (New York, 1971), p. 285. Contrary to a widely circulated view in the United States, the basic supply of Soviet arms came from Soviet sources. For the first two years of the war, the United States sent but a trickle of arms into the U.S.S.R. (Ibid, p. 392; G. Deborin, *The Second World War*, trans. Vic Schnierson, Moscow, n.d., pp. 189-90). Only when it became apparent that the Soviet armies might weaken German imperialism did the rival imperialist regime in the United States begin to send arms on a meaningful scale. The massive transfer of Soviet factories westward (ibid., p. 163) was vividly shown on the television series, *The Unknown War*, presented in the United States in 1978-79, which also show that following the main offensive in Europe, the Soviet army shattered the Japanese forces in Manchuria in a massive and rapid operation. The title indicates that the major aspect of World War II, the struggle between German imperialism and the U.S.S.R., was and is "unknown" in the United States, hidden from the people by bourgeois historians and publicists. On the panic in Moscow see Grey, *Stalin*, p. 337.

5. Stalin, *Great Patriotic War*, pp. 36, 38, 77, 148.

6. *Leninism: Selected*, p. 441; quoted in Grey, *Stalin*, p. 310; quoted in G. Deborin, *Secrets of the Second World War* (Moscow, 1971), p. 239.

7. Joseph Stalin, *For Peaceful Coexistence: Postwar Interviews* (New York, 1951), pp. 9, 38, 39. The Soviet government official figures at the time listed 7,000,000 dead, but these figures were designed to hide the U.S.S.R.'s weakness from its imperialist "allies." (Deutscher, *Stalin*, p. 575.) The actual number was 20,000,000, as was later confirmed by Leonid Brezhnev.

Chapter X

1. See Mahlon B. Hoagland, *The Roots of Life* (New York, 1977), p. 58-59, 87. A friend of mine, a well-known biological scientist, writes to me that the Soviet "science base in the non-math, non-physics areas has been thoroughly eroded and will take many years to recover." He visited Soviet biological laboratories in 1959 and 1969.

2. Joseph Stalin, *Marxism and Linguistics* (New York, 1951), pp. 9, 10, 12. For the background of the controversy and other views, see *The Soviet Linguistc Controversy*, trans. John V. Murra, Robert M. Hankin, Fred Holling, Columbia University, Slavic Studies (New York, 1951.)

3. G. V. Plekhanov, *Fundamental Problems of Marxism*, 1908 (Moscow, 1974), p. 70; Nikolai Bukharin, *Historical Materialism, A System of Sociology*, 1921 (New York, 1925), pp. 154, 156, 169, 190, 203, 208; *A Handbook of Marxism*, ed. Emile Burns (New York, 1935), pp. 543-44; V. I. Lenin, "The Three Sources and Three Component Parts of Marxism," March 1913, *Marx, Engels, Marxism*, p. 52 (see also pp. 12-13, 86). Although Marx does not use the term "the superstructure" without qualification, Engels does in a well-known passage in a letter to J. Bloch of Sept. 21, 1890 in which he expounds Marx's theory. This probably provides the source of much later confusion. *(Correspondence*, p. 475). On these matters, see my article "The Fallacy of 'the Superstructure,'" *Monthly Review*, XXXI (January 1980), 27-36, and my book *Marxism, The Science of Society: An Introduction* (South Hadley, Mass., 1985), pp. 25-28.

4. Examples of semi-theological intellectual contortions occasioned by an acceptance of the superstructure doctrine may be seen in Maurice Cornforth, *Historical Materialism*, a work still in print (New York, 1954), pp. 97-117, and in the standard Soviet textbook *Fundamentals of Marxism-Leninism* (Moscow, ca. 1959), pp. 150-54. This textbook, edited by a corps of leading Soviet intellectuals, was supposed to repudiate some of Stalin's views. The section on "basis and superstructure," however, simply reiterates Stalin's superstructure doctrine without reference to Marx or Lenin (or Stalin either).

Cornforth (pp. 104-05) quotes Stalin's statement—and is perhaps uneasily aware of problems inherent in it—that "the superstructure" contains the "views" and "institutions" of society. Then he arbitrarily states that this means only "the dominant views and institutions." The Soviet textbook, however, boldly states (p. 152) that "the superstructure also contains the ideas and organizations of the oppressed classes." Cornforth divides human consciousness into two parts, superstructural and non-superstructural; the Soviet experts throw almost everything, including the class struggle, into "the superstructure." We might also note the following in A. P. Sheptulin, *Marxist-Leninist Philosophy* (Moscow, 1978), p. 348: "Production relations are considered the economic basis of society while the views and corresponding institutions determined by them are considered society's superstructure." This is, of course, straight from Stalin. Sheptulin also wrestles with the (false) question of the extent of "the superstructure": "Though the superstructure of antagonistic society does contain the ideas and corresponding institutions of both the ruling and oppressed classes, it is nevertheless only the ideas and institutions of the ruling class that play the leading part in it." On Mao, see, for instance, *Selected Works* (Peking, 1977), V, 388.

5. *Marxism and Linguistics,* p. 33.

6. *Leninism: Selected,* p. 419. See also *Works,* I, 314. It is, however, only fair to Stalin to note that the germ for the slave-feudal-capitalist historical succession appears in Marx's general statement (1859): "In broad outlines, Asiatic, ancient, feudal, and modern bourgeois modes of production can be designated as progressive epochs in the economic formation of society" (Karl Marx and Frederick Engels, *Selected Works,* Moscow, 1973, I, 504). By the "ancient," Marx meant the slave-commerical society of Greece and Rome. By the "Asiatic" he meant the joint-landowning and peasant village systems of Asia (which were also basically feudal). On this latter question, see Kenneth Neill Cameron, *Humanity and Society: A World History* (New York, 1977), pp. 95-96, 247-49. The (completely incorrect) notion that China progressed from slavery to feudalism perhaps originated in Mao. See *The Political Thought of Mao Tse-tung,* ed. Stuart Schram (New York, 1971), p. 164. See also *An Outline History of China* (Peking, 1958), p. 20. Feudalism in China grew out of farming society.

7. Joseph Stalin, *Economic Problems of Socialism in the U.S.S.R.* (New York, 1952), pp. 19-20.

8. *Economic Problems,* pp. 18, 44 (see also p. 22), 51, 24 (see also *Leninism,* II, 70-71), 52.

9. Rise like Lions after slumber
   In unvanquishable number—
   Shake your chains to earth like dew
   Which in sleep had fallen on you—
   Ye are many—they are few.
   (P.B. Shelley, *The Masque of Anarchy,* 1819).

Chapter XI

· 1. *Twenty Letters*, p. 201; *New York Times*, March 5, 1953.

2. Nikita Sergeyevich Khrushchev, *The "Secret" Speech* (Nottingham, 1976), pp. 33-34; *Materials for the Study of the Soviet System*, pp. 205-06. Khrushchev's speech was delivered at a closed session of the 20th Congress of the CPSU on Feb. 24, 1956. The speech was not published in the U.S.S.R. but printed copies were sent to regional Party committees and to the heads of foreign Communist Parties. The *New York Times* and other bourgeois papers obtained copies and published the speech. The special amendment to the Criminal Code was abolished in 1956. *(New York Times, May 5, 1956)*.

3. *Secret Speech*, pp. 68, 26, 46.

4. Ibid., pp. 48, 49-50, 54-55. On Kharkov see Grey, *Stalin*, pp. 346-347.

5. *Khrushchev Remembers: The Last Testament*, ed. Strobe Talbot (Boston, 1974), pp. 13-14. The Presidium was set up in 1952 to take the place of the Political Bureau.

6. *Khrushchev Speaks: Selected Speeches, Articles and Press Conferences, 1949–1962* (University of Michigan Press, 1963), pp. 436, 440-41; *Secret Speech*, Introduction, p. 14.

7. *Secret Speech*, p. 71.

8. Davies, *Mission to Moscow*, pp. 191-92 (see also pp. 67-68), 343; Zhukov, *Memoirs*, pp. 283, 495. Enver Hoxha, *With Stalin*, p. 78; *Twenty Letters*, pp. 209, 201, 195. Although Stalin later quarreled with Svetlana when she took up a Bohemian lifestyle and became a religious mystic, his early letters to her show him as an affectionate father. See *Twenty Letters*, pp. 97, 149, 151, 192, for example (p. 97, where he jokingly calls her his "housekeeper"):

To My Housekeeper, Setanka:

You don't write to your little papa. I think you've forgotten him. How is your health? You're not sick, are you? What are you up to? Have you seen Lyolka? How are your dolls? I thought I'd be getting an order from you soon, but no. Too bad. You're hurting your little papa's feelings. Never mind. I kiss you. I am waiting to hear from you.

Little Papa

9. Zhukov, *Memoirs*, pp. 464, 281. See also pp. 267, 284, 297, 480-481, 512-514, 551, 657-659 and Appendix I, below. *The Land of Socialism Today and Tomorrow: Reports and Speeches at the Eighteenth Congress of the Communist Party of the Soviet Union (Bolsheviks)*, March 10–21, 1939 (Moscow, 1939), p. 381 (see also p. 382). Ten years later Khrushchev reiterated his support of Stalin:

Millions of persons turn to Comrade Stalin with the most profound feelings of love and devotion because he, together with Lenin, formed the great party of the

Bolsheviks and our socialist state, because he enriched Marxist-Leninist theory and raised it to a new, higher level. . . . The despised enemies of our people have more than once attempted to shatter the unity of the Bolshevist party, to ruin Soviet rule. A great service of Comrade Stalin is that he, in mortal combat with the enemies of the people—Mensheviks, S.R.s, Trotskyites, Zinovievities, Bukharinites, bourgeois nationalists—upheld the purity of Lenin's teaching, the unity and iron solidarity of our party's ranks. Led by the great Stalin, the party of Bolsheviks guided with confidence the peoples of our country along the Leninist-Stalinist path to communism. (*Khrushchev Speaks*, pp. 12-13; see also pp. 14, 17, 20).

10. Zhukov, *Memoirs*, pp. 226, 391 Davies reported to the United States State Department from Moscow at the time that Tukhachevsky and his group were probably guilty. (*Mission to Moscow*, pp. 236, 176-79.) Davies had known Tukhachevsky personally (ibid., p. 120). Grey (Stalin, p. 281) comments—in Gothic-fiction style—that the "evidence" was "probably not enough to deceive Stalin, but it aroused his pathological suspicion, which quickly turned to conviction of their guilt." Zhukov praises Tukhachevshy as "a clever erudite professional" (p. 113) but offers no opinion on his guilt or innocence.

11. Roy A. Medvedev, *Let History Judge: The Origins and Consequences of Stalinism* (New York, 1971), p. 239; Robert Conquest, *The Great Terror: Stalin's Purges of the Thirties* (New York, 1973) p. 706; Merle Fainsod, *How Russia Is Ruled* (Cambridge, Mass. 1957), p. 386; Conquest, pp. 707, 705. Medvedev submitted his manuscript to Khrushchev's Central Committee to obtain its seal of approval. (*New York Times*, Feb. 23, 1979).

12. Conquest, p. 712.

13. Albert Rhys Williams, *The Soviets* (New York, 1937), pp. 433-38, 442-43, 427-28.

14. Medvedev. pp. 225-34.

15. *Land of Socialism Today and Tomorrow*, pp. 189-91, 3.

16. V. I. Lenin, "Letter to American Workers," August 20, 1918, *Collected Works*, XXXVIII (Moscow, 1965), 71; E. H. Carr, *The Bolshevik Revolution, 1917-1923* (Penguin Books, 1956), I, 176, 175.

17. *Leninism: Selected*, pp. 459, 469-70.

18. *Leninism: Selected*, p. 465; *Land of Socialism Today and Tomorrow*, pp. 33, 41, 207, 203, 31. Jean Elleinstein in *The Stalin Phenomenon* (London, 1976), p. 116, claims that the fact "that there was no growth in steel output between 1937 and 1939" indicates "the disappearance of thousands of qualified managerial staff." Elleinstein fails to note that there was a considerable general economic increase between 1937 and 1939 and that the number of "engineers and technicians" rose from 722,000 to 932,000 between 1937 and 1940 (*National Economy of the U.S.S.R.: Statistical Returns*, Moscow, 1957, pp. 40-42). Why steel lagged behind the national average is not clear. We might note (p. 58) that pig iron output also failed to

increase, although coal (p. 64) increased as did power output (p. 66) and consumer goods in general.

19. In 1957 Khrushchev wrote—without seeing the contradiction between his comments and his 1956 denunciation speech:

> What an amazing flourishing of the economy and culture we have in our Soviet republics! What wonderful people have grown up and developed there under the conditions of a Soviet society, under the leadership of the Communist Party, in the course of the historic struggle for communism! (*Khrushchev Speaks*, p. 276).

It was indeed "amazing" that a country which had been paralyzed by the Stalinist "terror" until 1953 should make so dramatic a recovery, including developing a new generatiion of "wonderful people" in four years.

20. *Twenty Letters*, pp. 166-67.

21. Albert Szymanski, "The Class Basis of Political Processes in the Soviet Union," *Science and Society*, XLII (Winter 1978-79), 437-48. See also: Victor and Ellen Perlo, *Dynamic Stability: The Soviet Economy Today* (New York, 1980), Chapter VIII, "Democracy and Cultural Freedom." We might note, too, that Zhukov, who had fallen out of favor with Khrushchev was brought back by Brezhnev—in a meeting of 6,000 in 1965 at which both he and the memory of Stalin were applauded. (Otto Preston Chaney, Jr., *Zhukov* (Norman, Oklakoma, 1971), pp. 426-427.

NOTES TO APPENDIX II

1. Joseph Stalin, *Leninism: Selected Writings* (New York, 1942), p. 406.

2. Karl Marx, "Afterword to the Second German Edition of the First Volume of Capital", Karl Marx and Frederick Engels, *Selected Works* (Moscow, 1969), II, 97-98.

3. Stalin, *Leninism: Selected Writings*, pp. 407-08, 412, 414, 416; Frederick Engels, *Anti-Dühring* (New York, 1939), p. 29. Engels, following Hegel, used "metaphysical" to denote thinking in terms of set categories, established most notably by Immanuel Kant.

4. Karl Marx, "Theses on Feuerbach," *Selected Works,* I, 13; Karl Marx, *Preface to a Contribution to the Critique of Political Economy,* 1859, quoted in Lenin, "The Teachings of Karl Marx," in *A Handbook of Marxism,* ed. Emile Burns (New York, 1953), p. 543. I prefer the *Handbook* translation—with its (correct) "human beings" instead of "men"—to that in *Selected Works,* I, 503 and elsewhere. In considering Stalin's division of consciousness theory, it is only fair to note that, strange though it may seem, he was probably misled by faulty formulations by Lenin. As he moved from "dialectics" to the historical materialism section in his encyclopedia essay on Marx (1914), Lenin wrote:

> If materialism in general explains consciousness as the outcome of existence, and not conversely, then materialism as applied to the social life of mankind must explain social consciousness as the outcome of social existence *(Marx, Engels, Marxism,* New York, n.d., p. 11)

And again (1913) in *The Three Sources and Three Component Parts of Marxism:*

> Just as the cognition of man reflects nature (i.e., developing matter) which exists independently of him, so also the social cognition of man (i.e., the various views and doctrines, philosophic, religious, political, etc.) reflects the economic order of society. *(Marx, Engels, Marxism,* p. 52)

There is no "existence," in this context, separate from "social existence," no "consciousness" separate from "social consciousness," and no general "cognition" reflecting "nature" separate from "social cognition." True, consciousness has biological (evolutionary) roots but it is primarily formed by social forces and the fact that it reflects both nature and society does not mean that it consists of two separate components, one natural or general and one social. Certainly there is no such division in Marx. Consciousness, arising from "social existence," reflects both nature and society. Lenin was, of course, aware of this but apparently made faulty formulations in attempting to distinguish between philosphical and social matters.

5. *Leninism: Selected,* pp. 407, 410, 417; V. I. Lenin, "On the Question of Dialectics," 1915, *Collected Works,* XXXVIII (Moscow, 1972), 359. Stalin in his essay (p. 407) quotes Engels: "nature is . . . in a state . . . of constant renewal and development" (*Dialectics of Nature,* London, 1940, p. 13). This passage and other faulty formulations by Engels apparently helped to mislead him.

6. Lenin, *Collected Works,* XXXVIII, 360; Lenin, "Karl Marx," *Marx, Engels, Marxism* p. 11. Lenin wrote this article on Marx for a Russian encyclopedia in 1914. On the negation of the negation see Engels, *Anti-Dühring,* pp. 148-56. Lenin places "struggle" in quotes to indicate that he here intends it to designate an objective process.

7. Stalin, *Works,* I (Moscow, 1952), 374, 376, 382, 384-85; David Guest, *A Textbook of Dialectical Materialism* (New York, 1939), p. 87.

8. *Works,* I, 319; *Handbook of Marxism,* p. 544; Karl Marx, *The Poverty of Philosophy,* 1847 (London, n.d.), p. 89.

9. *The Fundamentals of Marxist-Leninist Philosophy* (Moscow, 1974), Chapter Five; ibid., p. 126; Lenin, *Marx, Engels, Marxism,* p. 11. Soviet scientists and political leaders have sometimes repudiated Soviet philosophers. One scientist is reported as having said that if they had "paid attention to the philosophers" they would never have had a space program. In 1947 Zhdanov made a sweeping attack on Soviet philosophy. Richard T. De George, *Patterns of Soviet Thought* (Ann Arbor, Mich., 1966), pp. 188, 208.

10. *Marxist-Leninist Philosophy,* pp. 125, 131; Marx, *Selected Works,* II, 98. See Lenin, "Once Again on the Trade Unions . . ." *Selected Works,* IX (Moscow, 1937), 65-67, in his attack on "Bukharin's lifeless and vapid eclecticism," in which he amusingly but illuminatingly discussed all the ways in which a water glass could be viewed: "the demand for all-sidedness is a safeguard against mistakes and rigidity."

11. *Marxist-Leninist Philosophy,* p. 135.

12. *Marxist-Leninist Philosophy,* p. 143; Marx to Johann B. Schweitzer, Jan. 24, 1865, Marx and Engels, *Selected Works,* II, 30.

13. *Marxist-Leninist Philosophy,* p. 157. We might note the following in Hegel: "the whole is the essence perfecting itself through its development"; "this dialectic . . . is matter's very soul putting forth its branches and fruit organically" (Raymond Plant, *Hegel,* Bloomington, Indiana, pp. 137, 141). It was in response to concepts such as these that Marx wrote: "My dialectic method is not only different from Hegelian, but is its direct opposite" ("Afterword to the Second German Edition of Capital," *Selected Works,* II. 98).

14. Marx to Johann B. Schweitzer, Jan. 24, 1865, *Selected Works,* II, 26; Frederick Engels, *Dialectics of Nature* (London, 1940), p. 224; Lenin, *Philosophical Notebooks, Collected Works,* XXXVIII, 256, 93, 94.

15. *Marxist-Leninist Philosophy,* pp. 163, 131, 165, 162, 163.

16. Engels, "Socialism: Utopian and Scientific," *Selected Works,* III, 131. All that would be left of "all earlier philosophy," Engels argued, would be "the science of thought and its laws—formal logic and dialectics. Everything else is subsumed in the positive science of Nature and history." *Marxist-Leninist Philosophy,* pp. 162, 130, 133, 181.

17. *Marxist-Leninist Philosophy,* pp. 163, 166, 191. The "cup" image, in fact, seems to be taken directly from Plato: "Thus he ["the creator of the universe"] spake and once more into the cup in which he had previously mingled the soul of the universe he poured the remains of the elements." *Timaeus, The Portable Greek Reader,* ed. W. H. Auden (New York, 1955), p. 111).

18. *Marxist-Leninist Philosophy,* pp. 215, 216, 234.

19. Sheptulin in *Marxist-Leninist Philosophy* has a long chapter entitled "Categories of Materialist Dialectics" preceding the chapter "The Basic Laws of Dialectics," which by itself implies the primacy of the categories over the laws; in fact "law" is one of the categories. In Kharin's *Fundamentals of Dialectics* we find (p. 233): "Essence is a category denoting the internal basis of a thing . . . the category appearance reproduces the outward side of a thing." Thus essence and appearance are regarded not primarily as objective phenomena whose subjective counterparts denote different levels of penetration into reality but as mental constructs. The same confusion appears throughout, for example (p. 237): "Unlike formal logic, which pinpoints stability in the objects of thought, dialectical logic is tantamount to thinking in terms of categories within the unity of opposites. It is a doctrine of how human ideas and concepts reflect the infinitely developing and changing objective world." Thus dialectical materialism becomes a "doctrine" acting within a system of abstract categories. The same idealist outlook underlies Alexander Spirkin's *Dialectical Materialism,* Moscow, 1983. In fact new categories are added: Space and Time (as in Kant), System and Structure, Essence and Phenomenon, Negation and Continuity, Contradiction and Harmony. Modern Soviet philosophy must have sprouted at least fifty categories. The "system" becomes more immense each year, and its "mastery" correspondingly more difficult—and more remote both from reality and the materialism of Marx, Engels and Lenin. Finally, these philosophers seem to know little or nothing of modern brain research or animal-society research, which show us the evolutionary roots of human behavior and thought, but continue to discuss "man" and "consciousness" in outmoded abstract constructs.

BIBLIOGRAPHY

Alliluyev Memoirs. Trans., ed., David Tutaev; New York, 1968.

Alliluyeva, Svetlana. *Twenty Letters to a Friend*. New York, 1967.

Ash, William. *Pickaxe and Rifle*. London, 1974.

Benns, F. Lee. *European History Since 1870*. New York, 1955.

Beria, L. *On the History of the Bolshevik Organizations in Transcaucasia* (1935). New York, n.d. (?1939).

Bettelheim, Charles. *Class Struggles in the U.S.S.R.: Second Period, 1923–1930*. New York, 1979.

Bolsheviks and the October Revolution: Minutes of the Central Committee of the Russian Social-Democratic Labour Party (Bolsheviks), The. London, 1974.

Bukharin, Nikolai. *Historical Materialism, A System of Sociology* (1921). New York, 1925.

Bunyan, James and H.H. Fisher. *The Bolshevik Revolution, 1917–1918, Documents and Materials*. Stanford, California, 1934.

Cameron, Kenneth Neill. *Humanity and Society: A World History*. Bloomington, Indiana, 1973; New York, 1977.

————. "The Fallacy of 'the Superstructure.'" *Monthly Review*, XXXI (January, 1980), pp. 27–36.

————. *Shelley: The Golden Years*. Cambridge, Mass., 1974.

————. *Marxism, The Science of Society: An Introduction*, South Hadley, Mass., 1985.

Carr, E.H. *The Bolshevik Revolution, 1917–1923*. 2 vols. Penguin Books, 1956.

Chamberlin, W.H. *The Russian Revolution*, 2 vols. New York, 1935.

Chaney, Otto Preston, Jr. *Zhukov*. Norman, Oklahoma, 1971.

Ch'en, Jerome. *Mao and the Chinese Revolution*. New York, 1965.

Clough, Shepard Bancroft and Charles Woolsey Cole. *Economic History of Europe*. New York, 1952.

Cohen, Stephen F. *Bukharin and the Bolshevik Revolution*. New York, 1975.

Cornforth, Maurice. *Historical Materialism*. New York, 1954.

Conquest, Robert. *The Great Terror*. New York, 1973.

Davies, Joseph E. *Mission to Moscow*. New York, 1941.

Deborin, G. *The Second World War*. Trans. Vic Schnierson. Moscow, n.d.

————. *Secrets of the Second World War*. Moscow, 1971.

Dedier, V. *Tito Speaks*. London, 1953.

Deutscher, Isaac. *The Prophet Armed: Trotsky, 1897-1921*. New York, 1954.

————. *Russia, What Next?* New York, 1953.

————. *Stalin: A Political Biography*. New York, 1967.

Dimitrov, Georgi. Report. *VII Congress of the Communist International: Abridged Stenographic Report of Proceedings* (1935). Moscow, 1939.

Djilas, Milovan. *Conversations with Stalin*. New York, 1962.

Elleinstein, Jean. *The Stalin Phenomenon*. London, 1976.

Essential Works of Chinese Communism (revised ed.). Ed. Winberg Chai. New York, 1972.

Florinsky, Michael T. *Russia: A History and Interpretation*. 2 vols. New York, 1953.

Fundamentals of Marxism-Leninism. Moscow, n.d. (?1959).

Goldfield, Michael and Melvin Rothenberg. *The Myth of Capitalism Reborn*. San Francisco, 1980.

Grey, Ian. *Stalin: Man of History*. London, 1982.

Handbook of Marxism. Ed., Emile Burns; New York, 1935.

Historical Statistics of the United States, 1789–1945. Bureau of the Census, Washington, D.C.

History of the Communist Party of the Soviet Union (Bolsheviks), Short Course. New York, 1939.

History of the U.S.S.R.: The Era of Socialism. Moscow, 1982.

Hoagland, Mahlon B. *The Roots of Life*. New York, 1977.

Hoxha, Enver. *Selected Works*. Tirana, 1974.

————. *The Khruschevites: Memoirs*. Tirana, 1980.

————. *With Stalin: Memoirs*. Tirana, 1979.

de Jonge, Alex. *Stalin and the Shaping of the Soviet Union*. New York, 1986.

Khrushchev, Nikita Sergeyevich. *Khrushchev Remembers: The Last Testament*. Ed, Strobe Talbot. Boston, 1974.

————. *The "Secret" Speech*. Nottingham, 1976.

Khrushchev Speaks: Selected Speeches, Articles and Press Conferences, 1949–1962. Ann Arbor, Michigan, 1963.

Krupskaya, N.K. *Reminiscences of Lenin*. New York, 1975.

Land of Socialism Today and Tomorrow: Reports and Speeches at the Eighteenth Congress of the Communist Party of the Soviet Union (Bolsheviks), The. March 10–21, 1939. Moscow, 1939.

Lenin, V.I. *Against Trotskyism*. Moscow, 1972.

————. *Collected Works*. 45 vols. Moscow, 1963–1977.

————. *Marx, Engels, Marxism*. New York, n.d.

————. *Selected Works*. 10 vols. Ed. J. Fineberg. New York, n.d. (?1943).

Mandel, William M. *Soviet Women*. New York, 1975.

Mao Tse-tung. *Chairman Mao Talks to the People*. Ed. Stuart Schram. New York, 1974.

————. *Selected Works*, New York, 4 vols., 1954–1956.

————. *Selected Works*, V. Peking, 1977.

Marx, Karl. *A Critique of the Gotha Program*. New York, 1933.

Marx, Karl and Frederick Engels. *Correspondence, 1846–1895*. London, 1934.

————. *Selected Works*, 3 vols. Moscow, 1973.

Marmullaku, Marmal. *Albania and the Albanians*. London, 1975.

Materials for the Study of the Soviet System. Eds., James A. Meisel and Edward S. Kozera. Ann Arbor, Michigan, 1953.

National Economy of the U.S.S.R.: Statistical Returns. Moscow, 1957.

Outline History of China, An. Peking, 1958.

Pano, Nicolas: *The People's Republic of Albania*. Baltimore, 1968.

Payne, R. *The Rise and Fall of Stalin*. New York, 1965.

Perlo, Victor and Ellen. *Dynamic Stability: The Soviet Economy Today*. New York, 1980.

Pittman, Margrit. *Encounters in Democracy*. New York, 1981.

Plekhanov, G.V. *Fundamental Problems of Marxism* (1908). Moscow, 1974.

Political Thought of Mao Tse-tung, The. Ed. Stuart Schram. New York, 1971.

Pollo, Stefanaq and Arben Puto. *The History of Albania*. Boston, 1981.

Popov, H. *Outline History of the Communist Party of the Soviet Union*. 2 vols. New York, n.d.

Prifti, Peter R. *Socialist Albania Since 1944: Domestic and Foreign Developments*. Cambridge, Mass., 1978.

Pritt, D.N. *The Zinoviev Trial*. London, 1936.

Reed, John. *Ten Days that Shook the World*. New York, 1934.

Report of the Court Proceedings in the Case of the Anti-Soviet "Bloc of Rights and Trotskyites." Moscow, 1938.

Report of the Court Proceedings in the Case of the Anti-Soviet Trotskyite Center. Moscow, 1937.

Schram, Stuart. *Mao Tse-tung*. Penguin Books, 1970.

Segal, Ronald. *Trotsky: A Biography*. New York, 1979.

Sheptulin, A.P. *Marxist-Leninist Philosophy*. Moscow, 1978.

Soviet Linguistic Controversy, The. Trans. John V. Murra, Robert M. Hankin, Fred Hollings. Columbia University Slavic Studies, New York, 1951.

Stalin, Joseph. *Economic Problems of Socialism in the U.S.S.R*. New York, 1952.

————. *For Peaceful Coexistence: Postwar Interviews*. New York, 1951.

————. *Leninism*. 2 vols. Trans. Eden and Cedar Paul. London, 1932, 1933.

————. *Leninism: Selected Writings*. New York, 1942.

————. and H.G. Wells. *Marxism vs. Liberalism, An interview*. New York, 1950.

————. *Marxism and Linguistics*. New York, 1951.

————. *Marxism and the National and Colonial Question*. New York, 1934.

————. *October Revolution, The*. New York, 1934.

————. *On the Great Patriotic War of the Soviet Union*. Calcutta, 1975.

————. *Works*, 13 vols. Moscow, 1952–1955.

Statesman's Yearbook, 1955, The. London, 1955.

Suyin, Han. *The Morning Deluge: Mao and the Chinese Revolution, 1893–1954*. Boston, 1972.

Sverdlova, K. *Yakov Sverdlov*. Moscow, 1981.

Szymanski, Albert. "The Class Basis of Political Processes in the Soviet Union," *Science and Society*, XLII (Winter, 1978–79,) 437–48 .

————. "Socialism or Capitalism in the U.S.S.R.," *Science and Society*, XLI, Fall, 1977.

Trotsky, Leon. *My Life*. New York, 1930.

————. *The Age of Permanent Revolution*. Ed. Isaac Deutscher. New York, 1973.

————. *The Challenge of the Left Opposition (1923–1925)*. Ed., Naomi Allen. New York, 1975.

————. *The History of the Russian Revolution*. Trans., Max Eastman. Ann Arbor, Michigan, 1964.

————. *The Russian Revolution*. Ed. F.W. Dupee. New York, 1959.

————. *The Stalin School of Falsification*. New York, 1937.

Tucker, Robert C. *Stalin as Revolutionary*, 1879–1929, London, 1973.

Ulam, Adam B. *Stalin: The Man and his Era*. New York, 1973.

Vernadsky, George. *A History of Russia*. New Haven, 1961.

Woman Question: Selections from the Writings of Karl Marx, Frederick Engels, V. J. Lenin, Joseph Stalin, The. New York, 1951.

Yaroslavsky, E. *Landmarks in the Life of Stalin*. Moscow, 1940.

Zhukov, J.K. *Memoirs*. New York, 1971.

INDEX